THE WEEK-END CRICKETER

A. C. L. Bennett

THE
WEEK-END CRICKETER

by
A. C. L. (Leo) BENNETT

With a Foreword
by
SIR DONALD BRADMAN

With 28 Illustrations

HUTCHINSON'S LIBRARY OF SPORTS AND PASTIMES
London   New York   Melbourne   Sydney   Cape Town

First published 1951

Printed in Great Britain
by The Anchor Press, Ltd.,
Tiptree, Essex

CONTENTS

LIST OF ILLUSTRATIONS

FOREWORD

In the modern world there is a constant search for excitement. Attention is focused on the more glamorous events, which thereby gain a position of prominence in the public mind—very often out of all proportion.

I sometimes think this happens in cricket.

Test Matches are really the culminating achievement of thousands of club players.

In Australia, for instance, all first-class cricketers make their *début* from the Saturday-afternoon club ranks—excluding the occasional country recruit.

I believe, therefore, that club cricket is vitally important, and I commend the efforts of the writer, who, among other things, has endeavoured to stimulate competition as well as provide entertainment.

Don Bradman

INTRODUCTION

THIS is not a book on how to play cricket. Let me make that clear at the outset. True, it includes some practical guidance that I hope will prove useful to the younger or less-experienced club player, but I had no intention of producing another variation on the 'how-to-play' theme. That has been dealt with admirably and adequately, in books by experts of far greater authority than I.

What I have set out to do is to fill a gap in the library of the sport by writing about club cricket for club cricketers. So, in these pages, all the emphasis is upon the game as the week-end, or spare-time, player knows it (and in him, if anywhere, is the perfect illustration of the old tag, 'I know what I love, and love what I know!').

The keynote, then, is the Club: in general, its players, ground, pavilion, equipment, organisation, administration; in particular, the stories of as many individual clubs and their players as I have been able to assemble. Some hundreds of clubs and well over a thousand players, in the Northern leagues as well as in the clubs of the South, are reflected, but, even so, I am only too well aware of the gaps that, for reasons outside my control, I have been obliged to leave. To all who should have been represented here, but are not, I express my sincere regrets, and the hope that there will be another opportunity of making good the deficiencies.

I engage at some length in the seemingly endless controversy about competitive cricket. Though I am a member of what is perhaps its most rigid opponent, the Club Cricket Conference (itself the subject of a chapter), I feel strongly that no club player can be indifferent to the question, and its 'pro's' and 'con's', therefore, are argued in detail—and I have been privileged to quote some expert and stimulating opinions.

And because the story of club cricket is international, there is a chapter about the way it is organised and played in Australia, New Zealand, South Africa, India, Ceylon, and the West Indies.

It is usual in an introduction to express the author's gratitude for help given him in his work. As this book could not have been written without the co-operation of the clubs themselves, I cannot hope to settle in that way my great debt of gratitude to the countless officers and players who took such trouble to meet my demands for information. My hope is that the book itself will speak for me.

It would be graceless, indeed, though, to omit to record my sincere thanks to the pre-eminent cricketer of our day for his foreword; to the information officers at the London headquarters of Australia and New Zealand for their personal interest and co-operation; and to John Arlott, Ken Ablack, Allan Rae, and Berry Sarbadhikary for their individual contributions.

My final 'thank you'—I was going to say my 'gratitude', until I looked up the definition: 'the lively anticipation of future favours !'—is to two people without whose help, advice, co-operation, and untiring efforts this book would have remained just an idea.

To Peter Goodall—for his forthright efforts and downright hard work, for supplying me with so much indispensable material, and for carrying the technical burden of the picture pages.

To Wilfrid Goatman—for keeping me on the literary path, for some of the brilliant flashes of expression that come only to the trained journalist, and for keeping me at it when the writing of this book seemed anything but a labour of love.

A. C. L. B.

Chapter One

THE CLUB

Organisation—Policy—Politics—Team spirit—The fixture list—Value of the non-playing member—What makes a good club man?—The 'utility' man—The women.

IT seems logical for a book like this, written for and about the week-end cricketer, to open the bowling from the pavilion end —in other words, to deal first with the organisation, policy, and politics of the week-end cricketer's club.

The club is the orbit, the cohesive force, of everyone interested in this great national game of ours—whether player, spectator, official, or even club steward. This is true even of 'wandering' clubs—those unfortunate enough not to have a ground of their own.

By club, I don't mean, of course, the bricks and mortar that make the club-house or pavilion, but the organisation, policy, and team spirit without which the game could not survive for long. I can tell you of many games I have played that could have been won had there been anything of the zip automatically instilled in a team that is together in spirit as well as physically.

Without exception, a side successful on the field is the direct result of a first-class organisation behind it. Few teams have gone out to play a match and won when there has been trouble 'behind the scenes'.

A committee must, of necessity, vary in size. Clubs—such as the Banks—that run six and seven XIs each Saturday must have larger committees than the club with, say, only two Saturday teams to consider.

The size of your own particular committee doesn't matter. What does matter is that you have the right men filling the various positions—in other words, the right man for each job. All too often, one finds a club member has been elected at the Annual General Meeting to fill a certain office, when it is abundantly clear that his strong point lies in another direction and he could serve club and members much more efficiently and profitably if he only were used in that way. All too often, also, an excellent clubman is not on the committee at all. Perhaps he feels the tie of doing some official job would be too much for him. Perhaps he's just too lazy. If a player really has his club at heart, then he should be only too ready to come forward and help in whatever way he can.

Only recently there were two instances of bad feeling in clubs near London, one of which concerned the president, and the other the captain.

Similarity between the two cases was in the manner of the removal of those officials. Both men were deprived of office without warning, by the last-minute nomination of a rival at the club Annual General Meeting. Before the nomination of new men was made, opponents ensured strong enough representation at the Annual General Meeting to prove the issue.

How silly are these subterfuges! In both cases, the officers would have been quite prepared to stand down if they had been given any intimation that their services were not wholly accept-able to everybody. But to be voted out by what was little more than intrigue and with no warning of any sort naturally went against the grain.

Even more important, from the club's point of view, is the inevitable unrest caused among supporters of the deposed men.

Indeed, only the 'disinherited' captain of a side can save the position for his club in the following season. He must insist on playing under the new skipper at a time when many first XI members are 'on strike'. His example can save the day. But if he can bring himself to do that for the sake of the club, he would seem to have deserved better treatment in the first place.

It is usual for the committee of a cricket club to consist of a chairman, the captains and vice-captains of each of the XIs, the honorary secretary, the honorary treasurer, the match secretary, the team secretary, and perhaps two other members. The duties of honorary secretary and honorary treasurer are sometimes combined. So are those of match secretary and team secretary.

The selection committee usually consists of the captains and vice-captains of each XI, the honorary secretary, the honorary treasurer, and the match and team secretaries.

The full committee should meet during the cricket season at least once a month. During the close season you will usually find that three or four meetings are enough to deal with the affairs of the club. These are in addition, of course, to the Annual General

Meeting, which is held either at the beginning or end of a season.

Personally, I favour holding the Annual General Meeting in October or November—or as soon after the end of the season as is possible. At the Annual General Meeting the new committee is elected, and I think it only right and proper that they should be responsible for doing all the dirty work for the next season. In any event, I am sure most committees would rather have all the arranging to do for the year during which they are in office, rather than take on commitments and responsibilities entered into by the outgoing committee.

In my own particular case, I know I would very much rather be responsible for next season's fixtures, tour, and the hundred-and-one odds and ends that must be settled before the nets are brought out of the groundsman's shed.

The club's policy is laid down at the Annual General Meeting and at committee meetings. From experience on and off the field, the committee will be able to draw up its own rules for ratification at the Annual General Meeting. Thus, over a period of years, policy takes a definite shape, and it is the responsibility of the committee to see that it is applied. I have been amazed at the number of well-established clubs with big names, who cannot define their policy or—beyond winning matches—their real aims. I know the ultimate aim of all cricket clubs and players is to win matches, but a sound and sensible policy must be laid down, otherwise how can there be an efficient organisation in the club?

I think, too, that clubs are very lax in the matter of conveying their policy to members. On the other side of the fence, I often find that members, ignorant of procedure when a problem arises, fail to take the correct action, and the 'usual channels' (I hate the phrase, but here it is the only really descriptive term) are ignored: members will not voice their grievances or criticisms to a member of the committee, or address a note to the chairman for ventilation in committee.

What usually happens is that the vice-captain of the third XI hears someone saying that someone else has complained bitterly that they never have new balls in their matches, or a committee man discovers through the bar steward that there is unrest about the exclusive right of the first XI to have 'covers' for their 'square'. A well-organised club has, of course, perfectly sound answers to all these points, and to the hundred-and-one others that arise every season, but I am not interested in the answers. The point I make is that there is a correct procedure for all complaints—bring it to the notice of your committee.

Ideally, of course, the committee must be strong enough to detect trouble before it has gained ground, and having tracked it down, to deal with it effectively and decisively.

The match secretary is the man who has the job of arranging the season's games for each of the XIs. There are many ways, of course, in agreeing your fixture lists for the following year, but not a bad one is to get the committee regularly—say, once a month from May to the end of September—to decide whether it wants to renew fixtures against the opponents played in the preceding month. In that way, the match secretary's work is considerably eased, and he hasn't the heavy task of dealing with all the next season's fixtures at the end of September.

The opponents will vary from year to year. It is usual for about half a dozen new matches to be arranged annually, but this is by no means the rule. I recommend the policy of retaining those clubs with whom you have had a good game—no matter what the result—and, if possible, of bringing in one or two new, and preferably stronger, opponents.

I am continually reminded of, and intend to refer frequently to, the great value of the non-playing member. Sometimes he is referred to as the 'utility' man, who does everything 'behind the scenes' and often in front, though never actually playing. Or he may be just a spectator, who turns up every Saturday to watch his side play.

If the players are the backbone, it would not be untrue to say that the non-playing member is the spinal nerve of any club. He assists in keeping the club's finances in a rosy state, and perhaps takes his turn behind the bar. Often he looks after either the scoring, the ground, the wicket, or the equipment. Perhaps all of them. How can any club get along without him? His car is always ready to dash off to hospital with some 'unfortunate'. He will organise and run the Derby sweep, or arrange the annual dinner or fête, or stand in when the secretary is ill.

Anyone who has played on Brondesbury's delightful ground at Cricklewood, not more than two throws of a cricket ball from the Hendon Way, in London, will know exactly what I mean. They are lucky. They have three such men there. R. E. Driskell

D. Landon well caught by K. N. Harris in a Kodak C.C. Trial Match. The wicket-keeper is L. Kemp

Frank Ahl (Brentham)

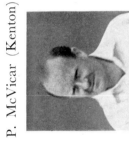

P. McVicar (Kenton)

R. H. Thornhill (Ashford, Middlesex)

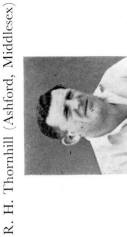

Len Newman (Alexandra Park), in his sixtieth year,
still makes his centuries

means more to that club than he would admit. 'Dris' can be seen any Saturday or Sunday afternoon in the season climbing on to the roof of the pavilion, score-book in hand, prepared to record faithfully details of the day's play. Later, the tea interval, and there he is attending to the refreshments. After the match, drinks are provided and the man who serves—Driskell. And when the rest have gone home, who shuts up the premises? Driskell, the genial, hard-working man who has played little cricket at all.

From the house around the corner comes another stalwart, sixty-five-year-old 'Todge' Woodward—first XI skipper for twenty-seven years. He looks after the outfield and wicket. Members know that without him there would be no 'Brondes-bury' now. Towards the end of World War II, he reconditioned the half derelict grounds entirely on his own—a wonderful feat for a man of his age. But age seems a secondary consideration to 'Todge'. He is invaluable still in the second XI, and bowls the youngsters out with no bother at all.

The third man is secretary Freddie Payne, former Casual footballer. He, too, is prepared to do almost anything for the club. Apart from all the catering arrangements, and the usual innumerable secretarial duties, Freddie's latest achievements are in the decorative line. A while back, he repainted the whole of the pavilion and the bar.

Now please don't think Brondesbury are unique in their good fortune. They are instanced only because they provide such a good example. All clubs have men of this kind. Without them, cricket would indeed suffer. If, later, I omit to mention any 'utility' men in any other club, believe me, it is quite unin-tentional. They deserve more credit than they ever seem to get, even from their own members.

My mentioning the 'utility' men, as I have chosen to call them, does not mean that I have forgotten the women—wives, *fiancées*, and girl-friends of the players, who usually provide all the meals. Paid servants are beyond the financial resources of most clubs, so how could we do without the ladies?

At the same time, I don't think we show enough appreciation of these enthusiastic and loyal supporters of the club. They are invited to the annual supper, and that's about all. We could, and should, do more to acknowledge their indispensable aid.

On the other hand, I must add a gentle warning here to the younger members. The day will surely come when a girl—perhaps

B

the girl—will want you to miss matches. Well, don't miss matches, even if there *is* a good film on at the 'local'! After all, the cricket season is with us all too short a time—a mere five months of the year. Surely the pictures and car rides can be enjoyed in the week-day evenings, or out of the cricket season?

Married men with families have good enough reason to miss the odd game here and there. The young and single men have not. Yet the average club today consists of comparatively old men—I know of few in which the average playing age is under thirty. Yes, I recognise that there has been a major war, that we have compulsory military service, that money is tight. But none of these factors really explains why recruitment is still below pre-war standard.

The club game is heading for disaster unless there are more keenness, enthusiasm, and loyal support by the younger members. I, in my middle thirties, can remember travelling in the backs of vans and tramping miles with my bag to play cricket. Nowadays, I find that unless someone takes some of the bags with him in his car, then all kinds of mysterious reasons are offered by otherwise regular players for being unable to play in 'away' games. I leave you to draw your own conclusions. Most of you will know exactly what I mean.

And here are other ways to kill a cricket club:

Don't go to the club meetings, but if you do, go late.

If the weather doesn't suit you, don't think of attending.

If you do attend a meeting, find fault with the work of the officers and other members.

Never accept an office, as it is easier to criticise than to do things. Nevertheless, get sore if you are not appointed on a committee; but if you are, do not attend committee meetings.

If asked by the chairman your opinion of an important matter, tell him you have nothing to say. After the meeting, tell everyone how things ought to be done.

Do nothing more than is necessary, but when other members roll up their sleeves and willingly, unselfishly, use their ability to help matters along, howl that the club is run by a clique.

Hold back your subscriptions as long as possible, or don't pay at all.

Don't bother about getting new members; let the secretary do it.

When a dinner is given, tell everybody money is being wasted.

If you receive a bill for your subscription after you have paid, resign from the club.

Don't tell the club how it could help you; but if it doesn't help you, resign.

If you receive service without joining, don't think of joining.

When you attend a meeting, vote to do something and then go home and do the opposite.

If you move a resolution and it is lost, say the other members are fools, and make personal explanations about it on every occasion.

Agree to everything said at the meeting and disagree with it outside.

When asked for information, don't give it.

Curse the club for the incompleteness of its information.

Talk co-operation for the other fellow, but never co-operate with him.

When all else fails, curse the secretary.

Chapter Two

THE WANDERING CLUB

Politics—Team spirit—Its value against the static club—Advantages and disadvantages—Wandering clubs and their players.

SINCE the end of World War II, the number of wandering clubs has grown considerably—mainly, as I explain in Chapter Eight, because of the loss of grounds to educational and planning authorities and to local councils.

The councils come into the picture chiefly because they still control many wartime allotments, and refuse to release ground still under cultivation.

But surely this problem of 'releasing' grounds is almost entirely a matter for local residents? They are the people who should petition and press for de-control. But too few are really concerned about the unfortunate fate of the local playing-field. More often than not, their only interest in cricket seems to be as a cause for complaint—because balls are knocked over their fences, because a roof-slate is removed as the result of a glorious six, or, as happened to my club, because half-dressed cricketers are supposed to have been seen standing near the dressing-room windows!

If the week-end cricketer happens to bring down his children to watch the match, then it is the noise that upsets the nearby resident.

No, the majority of them, I fear, are not nearly as interested as one might expect them to be. By not backing up a local club's request for derequisitioning, quite a few of them now overlook rows of prefabricated houses instead of an attractive sports ground. Poor exchange!

Under present-day conditions, 'wanderers' are inevitable— and invaluable. Without them, there would be fewer people playing the game. The more famous of them earn our gratitude by taking first-class players to play against clubs that, otherwise, would never see top-flight cricketers.

Here, of course, one thinks of *I. Zingari*, the *Free Foresters*, and *The Wanderers* as among the best-known and longest established of the wandering sides.

I have often been asked what I. Zingari stands for, and until recently I must admit I didn't know. It appears that the club has its roots in the old Blenheim Hotel in Bond Street, London. One evening in July 1845, the 6th Earl of Bessborough (then F. G. B. Ponsonby, afterwards Sir Spencer Ponsonby-Fane), J. L. Baldwin, and R. P. Long thought of creating a wandering cricket club.

There and then rules were drawn up and the intriguing title of I. Zingari was adopted. It comes from the Italian and, literally translated, means 'the gypsies'. The next day, some twenty or so members were recruited and I. Zingari was in being.

Its members have always taken pride in their unique organisation. Apart from the name, the club's rules and colours are proof enough of this quality. The rules say, for instance, that the 'entrance be nothing, and the annual subscription do not exceed the entrance', and that any Zingaro guilty of playing against the club incurs a penalty of 'immediate expulsion'.

The club colours—gaudy, if you like, but distinctive—are black, red, and gold, indicating 'out of the darkness through fire into light'. Some time after the end of World War I, Germany incurred the displeasure of I. Zingari by adopting the same colours for its national emblem. Indeed, so put out was the club that it published, in the form of a poem, an emphatic protest against the 'degradation' of its colours!

In 1856—eleven years after I. Zingari—the Free Foresters Club was founded in the Midlands. Each member during the early years of its existence came from Warwickshire or Staffordshire.

The choice of red, green, and white as the Free Forester colours all but led to a 'diplomatic incident'.

It appears that the wife of a Free Forester, while on a visit to Rome, proposed visiting the Vatican, or some other territory over which the Pope had jurisdiction. Before the visit, a search was made of her luggage. Among her belongings was a gown trimmed with Free Forester ribbon. The colours were identical with those of Garibaldi, then under something of a cloud in the Papal State, the boundaries of which he had appreciably curtailed.

The official searchers immediately thought the owner intended wearing the gown at a carnival in Rome to enlist support for Garibaldi's cause!

Explanations were given, but the Italians, not unnaturally, were suspicious. However, after a number of interpreters and other

officials had intervened on the lady's behalf, it was announced
that no further action would be taken after the confiscation of the
ribbon. But the lady is still convinced that she was kept under
police surveillance throughout her stay in the territory!

In 1881, *The Wanderers* came into being. They were founded
by one of cricket's best-known personalities—the late Stanley
Coleman, of Surrey. Stanley must have done more for The
Wanderers than any other person for any other club. He is said to
have appeared in 2,500 matches, and, for fifty-six years, personally
collected the side for every match. What an achievement!

Such names as these appear in The Wanderers' score-books
(which contains the results of the earliest games): Alf Gadsby;
George Parker, who is their present match and honorary
secretary; Jackie Brown (Richmond); A. S. ('Bert') Soole;
Hubert Cath (Paignton), secretary of the Devon Cricket Association and president of The Wanderers in 1950; 'Monty'
Garland-Wells; Jack Seward (Malden Wanderers); Wally Burton
(skipper of Hampton Wick in 1950); and Reg Henty. These
are but a few of the hundreds of interesting and well-known
cricketers who have turned out for this celebrated club.

Young Peter Turton (West Surrey), who played for the C.C.C.
against the Universities Athletic Union at Motspur Park in 1949,
is probably the youngest Wanderer ever to be invited to become a
member. County cricketers Alf Gover (England and Surrey),
Eddie Watts (Surrey), and Vic Ransom (Hants) have also represented the club, which always turns out a strong XI of grand
chaps and fine cricketers.

Other well-known 'wandering' clubs include the *Incogniti*,
the *Butterflies*—membership of which is restricted to Old Boys
of Eton, Harrow, Winchester, Westminster, Charterhouse, and
Rugby—and the *Stoics*, which were founded as early as 1877,
by O. R. Borradaile, who did so much for Essex cricket.
Originally, it was intended that club membership should be
confined to the old boys of Borradaile's School, Westminster, but
before long the club was closely connected with the Essex
C.C.C. But nowadays the county influence has largely passed
from Essex to Surrey, and certain Stoics matches are played at the
Oval.

In the fifty-three years from 1896 to 1948 there were only three
presidents of the club: A. E. Stoddart (1896–1907), O. R.
Borradaile (1907–1935), and the late Edgar Walmisley (1935–

1948). (Walmisley was possibly one of the heaviest men ever seen on a cricket field.) In more recent years Joe Moore, the old Dulwich cricketer, has taken on the presidency.

Among the thirty or forty Stoics who have played for a county are A. P. Lucas, H. G. Owen, C. J. Kortright, A. E. Stoddart, R. W. V. Robins, H. L. Dales, C. D. Gray, G. W. O. Smith, J. H. Lockton, W. I. Cook, A. Jeacocke, V. G. Grinter, B. K. Castor, A. E. S. Rippon, J. G. O'Gorman, C. D. McIver, C. S. Davies, H. J. J. Malcolm, A. C. Burnett, N. H. Bennett, and D. L. Newman.

Membership is restricted to 100 playing members and their activities are confined almost exclusively to mid-week cricket.

In 1927 some interesting correspondence took place with the Headmaster of Stowe School about the use of the name 'Old Stoics', and I'm glad to hear an amicable agreement was reached that it should be used only by the 'Old Society' of the school, and would not be used for a cricket club composed of old members of Stowe School.

Some of the Stoics' outstanding performances have been D. Robertson's 1,000 runs and 100 wickets in 1911, V. G. Grinter's average of over 100 in 1922, and Henry Malcolm's average of over 100 in 1948, which included a score of 210 before lunch at the Oval against H.M.S. *Dolphin*.

In *Wisden's* is the record of a most interesting game in 1886 against Hampstead. Hampstead made 668, of which A. E. Stoddart contributed 485 (still a record for one-day cricket), but as no declarations were allowed in those days, the Stoics had no time to bat!

R. Andrews was secretary until his death in 1947, but since then these important duties have been carried out by V. G. Bromage, who is better known as the Finchley C.C. cricketer and mine host of the Crown Hotel in Brewer Street, London. I have never been into 'Brom's' pub without hearing some amusing story about cricket. One he told me not long ago occurred in a match against The Wanderers at the Oval. The rules of cricket were adhered to very strictly. Stanley Coleman, captaining The Wanderers, insisted that Edgar Walmisley, captaining the Stoics, should list the team by 11 a.m. The Stoics were then two short and Walmisley had to include two of the ground staff. By 11.15 his two original players had arrived, but Stanley Coleman refused to allow them to play. All went well until Coleman himself came in to bat, with a runner. Immediately Edgar Walmisley protested and rightly pointed out that as Coleman had not incurred injury during the game, he was not entitled to a runner. Exit the runner, and honours were again even!

R. B. Bisgood has been treasurer of the club since taking over in 1948 from J. N. D. G. Bettley. Recent elections to the ranks of the Stoics include T. Q. Abell, P. S. M. Auld, J. E. A. Blatherwick, L. Calderwood, D. Callender, Rev. J. Deigen, A. Fletcher, G. Hammond, F. W. Hobbs, E. Hayward, P. Markham, F. J. Payne, L. H. Phillips, H. N. Greene, and R. Subba Row, the nineteen-year-old ex-Whitgift School boy, who has played for the Young Amateurs of Surrey, and who is showing great promise. In previous elections we find the names of J. W. Harrison, one of the famous Old Whitgiftian brothers, Jack Livesey the actor, Pat Sherwood, and another Old Whitgiftian, Martin Turner, the Rugby international.

From the point of view of the static cricket club, the wandering teams have one real asset: they help to fulfil fixtures at a time when the club's usual opponents are not available, and especially during cricket weeks. Usually, at least two or three matches during a club 'week' are against homeless clubs, or scratch teams.

And don't forget there is still another side to the question. Many of the clubs included in the 'wandering' list have lost their grounds through no fault of their own, and though many of them are prepared to spend a substantial sum of money on preparations and equipment, the almost insuperable difficulty of finding enough free land in their immediate areas defeats them.

The C.C.C.'s Preservation of Sports Ground Committee, mentioned in Chapter Fifteen, is continually fighting on behalf of such clubs, and, in a number of instances, has been successful.

True, before World War II many wandering sides had chances of getting hold of a ground, but refused. Why? The only reasonable answer, to my mind, is that members wanted to continue playing cricket 'on the cheap'.

Clubs of this nature, given a reasonable playing strength, can easily fill their fixture lists. The cost of membership need be only a few shillings a year, as there is no ground upkeep, no rent, and no ground-staff wages. Add travelling expenses, which, of necessity, are higher than those of an ordinary club player who plays at least half his matches 'at home'; and then add a bit more for repairs to personal gear, and that is about all a 'wanderer' *need* pay for a season's cricket.

The better 'wandering' clubs have their own umpire, whom they may pay slightly more than the official rate. This is their one weekly commitment.

Apart from having no overheads, a great number of these clubs do not buy many new balls. At 36s. a time, this is a big item, and it has become a particularly sore point with ground-based clubs who, after all, have high expenses of their own.

Surely the least these wandering sides can offer is a new ball for each match? Most of the wanderers that play on the BBC ground make this gesture, but from other clubs I learn that this is the exception rather than the rule. The home side should not be put in the position of having even to suggest, let alone ask for, such a contribution to the cost of the game.

In the South, officialdom intervened in this matter in 1949, when the Club Cricket Conference made a request at their Annual General Meeting that wandering clubs should provide a new ball at most of their matches.

So far, so good. But, as I have pointed out, I shouldn't like to have to ask my visiting captain to produce a new ball, if it is not offered automatically.

The alternative? Let all other club cricket associations and other ruling bodies put the following motion to their A.G.M.s: 'The visiting side (wandering clubs only) shall produce a new ball before play begins.' I'd like to bet quite a lot of money that such a resolution would go through.

Too much officialdom? Perhaps. But who would quarrel with such a rule? Clubs that didn't like it could always resign. I'll have another bet here: they wouldn't. They depend too much on membership of the big 'Conferences' or similar organisations for their fixtures.

The new ball would add about 3s. a head to the cost of the game—and the goodwill that expenditure would buy as well would make it cheap at the price.

And that brings me to the delicate subject of the general expense of playing cricket as a 'wanderer'. If, to the contribution towards the ball, we add, say, 2s. for entertainment after the game, there remain the cost of meals and travelling expenses. Let us say £1 all in, for a week-end. Surely that is a moderate investment for two days' entertainment?

I have not forgotten the junior members either, and although 10s. is little more than pocket-money to present-day youngsters, if there is any difficulty, I feel the senior members of the club should regard its solution as their responsibility. That, indeed, applies to any club, not specifically to wandering sides.

As in all cricket teams playing away from home, it is a matter for agreement and settlement before the season begins. Don't leave it to sort itself out, as so many clubs do. Thrash it out and arrange something that will work before the first match is played. No club, wandering or otherwise, can afford to drop promising juniors just for the sake of a few shillings a week. More important, the game cannot afford to lose such players.

Here is a solution that appeals to me. In quite a number of clubs younger members get meals at half-price and pay a half-contribution towards the visitors' 'entertainment' kitty. Some clubs omit the latter contribution altogether.

By paying half the expense, these young members would feel that they are contributing something towards their cricket—a sense of responsibility that must be encouraged. (Too many of them these days have too great a tendency to regard sport—not to say life in general—as all 'take' and no 'put'.)

These matters *must* be sorted out during the close season. It is so short-sighted to wait until there are, perhaps, two outstanding young players in a club who cannot play regularly because they cannot afford it. And to improvise some sort of collection becomes too much like a weekly charity. It doesn't happen in all clubs. But when a committee does let things slide, the problem, sooner or later, becomes acute.

Here again the wandering clubs are at a disadvantage. They have no 'home'. For the majority, 'team-work' off the field con-sists of informal meetings held at infrequent and irregular intervals.

Don't misconstrue these criticisms. There are innumerable wandering clubs that are an asset to the game, and it is deplorable that so many reputable sides are classed with the 'play on the cheap' clubs, simply because they, too, are 'wanderers'.

Now read about some of the popular 'wanderers'.

I have always looked upon the *Stage Cricket Club* with great affection, not only because of the fine cricket they play, but because in the early days of my own BBC club the Stage did almost more than any other side to put us on our feet, often bringing a side down to our ground at Motspur Park at short notice. This is one of the wandering sides for whom I have the highest admiration, and against whom none of the accusations I have made of playing cricket 'on the cheap' could ever be levelled.

To my mind there have been, and still are, two outstanding personalities behind the Stage Cricket Club—the founder, W. Earle Grey, and Garry Marsh, the film star. Madly enthusiastic about cricket, Earle Grey used to get together scratch games with stray teams on hired pitches; in 1930, together with two other actors, Neil Porter and Abraham Sofaer (Sofi to his friends), he organised a permanent team and the Stage Cricket Club was launched. Often, Bill Grey would visit West End theatres while performances were on to get actors to turn out for him at the week-end. In this way he collected a number of notable club personalities. For instance, John Turnbull, now president, was the club's first captain. He handed over to Garry Marsh, who, with the exception of one or two seasons, has held office ever since. Other founder-members who still play regularly are three old friends of mine, Kenneth Buckley, Leonard Brett (with Television at Alexandra Palace), and Abraham Sofaer, the present hon. sec. In addition there are Huntly Gordon and Bernard Gordon.

How many clubs can boast of having had such celebrated actors playing for them as Rex Harrison, Donald Wolfit, Sir Laurence Olivier, Jack Hawkins, Jack and Roger Livesey, Trevor Howard, Robert Douglas, and Leo Genn?

Oliver Gordon, better known to a lot of cricketers as O. G. Battcock, the Bucks player, led the side in 1940, but that was the only cricket the Stage played until the end of the War.

Resurrected in 1946, the Stage C.C. has got back to a fixture-card of over forty well-known clubs. Perhaps an almost unique record is that of Mrs. May Buckley, mother of Kenneth Buckley, who has been official scorer for the club for over twenty years, as well as its treasurer. If a member turns up late, or transgresses in any other way, it has to be made right with Mrs. Buckley.

Garry and Sofi have probably told me more amusing cricket stories than any other two cricketers, and here is one I shall never forget. W. Earle Grey, who was a very dour kind of batsman, went in No. 9 in a match in which there had been a collapse. His doggedness seemed to inspire his partner, and spectators witnessed an hour's defence against fast bowling on a murderous wicket, during which time Bill was hit on every part of his body, and managed to score seven runs unintentionally. At this stage a few of his friends started barracking, which made him feel he should turn to aggression. Almost immediately he hit a turning ball on the off side slightly harder, and gave 'gully' an easy catch. Bill walked back to the pavilion with clenched teeth and thunder on his brow—he was bursting with self-condemnation. He strode into the dressing-room, threw his bat with disgust into his bag, and said scornfully: 'Weak! Weak! No concentration!'

I think the best story I have heard about Sofaer, who had been studying Ranji's book all the winter and advocated it—as only he could—with sonorous speech and thrustful dialogue, was during a match when Sofi had been waiting to bat No. 9. A battery of fast bowlers were playing havoc with the ribs and heads of the earlier Stage batsmen. Many received nasty knocks, but Sofi scorned their injuries saying that if they had only read Ranji's book they would know how to hook those off their faces and chests. Eventually, his turn came and he faced the onslaught. A short one reared up under his nose and Sofi stepped back smartly to hook. He missed the ball, which smote his elegant nose severely, and Sofi was assisted from the field covered with blood. At the pavilion gate he was heard to say in his loud, bell-like voice, 'Either His Highness was wrong, or I have misread his instructions!'

There are several good stories told about the old *Concert Artistes' Cricket Club* which was founded in the early 1920s and expired, like so many other wandering sides, only because of the War.

Some stars of the side, which played on Sundays only, were Jim Cutmore (Essex), Webster Booth, Robert Easton, and Fred Yule, and a feature of their matches was the concert they always gave in the pavilion after the game. This often caused the fixtures to be a little one-sided in the early years, as clubs always turned out at full strength because of the show in the evening!

Dennis Castle, who reminded me of the club, first played when he was fourteen years of age. When on school holidays, he used to field for the club, racing round like a ferret after the balls that went through legs nearer the wicket. One stout baritone, having let his eighth ball pass him to the boundary, yelled out to the skipper, 'Isn't it about my turn to have that boy over here?'

The club became quite strong in the middle 'thirties, beating sides like Barclays Bank, Malden Wanderers, and Catford Wanderers. Cecil Tinsley (Cyphers) and Robertson Deans, skipper of the Club for several seasons, were always prominent.

A character in the Concert Artistes' side was the late Frank Damer, a baritone. Once, when playing a London club, the C.A.A. were in the field and a chap walked to the wicket wearing a Harlequin cap. (Jardine had publicised the cap in Australia the year before, and the batsman wore it on this occasion with a swagger and air of confidence.) He took guard, had the screen moved, retook his guard, and glared round the field. The first ball shaved his off stump, and he made the worst of school-boy strokes at it—a sort of tentative prod towards gully. The second and third beat him all ends up, and each missed the stumps by the merest fraction. Then he connected with a desperate slice that chipped the end off his bat.

After delay, while he selected one of eight bats brought out to him by his team mates, he played out the rest of the over, giving a chance to gully, and surviving a very confident l.b.w. decision. At the end of the over he confidently readjusted his cap.

As they crossed over, Frank Damer said to the bowler, 'Must be Jardine's chauffeur, old man!'

Fred Yule, so often on the BBC, was an early member of the C.A.A. Dennis Castle was batting with him when he came in last against East Molesey on their picturesque riverside ground. L. McCanlis was bowling, and Fred, stout and staunch, made a lusty jab at a ball going away to slip and effected a magnificent late cut—in appearance. For some reason there was no third man and the ball sped away to the furthermost point on the ground towards the racecourse. The fielders did not chase it, as it looked to be a certain boundary. Here I must call upon Dennis to continue the story:

'Fred ran as fast as he could. Things became complicated as I found myself running alongside him and going the same way. This was amusing only until we realised that the crowd were shouting that the ball had stopped just short of the line. There was complete chaos in the middle. Fred turned and began to retrace his steps. I yelled for him to go on. He turned back and cannoned into me. By this time the ball had been retrieved and I could see the throw-in in the air. I yelled for Fred to go back and dashed into my ground. Fred came towards me and then began to totter back down the pitch. He was sixteen stone and quite speechless by this time. It was a race of man *versus* ball. Apparently Fred's eyes were dilated with terror at the thought of being run out, but he could only totter. Then, as the ball struck the wicket-keeper's gloves, Fred fell like a crashing boulder. His bat waved limply in the air, just a foot short of the crease. Came a huge groan—the last sound Fred could make.

'The wicket-keeper did not remove the bails. Firstly, laughter made it hard for him to do so, but secondly, the crowd were all against losing Fred so quickly. Fred was hauled to his feet, dusted down and stood at his crease. But his bolt had been shot. We had run seven according to the scorer, and that had taken all Fred's wind. The next ball he received shattered his wicket, and we got him back to the pavilion in easy stages!'

The bowler in that story was Laurence McCanlis, who died at the age of thirty-eight in December, 1949. He was the brother of K. McCanlis, whom I often meet as a first-class umpire when I play county cricket. Laurence was connected with the stage, and played rugger for London Scottish and London University Vandals. I remember him as a club cricketer and one of the founder members of *The Ducks*, another well-known wandering club.

For The Ducks, Laurence was quite tireless, both off the field, as secretary, and on, with his dazzling left-handed batting and brilliant fielding. His slow-medium bowling, too, was often very useful. It was McCanlis who first realised the talent of C. E. Winn—the Oxford Cricket Blue and English Rugger Trialist.

Kenneth played regularly for Surrey second XI from 1934–1936 as a fast bowler, and turned to umpiring in 1946. And what a success he has made of that exacting job! The McCanlis brothers also devised a new system of scoring, which has been tried out in nearly every cricketing country in the world. The main characteristic is that the batsman, in addition to having the number of runs scored put down against his name, also has the number of deliveries shown, so that a comparison can be worked out between balls received and runs scored.

The Ducks have a great reputation as trainers in tactics, and many members have enjoyed great success.

Founded in 1899, the *Early Birds Cricket Club* used to play early in the mornings in Battersea Park. When it got near breakfast time they would go back to their respective jobs, the game being completed the next morning. From these early beginnings the club naturally derived its name.

Before World War II, the Early Birds had their own ground at Paddington, where they had a large following, but like so many others, lost their ground as the result of hostilities.

F. Helyer, who has been a member for thirty years, is considered to be the 'backbone' of the club. For twenty-five years general secretary, he then became chairman. Skipper at present is Sidney Rutty, a fine forcing batsman, who scores many centuries for the club. Ronald Swanson, an extremely good fast bowler, has many excellent results to his credit, perhaps his best in recent years being his 8 wickets for 8 runs against Laleham C.C.

The Early Birds have Sir Raymond Evershed, now Master of the Rolls, as their president, T. Hinton as fixtures secretary, and R. R. Madgwick as treasurer.

Secretary Arthur C. Simpson told me this amusing story about one of the club's tours. Apparently the Birds usually join forces with another club. One year, to fulfil a certain fixture, some members travelled all night from Devon and met the rest of the side at the ground. The Early Birds' team batted first. At lunchtime down came the rain, which held up play for some time. An exceedingly good lunch was taken plus a few extra drinks! By 3.30 p.m., however, it was decided to carry on with the game.

Sidney Rutty, by that time in a very happy frame of mind, proceeded to score a fine century. When asked afterwards how he did it, he said he had to pick out the middle ball, and that every time it happened to be the correct one!

Whether they are of the feathered variety like 'The Early Birds' I don't know, but there should be something bird-like about *The Chinghoppers*. Their name rather implies it.

The club has been in existence since 1932. Well-known cricketing names turn out to play against some of the best opposition not only in London but throughout the southern counties. Opposition of the calibre of South Hampstead, Dover, Finchley, Winchmore Hill, Alexandra Park, the Mote, St. Lawrence, Canterbury, and Buckhurst Hill all appear on the fixture-card.

As far as the members are concerned, I have only to mention a few like Len Newman, Doug Insole (Cambs batsman and now the Essex skipper), Doug Newman (Len's son), Con Davies, who used to play for Warwickshire, Bertie Clarke (West Indian

Test player), Peter Smith, and Sonny Avery (Essex), to show just how strong a side they can turn out.

The Chinghoppers have a management committee to handle their affairs both on and off the field. F. G. Cheeswright is the life-chairman, while G. E. Kent does all the secretarial duties. L. S. H. Bayes, the treasurer, J. N. Putnam, J. Davis, and G. Downes are the other members of this committee.

Some of the rules are somewhat original. One, for instance, positively forbids the drinking of lemonade! Another: 'Any member failing to remember his roll number when challenged by a fellow-member, must buy his challenger a "strong" drink or pay a fine of 1s. to the club.' Yet another says: 'Personal excuses for batting, bowling, catching, and for fielding failures shall be subject to a fine of not less than 3d. at the discretion of the "Fines Committee"!'

The 'Fines Committee', incidentally, consists of three players appointed before each match. It can levy fines for not making a catch, or for being late at the start. An excellent idea, and one that many other clubs I know would do well to follow.

But no matter how successful 'Fines Committees' may be, you can't buy a ground if there is nothing suitable available.

L. W. Lowe, Secretary of the *Waverley (Kent) Club*, has told me how, although small in numbers, his club has struggled for survival as a wandering club.

Since World War II, he has had to beg, borrow, and all but steal to hire a ground. 'It is all so distressing,' he says, 'because you have only to walk round Dulwich on a Saturday or Sunday afternoon to see countless grounds not being used.'

Long before the War, the club was a church side called the St. James' C.C. After the war, on reformation, they found it difficult to carry on as a church side for lack of members. So, they reconstituted themselves as the Waverley C.C., became affiliated to the C.C.C., and tried, unsuccessfully, to get a ground. They had to fall back on park permits to enable them to play at all, only to find that they could have got permits more easily if they had remained 'St. James' C.C.'

In 1950, however, more members joined, including W. Bond, a 'natural' bat. Now, with Arthur Phebey (Kent) as its president, the club hopes to settle down at last.

Skipper E. Matthews is fortunate in having such a good fast

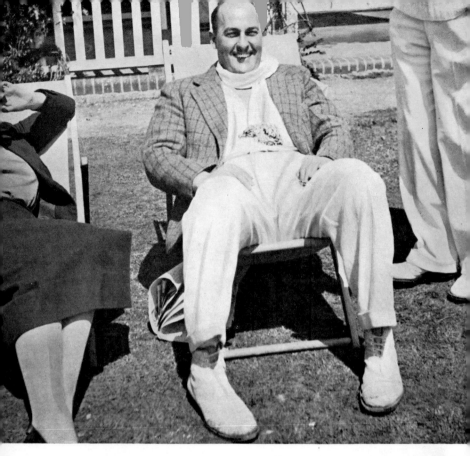

Garry Marsh, the genial captain and all-rounder of The Stage
Cricket Club

Maurice Begent
(Sevenoaks Vine)

R. Edwards
(Woodford Green)

Henry Malcolm (South Hampstead), generally recognised as perhaps the best all-rounder in the South of England

bowler as D. Matthews to support him. Vice-captain D. Lovett, until recently the chairman, is a sound player on whom the team depends a great deal.

Lowe told me about an incident when they were playing on a park pitch. During the game, a keeper came up to him and complained of 'casual betting'. This horrified Lowe, who couldn't understand what he was talking about, as the lads never had a bet on anything.

It was not until the argument was nearly over that anyone realised the keeper was a Devonshire man, with a broad accent. He had been complaining about 'casual batting'!

Lowe recalled another incident which occurred at one of their general meetings: he boldly announced that the next week-end game would have to be held on a Wednesday evening!

Good luck to Waverley and its members. I sincerely hope a ground comes their way in the near future.

Another club whose fortunes have been greatly affected by the War is *Langham Athletic Cricket Club*. Since 1939, this has been a wandering side, as its ground was requisitioned and has still to be released. J. C. Christen, the honorary secretary in 1940, had to rebuild his side under the great handicaps of having no ground and players' joining the forces, but with his enthusiasm and encouragement the youngsters held the club together throughout the War.

Although there is a total membership of 550 in the club, a mere twenty-five of these are active cricket members. But how they enjoy their cricket! During the War years they were travelling to play Dorking. They had just become affiliated to the Club Cricket Conference, and were playing against one of the Conference's oldest members, but Hitler and his bombers had no respect for the C.C.C. or cricket clubs, and I am told the team were heavily bombed both going and returning from the match!

A typical example of a 'permanent'-side-turned-wanderer is the *Hurlingham Oddfellows*. Its ground, in Poulter Park, Mitcham, once belonged to a stately home of England. From the 1920s to the outbreak of war, the ground had been hired by the Oddfellows from the Carshalton Council. The old mansion made a superb pavilion (except that it was 'dry'!). Then came the War, and the ground was lost. But the difficulties may be solved by using a square on the Hurlingham Polo Ground.

D. Kelly—one of the club's better known batsmen—always
seems to make a habit of getting out in the '90s'. At Lords, in a
wartime match, Alec Bedser dismissed Kelly for 98, when he
was playing for the London Fire Service against the R.A.F.

R. H. Crowe was in great form in 1945 and performed the
'double'. F. E. Hughes, an excellent fieldsman, took his 250th
catch in 1949.

Ronnie Rooke, the ex-Arsenal footballer, played regularly
for the club in 1947, and was always a great attraction, being a
big hitter and fine slip fielder.

R. Kingswell has been a stock bowler for years, taking 100
wickets season after season.

For such a small club—of its total membership of forty, only
thirty play cricket—Hurlingham Oddfellows have done very
well to maintain such a thriving state. F. E. Hughes has been
skipper of the first XI since 1935, and E. J. Lee, founder of
the club in 1900, has seldom failed to take the chair at Annual
General Meetings.

Hughes told me that, on the first day of the flying bombs, they
were playing a match against Tooting. A flying bomb appeared
and the local guns fired away at it so that shrapnel came down
like rain. They weathered that lot, but when, a little later, real
rain came, the players could not get to the pavilion fast enough!

It is not often that a game finishes by a bowler's taking the
last four wickets with successive balls, but this was achieved in a
game against Wembley by E. A. Strange, the club's fast bowler.

In another match against Shepherd's Bush the scores were
level, but the Bush had four wickets in hand. Again, the Oddfellows dismissed the last four batsmen for the addition of no more
runs! Some bowling!

Almost a next-door neighbour of ours at Motspur Park, is the
Raynes Park Cricket Club, which was formed as St. Matthew's C.C
in 1920 by a group of ex-servicemen from World War I, all
residents of Raynes Park.

One of the officials, George Whiting, despite injury to a leg in
a motor-cycle accident, has been a popular choice as captain
since 1928. While Raynes Park—the name was not adopted until
1933—prefers to keep only club records rather than make a song
about individuals, it takes pride in two outstanding performances
in 1949.

Eric Pollard, a left-arm spinner of immaculate length, took 119 wickets in 21 matches only—a magnificent performance, remembering the bone-hard wickets and the fact that he played so few games. H. C. (Joe) Whiting, opening batsman for years, and until recently club secretary, scored 125 when he and Dennis Richardson (66 not out) put on 187 for the fourth wicket against Devas C.C. at Mitcham. Joe Whiting also featured with his brother, R. J. (Roll), in the previous record stand of 175, some nineteen years back.

Playing the staff of a mental hospital, Raynes Park batsmen were faring rather badly, to the obvious disgust of the inmates watching the play. One patient gave vent to his feelings by yelling loudly enough for all to hear, 'Worst adjectival team we've seen here for years!' Fortunately Raynes Park retrieved the position later, but as Whiting comments, 'There's nothing like candour.'

Another small wandering club is the *Australia House* side. With a mere twenty-one members now, this popular pre-War team is struggling desperately to regain its former strong position.

Membership is confined to Australians resident in England and persons employed in this country in the Commonwealth Government offices. Each week, the team consists of at least eight or nine Australians, so they can justifiably claim that they are the only Australian side in the Club Cricket Conference.

The cricket caps they wear are of the Australian style and the blazers are similar to those of the Australian touring sides. The badge has been copied from the Australian coat of arms, with a red London dagger and the Southern Cross on a blue background.

It is to C. Twelftree and Val Stivens, on the public relations staff of the Australian Government, that I am indebted for augmenting my notes on club cricket in Australia.

Remember George Clark, who was a regular member of the London Counties XI during the War? Now he is the mainstay of the *Carmelite Club*, a small business-house team formed in 1946. Like other 'new' sides, it has been unable to find a ground, but has over fifty members. Clark played for Arsenal footballer Joe Hulme, when he captained the South of England *versus* North of England on the Old Trafford wicket just before the end of the War.

Few clubs have had a more varied career than the *Lauderdale*

Cricket Club. They began in Victoria Park, Hackney, in 1890, and competed in the local cup competition. They won it when it was run on league lines in 1894, and in 1897 obtained a private ground at Walthamstow, but returned to 'wandering' in 1900. They shared a ground from 1907 to 1914 with Pelham C.C. at Chingford, and thanks to the late Charles McGahey—then assistant secretary to Essex—played a few 1914–18 wartime games on the Leyton County Ground.

They had a second XI, too, from 1919 to 1927 and included tours of Kent, Sussex, Essex, Dorset, and Cornwall. Now, with one team since 1928, they are back to 'wandering'. Arthur Matthews, captain from 1929 to 1939, still holds the job, and is now chairman. Since the War, the club has found a number of useful players, including David Johns, an all-rounder, who now plays for High Wycombe and Bucks.

Three men to take all ten wickets are P. C. Sheen, for 20 *v.* Stock Exchange; C. A. Hurren, for 29 *v.* Anlaby, and H. Sherr, *v.* Ravensbourne. Hurren has been hon. sec. for over thirty years —first with the founder-secretary, the late Alfred Wren.

Andy Wilson, Gloucester's wicket-keeper, used to play regularly for Lauderdale. His comment one day is still a club legend. To a bowler he remarked, 'You've got your length; it's width that's the trouble!'

What more typical of this modern age than the *Lambeth Cricket Club?* It was founded in 1939 by the local Civil Defence Services, and members were given facilities for net practice by the Governors of Dulwich College. All early games were against teams from other defence areas and services. They shared Alleyn Old Boys' ground at Burbage Road, Dulwich, until the end of the War, and when Civil Defence was disbanded, it was decided to continue as a borough club.

First President was Alderman 'Bill' Lockyer, then Mayor of Lambeth and, appropriately, Chairman of the Civil Defence Emergency Committee. A link with the Oval was formed by Surrey's allowing the club to play one match there a year. This has become an annual fixture against Mitcham, and is attended by Lambeth's mayor, as club president.

F. C. Mansfield, the club secretary, who is also joint secretary of the Surrey Association of Cricket Clubs for the Dulwich area, rather shocked the Metropolitan Police one day. He hit a six through their pavilion window and put the next ball into the far corner, where it bounced on to the bowling green and hit the jack. Jack-pot?

Lambeth, incidentally, relies a lot on all-rounders C. Green and W. J. McIntyre, Green having had quite remarkable success. Still without a ground, the club plays a few matches on Ellerbank ground, Dulwich, by arrangement with the Johnson Matthey Sports Club.

Now to the *Caterpillars Club*, which has an interesting history. Although shown as being formed in 1927, there is no doubt that the club was preceded in the early 1920s by a side called the Athenians. Towards the end of 1926, at the Annual General Meeting, members were so late in turning up that the secretary likened them to caterpillars. The name stuck, and the Athenians went out of existence.

The sole life-member of the club is Charles H. Lush—secretary from 1941 to 1945. Since then, secretarial duties have been shouldered by Douglas Gray, who before joining the Caterpillars was one of Elmers End's bowlers. Against Wallington, he just missed 'all ten', as Wallington had already lost one wicket before he went on to bowl. He finished with 9 for 28 runs.

Doug Short, skipper since 1936 and a useful all-rounder, couldn't tell me enough about Gray's excellent work for the club. He said: 'Gray is one of the most efficient fellows I've ever met. The fine position in which the club finds itself today, is mainly owing to his untiring and unselfish work. His enthusiastic spirit infuses itself into all the members.'

How rare it is to find a club extolling the virtues of its secretary—and how refreshing!

The old Warwickshire player, A. S. Goodwin, is now chairman, scorer, and critic. Frank Shore, a dour Yorkshireman, is treasurer, and R. L. Downing team secretary and umpire.

Doug Short's vice-captain is H. T. Richards, a sound opening bat and excellent wicket-keeper. He is a master at St. Clement Dane School. In the first two weeks of the 1949 season he scored two centuries (119 *versus* Addiscombe, and 104 *versus* Standard Telephones).

Leslie Hammond is a more than useful all-rounder, being an excellent bat and a brilliant fielder. His century knock against Rickmansworth in 1949 has been acknowledged as one of the

finest seen on the 'Ricky' ground. I remember Hammond's
having C.C.C. trials in 1948 and 1950, when he batted and fielded
well. He shares the club record wicket stand with H. T. Richards,
and in 1950 headed the averages for the third year in succession.

Among those who excel with the ball are Geoff Summer-
hayes, Haydn Buttle, and Jack Searby.

In a keen match against Mill Hill Park, in 1948, Doug Short
went in to bat after the Caterpillars had lost two or three wickets
fairly cheaply. Len Turner bowled to Short, who promptly drove
him hard through the covers for three runs. Before the first run
had been completed, the wicket-keeper appealed for 'hit wicket'.
Both umpires said 'not out', as they hadn't seen what happened,
so Doug ran on to a useful '50'. In spite of his effort, the Caterpillars lost by one run off the last ball of the day!

Another wandering side for whom I have the highest admiration is the *West Indies*, comprising, as it does, West Indians resident
in and around London. They have built up a fine fixture-list and
play some of the leading clubs.

Naturally, with such personalities as Learie Constantine,
C. B. Clarke, Allan Rae, Ken Ablack, Ernest Eytle, Harold
Fraser, Frank Worrell, and Everton Weekes to make the opposition, clubs are always anxious to see the West Indians on their
grounds. It often happens, therefore, that the 'lesser lights'
cannot command a place in the West Indian side. Dennis Long,
of the Welfare Department of the British Council, mindful of the
position, wrote to a number of London clubs asking whether they
would allow West Indians, who normally don't get a chance of
playing, to become members of their clubs.

The response, I am delighted to say, was most favourable,
and I heartily commend these clubs for their friendly and sporting
gesture. It is a grand boost for club cricket—and it's more of this
spirit we want in cricket today.

Here is another example of a club's coming into existence
through the war. The *Putney Eccentrics Cricket Club* was formed in
1943, by a group of club cricketers in Civil Defence, when their
own club had closed down. L. V. Francis, their skipper and
secretary, told me that now, because of the happy atmosphere,
they find they can't disband, so the club continues 'madder and
merrier' than ever. But it is still compelled to wander.

High Court Judge Sir James D. Cassels is president, with A. Norman Rogers as vice-president.

Francis depends to a very large extent on J. P. Brown, the Private Banks medium-pace bowler, who played for Northumberland before the War. He always plays for the Eccentrics on Sundays. Besides being their star bowler, he also scores a lot of runs.

C. S. Lees, another all-rounder, joined the club on demobilisation and used to get the 'double' regularly, but now, unfortunately, has left the district. E. T. Askey is another attractive opening bat.

K. P. Emmett—now twenty-two years of age—is a 'home-bred' product. In 1949, for the first time, he scored over 1,000 runs, and gives promise of improving for many years to come. He is also a useful bowler.

A. J. Middlemass bowls slow leg-breaks and is a solid opening bat. L. C. Preece is a fast-medium bowler and aggressive bat. S. Bartlett—another stylish and forcing bat—is also a medium-pace bowler. Francis, the wicket-keeper, describes himself as 'indifferent', but I feel certain that's quite untrue.

K. C. Hope, like Brown, is another Private Banks Saturday player. He is a stylish opening bat, who scores a lot of runs.

Also in this team of all-rounders are F. G. McNeil, B. E. Coggins, P. Chappell, a Bancroft boy, J. H. Raine, who is a useful left-hand bat, and two other Private Banks players, J. P. Merredew and fast bowler M. J. Glitz.

I asked Francis about any interesting or amusing incidents that have befallen the club. He laughingly replied, 'Mostly unprintable, old man!'

The club's motto is *Messis Nostra In Herba Est*, which means 'Our Harvest is in the Blade'. May the Putney Eccentrics reap an excellent harvest for years to come, and may they soon find a ground of their own.

Chapter Three

CLUBS AND THEIR PLAYERS

Histories, outstanding players, and anecdotes of the clubs in Middlesex.

TO be confronted by the words 'Police Station', when you are about to enter a cricket ground is, to say the least, disconcerting, but that's the notice you see when you go to play against *Alexandra Park Cricket Club*.

The ground is in the middle of Alexandra Park Racecourse. On race days, the police often have to round up some of the unruly element. They then take them back to the A.P. pavilion, which is used as an improvised police station for the day.

Originally, the ground belonged to the Great Northern Railway, but was taken over when the latter moved to Gordon Hill.

The present president, E. A. Cawdron, founded the club in 1888, and was its first captain. Since those days, there have been only two other skippers—S. W. Brent and Len Newman. Club cricket, and Alexandra Park in particular, owes a very great debt of gratitude to Len Newman. I have known Len for many years. In every sense of the word, he has been, and still is, at sixty years of age, the complete cricketer. As a club batsman, he may never be surpassed. As a man, he is one of the most cheery people one could wish to meet. Another good friend of mine, and outstanding Alexandra Park player, is Con Davies. Together, these two have probably broken more club cricket records than any other two players. For instance, up to and including 1949, they had scored over 100 runs together for the first wicket more than 70 times and still hold A.P.'s first-wicket record by scoring 272 against South Hampstead in 1943.

Len himself has scored 245 centuries, including 12 double centuries since 1910. He has made the highest number of runs ever made by a club cricketer in one season—4,138, which, I believe, is a world record. In seasons 1934–36 inclusive, he scored 10,807 runs.

Con Davies, a colleague of mine on the Council of the C.C.C., has scored over 44,000 runs in all cricket, and has taken over

3,500 wickets. In 1943, against Cheshunt, he scored 107 runs and then took all 10 wickets for only 14 runs.

Con was a partner of Len Newman's when the latter, batting against Turnham Green, hit a ball from the square on to the steps of the Chiswick Empire. A rare feat! Con bowls left-hand spinners, but bats right-handedly. He used to play for Warwickshire.

Len's son, Doug Newman, has begun to emulate his famous father. He has a delightfully free style and is quick-footed. He got his Middlesex II cap in 1948, and played for the County first XI against Glamorgan. Doug got his C.C.C. cap in 1946. With his father as partner, he holds several batting records.

Having three such outstanding personalities in one club might tend to overshadow other members, but not so A.P.

H. T. Smith is one of their stock bowlers, who, in 1949, waited until August before bowling his first full toss that year! D. Solomons, a right-hand bat and excellent bowler, has strengthened the side since 1948. M. Penney is a good bat and has kept going since before the War. Incidentally, he is a fine artist, having had several paintings accepted for hanging in the Royal Academy.

Elliott Marten, skipper of the third XI, maintains that his is the finest side in the club, so great is his enthusiasm for his players.

A.P. run a colts side. J. E. Dyer, a slow leg-spinner, was sent to the club by the *Evening News* coaching scheme. He is in good hands.

In one match, Len Newman (with 96 to his credit) struck a ball firmly on the off side, the bat flew out of his hand and felled mid-on like an ox. Everyone crowded round the injured fieldsman and helped him off the ground. No one saw where the ball went.

Some ten minutes later, the game was resumed. The ball was missing—obviously a 'four' in view of the crack Len gave it. The umpire was loath to signal a boundary as he hadn't seen it cross the line, but he finally gave Len the four runs, which also gave him his century. Len says it was the longest time on record—some twenty minutes—between the stroke and the runs' being credited to give a batsman his 'ton'.

While on the subject of records, let us turn to the *Cockfosters Cricket Club*, one of the oldest-established North London clubs.

It has only recently lost the services, through retirement, of its famous slow spin bowler, R. A. Clarke. Most club cricketers will have heard of Clarke. He has probably taken more wickets than any other bowler in club cricket: since 1919, over 4,000, including five in an innings on more than 400 occasions. His most successful season was in 1934, when he dismissed 386 batsmen. Before 1937, he claimed his victims in Kent, but then moved to Cockfosters and joined the local club. At the club's annual dinner in October, 1949, he was presented with the ball, suitably mounted, with which he obtained his 4,000th wicket.

What I would have given to have had in my side Len Newman, to get the runs, and R. A. Clarke, to bowl them out, when they were both at the height of their careers!

It was John Walker, oldest of seven cricketing brothers, who levelled the ground opposite the old Weld Chapel and founded the *Southgate Cricket Club* in 1855. Six Walkers represented the 'Gentlemen', so it was hardly surprising that the family club quickly achieved eminence. The brothers were active players from 1855 to 1877, during which time the club played 192 matches, won 133, and lost only 27!

V. E. Walker, first Southgate president, was president of the M.C.C. and Middlesex, and captained England and the 'Gentlemen'. The brothers were intimately concerned with the founding of the Middlesex C.C.C. in 1864.

The club became a public one in 1873, and the ground, now known as the Walker ground, was placed in trust for the club by R. D. Walker in 1906.

Since the Walkers, Southgate has had many prominent players, of whom perhaps F. T. Mann (Middlesex), T. N. Pearce (former Essex skipper), and S. H. Saville (Middlesex), the great cover-point and England hockey captain, are representative.

The present side is a strong one. Five matches are played at week-ends and there is a flourishing junior section. During the War the club played Hornsey, a rival since 1872, at Lord's.

The skipper is F. C. (Cyril) Hawker, who has been in office since 1941. He used to play for the Old Citizens. Still a very good bat, Cyril is a first-class skipper, and chairman of the committee.

To help him on the official side is Secretary M. S. Glennie, who is a very useful wicket-keeper and batsman. Alan Fairbairn, the Middlesex player, played regularly for Southgate in 1947, when he made a startling *début* in county cricket by scoring centuries in each of his first two appearances.

G. J. Fish, captain, 1939–40, and joint captain with Cyril Hawker in 1941, is a compact left-handed bat, who delights in the straight drive. Before the last War, Fish played badminton for England.

W. R. Burton, secretary until 1948, has held office in some capacity or other since 1937. Like the late Eugene White, he has rendered unique service both to Southgate Cricket Club and to cricket generally.

S. C. Silkin, who was at Dulwich College in my day and did well at Cambridge, joined the club, but has now been forced to give up the game because of a shoulder injury.

J. F. H. Tyler, T. Crabtree, and D. G. Roper get a lot of the runs, and T. J. D. Walker (captain of Cambridge in 1944), W. R. Burton, the Rev. G. H. K. Sherlock (Devon), J. W. MacMahon (one season only before joining Surrey), and Dr. R. A. Shaddick (Middlesex) have been bowling out the opposition.

Among the all-rounders are H. Wass (Scotland), J. M. Broadley (Army and Kent II), and P. E. Bodkin (captain of Cambridge in 1946).

Tall G. A. (Tony) Turner, who has played rugby for the Saracens, had some bad luck in 1948 and 1949. First of all, he was knocked out when keeping wicket early in the season and had to go to hospital, and then he had muscular trouble, which kept him out of the game. Then, in the winter, he had double pneumonia and spent many, many weeks getting fit again. He was captain for several years, and a very free scorer.

A Southgate boy, J. M. Phillips, who played for the Northern Schools at Lord's, and captained the Young Amateurs of Middle-sex, is a batsman of whom the club thinks very highly.

At a charity match played at Southgate at the end of the War, between selected members of North London clubs, umpire Fred Canham (Southgate), the two batsmen, J. F. H. Tyler and F. C. Hawker (both of Southgate), and the two bowlers, P. Blackwell (Winchmore Hill) and Con Davies (Alexandra Park), all wore glasses and were in the game at the same moment.

And there was gentle rain falling at the time!

Another strong side in the same locality is the *Finchley Club*, established in 1860. It played on two other grounds before settling at its present 'Moat ground' in 1903. At that time, it had difficulty in raising two Saturday teams for forty-eight matches per season. Now it has over 130 fixtures.

The club was closed during the First World War, when L.D.V.s trained on the ground—and the cricket pitch. It was not until about 1921 that the 'table' really recovered, under the expert hands of groundsman Walter Watts.

High spot of the club was in the early 'twenties, when it was captained by the Middlesex player, Eric Martin. He was killed in a flying accident in 1924.

Then followed a very successful period under the captaincy of Tom Birkin, when men such as H. E. Carris, D. F. Surfleet, F. Allen, J. A. Nelson, P. J. M. Nelson, the Bishop brothers, D. Eves, C. F. Harvey (the present hon. sec.), W. B. Walton, J. Smith, B. Neville, and C. E. Butcher were playing for the club.

There was no stopping Finchley in World War II. They played throughout, owing chiefly to the enthusiasm of Percy Hind and Birkin. They have made a name for themselves by their 'discoveries', the most successful of whom, so far, has been Ian Bedford, the Middlesex spin bowler. In 1948, they 'found' R. Burville, a soldier, who bowled for the C.C.C. in August of that year, and 'Pip' Sawyer, another useful pace bowler.

Other personalities include my old pals, 'Josh' Levy, a fine all-rounder, Vic Bromage—both well-known as Stoics players—Frank Hobbs, who has borne the brunt of the batting for a number of years, M. Gobey, J. Norrish, R. M. Davidson, and Geoff Davidson, the cheery 'cover-point'.

Jack Vaughan (Middlesex II) is a very good No. 1 or No. 3; Jack Winchester, wicket-keeper, is also a useful left-hand bat, and Farrow and David Pike are both steady and reliable bowlers.

Not connected directly with the Finchley Club, but with several members in common and playing in the same part of London, is the *Old Finchleians Club*, which, with other sporting and social sections, has a total membership of 600. But the cricket section has only forty-five players to draw on for its week-end games.

Until 1945, the club, established as long ago as 1904, was a wandering side. Then the present ground at Southover, Woodside

Park, London, was purchased. The necessary funds were raised entirely by the members, who then set about building their own pavilion, and a fine job they made of it. In all, a notable achievement, owing mainly to the foresight and untiring efforts of the general club secretary, Reg J. Mander.

Since the resumption of cricket after the War, the club skipper has been H. W. Baker. His keenness and enthusiasm have attracted support, and to aid him there is Geoffrey M. Whaite, an opening bat and wicket-keeper. He amasses a pile of runs season by season.

F. C. J. Parkes, the present honorary cricket secretary, told me of an 'away' match on the ground of Richings Park C.C. J. C. Wells, a hard-hitting batsman, had the distinction of hitting two sixes off successive balls in the same over—one over each sight-screen! Now work that one out!

Not more than a mile away from Woodside Park are the clubs in the 'Crouch End' group.

First, there is one originally known as the Holborn Cricket Club: the *North Middlesex Club*, founded by John C. Caulfield in 1875. H. B. Kimpton and Arthur Jennings were the only other founder members.

The first ground used by the club was Page's, at Tufnell Park, where it remained until April, 1894. It then moved to Nightingale Lane, Hornsey, but in 1902 the present ground in Park Road, Hornsey, was taken over and with the change of headquarters came the change in name.

The present captain of the club, and the captain of the first XI and officer in charge of promoting and coaching the Colts XI, is K. C. P. Gunson. E. C. Tyler, skipper of the fourth XI, also shares the job of general secretary with T. Mundy. George Clarke is cricket secretary.

Perhaps the outstanding player of recent years has been K. Taylor, who, when a member of the club, was signed on by Warwickshire, and played for the county until the end of 1949.

Quite a number of members have made a name for themselves in circles beyond club cricket. It was while playing for North Middlesex that G. Burton, the old Middlesex slow bowler, first caught the experts' eye. E. T. Vieusseux and F. Henry have also played in the Middlesex XI, as have H. E. Pearce and S. G. Etheridge. C. V. Jenkinson played several times for Essex, as wicket-keeper.

Although many members have scored over a thousand runs in one season, in 1911 a record was created for the club when both C. W. Morrison and H. S. Morris performed this feat, and J. W. Dann took 100 wickets. In 1942, P. Attoe got the cricketers' double.

I was most interested to hear from George Veglio about the Colts' section, which was formed in 1948 by Ken Grierson. It has been a great success, and several promising youngsters have been discovered.

The ground was taken over during the War by a barrage-balloon unit, and there still remain the embedded concrete pillars, though they are now covered by grass. However, a lofted ball on one occasion was seen to fall on top of one of these now hidden concrete patches and bounce to a height of over twelve feet. The opponents apparently took a great deal of convincing that North Middlesex had not supplied a rather peculiar ball.

Years ago, when suffragettes were 'in form', as it were, their activities included the burning down of the pavilion. When the new pavilion was erected, the club took one of the charred bats and had it enclosed in a glass case with the words, 'Lest We Forget'.

Time has healed the wound, and ladies now form a large part of the Saturday crowd.

Though somewhat smaller than North Middlesex, the *Calthorpe Club*, sporting the blue colours of Oxford and Cambridge, goes back to 1874.

Honorary Secretary W. Morley told me that, although in its seventy-fifth year, they had a bar for the first time in 1949, and credit must go to non-playing member W. Lush for the work on this important installation.

Morley explains that, although private, the ground is called the Crouch End Playing Fields, which often gives strangers the wrong impression.

V. Saunders is the star batsman, having scored several centuries in 1949, and more often than not he manages to top the thousand before the season ends. F. Lafosse is the best bowler. He took 124 wickets in 1949, and in fourteen seasons has secured 100 wickets on ten occasions. Not many bowlers can claim to have been so consistent and successful.

After fifteen years with the club, G. Hollis left for Australia in

January, 1950. His loss has been felt by every member, but G. Thrift and J. Ford, originally score-boys, are now playing well, and will continue to improve.

J. Mitchell, though 't.t.' himself, will stand a 'round' with all, and no one expects him to depart from his rule of drinking only lemonade!

R. Fernie is the chairman, and S. Brewster is still playing, at over sixty years of age. Brewster helped to keep the club going after the War, and has been responsible for a great deal of the work done on the ground.

R. Rennie is the club secretary and is a fairly new member. Manual assistance from H. Harrison and W. Morley—to mention but two of the hard workers—has enlarged the cricket field at a cost of well over £100, which has been raised from social functions organised by Rennie—who, by the way, is only a tennis member of the club!

I asked Morley to tell me some interesting incident about the club. He thought for some time, then said: 'The only one I can think of isn't so funny, really. The pavilion was burnt down in 1945—after surviving the bombing—and all through a guy named Guy Fawkes!' He thought again, and added, 'Pym once took three wickets with the first three balls of the match, if that's any use?'

Useful enough, I should say!

President of the *North London Club* is Bert Goulding, who serves on the C.C.C. Council. He has been a member for thirty-five years, and in 1938 was elected president of the Club Cricket Conference.

The club, which is a strong one, was founded in 1877, under the name of the Old Holloway Collegians, by W. Roston Bourke, Headmaster of Holloway College. Originally at Tufnell Park, North London moved to its present ground in 1882, and changed to its present name in 1883.

A. R. Bourke, son of the founder, is now one of the vice-presidents.

A coincidence that doesn't often happen was the playing of three 'ties' in 1949. They were all played on their 'home' ground (known locally as the 'Shepherd's Cot') and within three weeks of each other—on August 1, *versus* Wembley; on August 13, *versus* Harrow Town, and the next day, against Ealing.

C. D. Catchpole has been a well-known all-rounder in North London for some time, and has been a member of the club since 1920. Then there is Jack Wells, with whom I have played a lot of representative C.C.C. cricket. He has been club skipper for some time. Supporting him, he has Joe Laurenzi, who took all ten wickets against Woodside Park in 1943, and C.C.C. Trial players K. Margree and G. Woods.

The honorary secretary is C. M. Powell, and match secretary, K. Margree.

The club has a story about a match during the 1947 'Week'. Playing for Frank Whitehead's XI, Len Newman and his son, Doug, put on 228 runs for the first wicket (Len, 103, and Doug, 109)—a record father-and-son partnership. Frank Whitehead's XI declared at 256 for 6 wickets, but North London won with 258 for 1 wicket on the board! (L. R. Battell 130 not out, and S. E. Machray 68 not out.) The most interesting part about the father-son partnership is that a previous record of 189 was made by Frank Whitehead himself and his son, when playing for Highgate Cricket Club!

R. A. Harkness has been president since the beginning, and has played a big part in helping to establish the Hendon Buccaneers, formed as recently as 1948.

C. M. Oliver has been honorary secretary all the time and has done a herculean job getting things going.

The club plays on a public ground in Sunny Hill Park, Hendon, which is hired by schools and clubs from the Hendon Borough Council.

J. A. Bass, who headed the batting averages in 1948 and 1949, has already made his mark. He is also the club's wicket-keeper. E. H. Mapes took 111 wickets in 1949.

A. R. Legg, the skipper, is a bowler who has consistent successes. In 1949, he took 114 wickets.

One of the best known and established clubs in N.W. London is the *South Hampstead C.C.*

Since 1875, when known as 'The Crescent Cricket Club' with its ground in Regent's Park, until the present day, there have been few clubs with more history and tradition behind them than this one. For ten years, South Hampstead's men played for 'The Crescent', but in 1885 they moved to Primrose Hill, Hampstead —the old Eton and Middlesex ground. Then, for a time, the club lost its ground and became a 'wanderer', using a ground in Walm Lane, Cricklewood, for practice.

In 1896 came another change, this time to a ground in St. Quintin's Avenue, North Kensington. Four years later, the present ground at Brondesbury Park was leased. Despite these moves the club took its pavilion with it every time!

Of the many notable club personalities, perhaps T. Y. Sherwell—a past president—is outstanding. Sherwell's son was P. W. Sherwell, who captained South Africa.

The club has 300 or so members and can count about half that number in the cricket section. Of these, about fifty are active playing members. A different story from that after the First World War, when membership dropped to three or four, but one side was kept going for fear that if the club did collapse it might never rise again.

Many attempts to turn the ground over to allotments or building have been frustrated, thanks to the general keenness of members to play their part in the running of the club. Several bombs and shells have left their marks, but today the club is stronger than ever before.

Last of the founder-members, H. W. Brooman—'the Guv'nor' —died in 1949. At one time or other he held the offices of president and secretary, and in his younger days was a great player. His sons W. P., Hubert (present chairman), and F. R. played for the club with distinction.

C. Pinkham—'Charles'—son of Sir Charles Pinkham, is the present president. He is a triple Blue, and was the finest of captains. 'Charlie', now a bowls player, was one of the best medium-pace bowlers in club cricket. Jack Tigg is the general secretary. Also on the executive side are the Rayners and the Watkins family.

Of the playing personalities I must first of all say something about H. J. J. Malcolm, present captain. Henry, or 'the Master' as he is sometimes known, is perhaps the best all-round player in London club cricket today. As a batsman, he is superb, possessing all the essential qualities so necessary to get out of the 'mediocre' class. I have seen him play many fine innings—perhaps one of his best being his century against the New Zealanders at Guildford in 1949. As a bowler he is first class; as a fielder, brilliant. One of Henry's pets is the South Hampstead coaching scheme. With other selected players, he passes the game on to youngsters from neighbouring schools.

D

Henry's two brothers, Doug and Allan, both help to keep the South Hampstead flag flying. Doug was captain of the Wasps rugby club, and at cricket, like Henry, is an all-rounder. So is Allan, but he has now moved from the district.

'Nosh' Robertson, the vice-captain, is yet another all-rounder in this extremely strong team. 'Horse' Woodbridge, a county hockey player, probably hits the ball as hard as anyone playing. H. L. (Herbert) Wallach, a past skipper, although the oldest playing member, still turns out regularly. Freddie Wallach is still a fine wicket-keeper.

Maurice Ferrara, born in the West Indies, is an accurate medium off-spin bowler, with a model run-up. Bill Western is a forcing bat, and also a very good fielder.

A past player and real character, Charlie Higgins, was one of the best new-ball bowlers in club cricket, but he was often not satisfied with his form, whereon his favourite comment was, 'I'm bowling like a dead horse!'

This story is told about the present president, C. Pinkham. He was so disgusted at the opposition's refusal to go for the runs in a match, that he took off his boots and bowled lobs in stockinged feet!

In a match against Middleton, while the club was on tour, a Middleton bowler delivered a ball to Henry Malcolm. In mid-air the ball suddenly swerved sharply away. It had hit a swallow in flight, and the bird fell dead on the pitch! It is in the Middleton pavilion today.

And now for one or two Middlesex clubs 'down by the river'.

First, the *Lensbury and Britannic House Club*, with its interesting history. The Lensbury Club was purchased originally for the staff of the Royal Dutch Shell Group of Oil Companies, and was opened in June, 1920.

Britannic House was originally bought for the staff of the Anglo-Iranian Oil Company and its associated Companies.

Although operating as one club, each has its own ground. The Lensbury ground is spacious and well situated at Teddington, while Britannic House's ground is at Lower Sydenham.

Secretary A. J. Hutchinson tells me that L. R. Ollis, the skipper from 1939 to 1947, and his successor, A. R. O. Bairnsom, have had the services of three former C.C.C. players, and of Pat

Dickinson, who scored a century in a 'Varsity match. Dickinson is now abroad, and his loss is felt very considerably.

The three C.C.C. caps are D. H. Richards, D. G. Henley, and A. K. Stacey. Richards is an excellent all-rounder, who in 1947 and 1948 failed by only a few runs to get his 'thousand', and took a lot of wickets. Henley, in 1949, captured 114 wickets at low cost; in 1950 he played for the C.C.C. Stacey gets more than his share of wickets year by year.

E. W. Burgess is responsible for the excellence of the club's fixture list.

Another riverside ground—in Duke's Meadows, Chiswick—belongs to the *Ibis Club*.

I have always had a very great interest in this club because a cousin of mine, Joe Burford, was the club's chief seam bowler for years before he settled in South Africa, where he goes on playing good cricket.

Ibis members are all on the staff of the Prudential Assurance Company. Ibis cricket goes back to 1860 and a public pitch in Battersea Park. In 1870 came its 'official' foundation, and then the club led a migratory existence, changing grounds almost yearly until 1882, when it came into possession of a ground in Dulwich, now used by Alleyn's Old Boys. In 1903, the club moved to Penge, and in 1939 to Chiswick.

The club was one of the pioneers of business-house cricket and its players have done many noteworthy things in the cricket world. Perhaps the two outstanding records are the huge total of 467 for 5 wickets declared, and the two double centuries by Ernest Dewey, who, until recently, was the deputy chairman of the company. This astronomical score, incidentally, followed a few weeks after the lowest—10, against Merton.

Against the Hawks, in 1896, Dewey scored 224, and followed this knock by 213 against Newlands Park two years later. In more modern times C. G. Cooper produced a record by taking all 10 wickets in 1933 against Private Banks, who were baffled by his leg-breaks.

The club entertained Sheffield Wednesday C.C. on its first appearance in London in 1901, and in 1903 'W. G.' brought his London County side to open the Penge ground. In 1936, the Ibis was the only private club to entertain the Canadian tourists.

Arthur Bartlett, the present honorary secretary and treasurer, told me about an Ibis bowler who took 9 wickets for 2 runs and performed the hat-trick on *one* batsman. First ball—caught off a no-ball; second delivery—bowled, also off a no-ball; third ball—bowled. The batsman agreed he had met his match!

A story told by the club against itself occurred in a match against the Cyphers. The latter were 11 runs short of victory at the beginning of the last over. Off the second ball the batsmen ran 4 runs, and in attempting a fifth run were presented with 4 overthrows. The fifth ball was driven hard back to the bowler, who deflected it on to the wicket, with the backer-up well out of his crease. The bowler's umpire was unsighted and the square-leg umpire was not looking. When the excitement had died down it was discovered that the ball had crossed the boundary, giving the Cyphers victory.

The mainstays of the club immediately before the War were C. G. Izzard, Hubert Cath, a prolific scorer who was the president of The Wanderers in 1949 and 1950, and Eric Dewey, a fellow Old Alleynian, who did very well at school before graduating to club cricket. In the post-War years, the main burden at the wickets has been borne by A. S. Goldsmith, the first XI captain, and S. W. D'eath. Gerry Rogers, honorary secretary for many years, was succeeded by a young veteran, George Clinton, who continued playing in a junior eleven up to the age of sixty-three, although carrying seventeen stone!

Like so many other business-house sides, the Ibis now runs four Saturday teams, and has, on occasion, turned out as many as eight.

The club has only recently got back its requisitioned ground, and is installed again in its pavilion—much to my delight, as on Boat Race days I am permitted to watch the race from there!

The *Sunbury Club's* ground is a private one, and provides a link between rugby football and cricket, as the club rents its ground from the London Irish Rugby F.C.

There is always an annual cricket match between the club and 'The Irish'. Sunbury usually wins, but by 'closing time' the Irishmen have done their best to convince Sunbury that it was very lucky!

The ground was originally used by another side affiliated to the C.C.C.—the Old Hamptonians. Strangely enough, many of Sunbury's founder members were Old Hamptonians themselves.

G. M. Kaye has been secretary since 1940 and for most of the War years was treasurer as well. The brunt of club work has been done by two playing members, who are also very useful performers. P. Sugg is the man who raises the money the club needs; A. Crook, the Walton and Hersham footballer, is the club handyman.

When the club used to play on the local recreation ground, Crook built a pavilion, which was promptly offered by the local Council to all and sundry, with the result that Sunbury left, taking their pavilion with them! The wood from the pavilion was then utilised to build two sight-screens and seating for spectators.

Jack Davies, former Harlequin rugger player, played for the club from 1938, when it was formed, until he left for Salford in 1947. He was skipper for three seasons, and an excellent all-rounder, usually taking 100 wickets every season. Top bat is Bob Schaffer.

John Smith, who joined the club in 1940, when he was fifteen, was the mainstay of the attack. In 1948 and 1949 he took more than a hundred wickets. Treasurer of the club is C. H. Simpkins, and the present captain is S. A. (Sam) Wood.

In 1946, during a Sussex tour, the club 'lost' three of its members, including Jack Davies. They were found in the middle of a bowling green discussing whether they should get the stumps out of the club bag and have a bit of practice. This happened to be on the green where the South of England championships were to be played the next day! They were hurriedly restored to the proper fold before any damage was done, but it was a narrow squeak.

Farther West, but still by the river, we come to Shepperton, where the *Sheppertonians* established their club in 1943.

In spite of its late arrival on the club-cricket scene, it can already boast of 102 members, which is a very good start for any club.

A. L. Curry, the secretary, has had a great deal to do in getting his club firmly settled, and is doing it very well.

Away from the river, and between Uxbridge and Rickmansworth, is one of the most enthusiastic clubs in Middlesex. The *Harefield Cricket Club* know and play real club cricket, in every sense of the word.

In a number of ways, the BBC is closely associated with the club. I myself had the honour to be made their first honorary vice-president; John Arlott and Andrew Timothy, the announcer, share the distinction. Then my good friend, Wilfrid Goatman, who works for the BBC's Overseas Service, is vice-chairman of the club, and a number of BBC cricketers have played both for as well as against it.

About 1810, in the reign of George III, when an act was passed for the enclosure of all common, moor, and waste land, John Trumper was appointed at Harefield to allot the land. His award is dated December 24, 1813. In his dispositions, Trumper set apart a piece of four acres for a cricket ground, so that we can say cricket has been played in this Middlesex village for 140 years.

Dick Wiles is the present chairman: with the aid of his wife —her sudden death in 1950 was a grievous blow to Harefield cricketers—Dick did a great deal to keep the club active during the War years.

The ground, as we now know it, was part of the estate of a local 'big house', which was bequeathed in the 'thirties by its owner to his two gardeners (who, incidentally, were brothers).

One of them, Walter Wood, a fervent cricketer and stalwart of the side, conveyed the land to the National Playing Fields Association (and, incidentally, prevented the driving of a main road across it) on condition that it was to be used by Harefield Cricket Club only, so long as the club existed.

N. K. W. (Jimmy) Wheatley, by his enthusiasm and hard work, has done a lot to keep the club together as skipper. Wilfrid Ward, an old-timer, has greatly assisted the youngsters, and some of the 'oldsters', to play cricket, and undoubtedly put the club's star all-rounder, Tommy Evans, on the right road.

Tommy, who is also the honorary secretary, scored over 1,000 runs and took 129 wickets in 1950. In 1949 he played for me against the Old Millhillians in a match during their Cricket Week, and bowled extremely well. Ron Owen is another very useful all-rounder.

Syd Knife, club treasurer, made 43 in twelve minutes in 1940 against Rickmansworth. 'Ricky' had batted first and were dismissed for 43 runs in the first innings, and when Syd went in to bat Harefield had 6 wickets down for only 12 runs!

In 1948 Bill Squires, another vigorous batsman, beat Syd's record by making 54 in ten minutes.

Not far from Harefield is *Pinner*, where the club, although only credited with an inception date of 1837, hold records showing that the first match played was in 1789, when Pinner beat Rickmansworth by 1 wicket. Since 1837, the club has played continuously on its present ground.

A. Vincent-Kemp, a former secretary, is now president, and is a very keen follower of all matches. Secretary is A. A. Weatherley.

Do you remember the Roncoroni brothers? Joe and Tony, both excellent all-rounders, used to play for the club and were also well-known on the rugger field. J. A. Massey, a captain of Pinner, has also played for Middlesex. E. C. R. Hopkins is a first-class bat and fielder. E. K. Cornes, who won the M.C. during the War, was captain 1947–48. He then went to South Africa, but returned to England in 1950 and is again playing for Pinner. While abroad he managed to play some cricket, although, he says, it was rather 'primitive'.

Pinner looks back on 1945 with pride. In that year it played an Australian Air Force XI consisting of several players appearing regularly at Lord's. It was a wet day, and Pinner, batting first, managed to get 110. During the tea interval the sun came out, the wicket got a little difficult, and the Australians were dismissed for 68!

Monty Garland-Wells always takes a side down on the Friday of the Pinner 'Week'. It is a good wind-up to an excellent week's cricket, as on the Sunday the Stage usually visits them. This match has been described by Weatherly as 'a carnival event of excellent entertainment'.

The Harrow area has always been rich in clubs and cricketers. The Sheriffs brothers have had a lot to do with the continued success of the *Harrow Town Club*.

Martin Sheriffs has been skipper since 1931, except for the War years, when his brother, Ian, carried on. Cricket was played every season—despite the N.F.S.'s taking over the pavilion, and the absence of a groundsman.

Originally named Harrow Derelicts, the club took over its present ground in 1921, and at the same time changed its name. Two members who helped to get the club going in its early days were the two Grants—George, now dead, and Jimmy, who is still playing.

Best known bowlers in those days were Basil Shaw and Ossie Potts.

Present players include Terry Carter, from Rickmansworth, Jim Donaldson, from Bessborough, and Bill Wignall, the Sunday XI captain, ex-Lord's ground staff, and now coach at Merchant Taylor's School. His experience is a big asset.

Top match in Harrow Town history is 329 for 3 wickets against Richmond Town in 1934—on a Whit Monday.

With younger members coming along in promising fashion, there seems every chance of improving even further their standard of play. The club has made a lot of progress in recent years, and David Lee, the match secretary, has been able to add top clubs to the fixtures. President of the club is Sir Cyril Norwood, a former headmaster of Harrow School, and the secretary is S. W. Allen.

The second club in this area is the *Harrow Club* itself, which, in 1948, held its Diamond Jubilee, celebrating with a redecorated pavilion, new flower-beds, a detailed score-board with rotating drums, and its own flag.

Harrow members owe a lot to F. J. Payne, E. H. Helliar, G. Cox, H. Weait, W. L. Genders, J. Butler, and E. Harrison, who kept the club going by running 'wandering' sides during the War. A. E. Fowler, who for twenty years was an active member, has been president for just over forty years.

Harrow now has two Saturday and two Sunday sides, and plays a few mid-week games. One, for instance, in June, 1927, was memorable. Playing Amersham, Harrow made 403 for 4 wickets in 140 minutes! W. C. Hands (149), W. W. Griggs (101), and G. W. Wood (101 not out) were mainly responsible for this big hitting. Amersham was all out for 140, in 110 minutes. H. J. Mayes took 6 for 53 runs for Harrow. C. G. Reeman, now an honorary life member, and D. R. Macdonald, now vice-president, both played in that game.

Present playing members include G. B. Thomson, who is skipper and gets a lot of runs as well; E. H. Helliar, who was top of the batting averages in 1947; and F. J. Payne, the vice-captain. Payne is an off-spin bowler and a more than useful bat.

The third club in the Harrow district, where there are no fewer than eight clubs affiliated to the C.C.C., is the *Harrow St. Mary's Club*.

Formed in 1901, the club played on a private ground, which was later handed over to the Harrow Urban District Council on trust, but the club retains right of management.

Now, with fifty playing members, skipper A. A. Adams has quite a pool from which to draw for his two Saturday teams. These include D. C. Wright, a good all-rounder, and G. Foster, whose batting is one of the mainstays of the club. He and G. Tomlins score a lot of runs. P. W. Abbott is seldom left out of the side.

Secretary and treasurer, W. H. Oram, and the chairman, S. W. Barnes, are both founder-members of the club.

Also in the Harrow district is the *Kodak Cricket Club*. The wicket-keeper of the Sussex County XI, Rupert Webb, is a product of Kodak's junior team. He secured rapid promotion and became their first XI wicket-keeper in 1938. Then his excellent work attracted professional attention, and he went to Sussex.

Webb is not the only Kodak player to gain high honours in the game. John Kohl, fast medium left-arm bowler—for many years their outstanding player—was an automatic choice for league representative honours before the War. His fine performance in a recent 'Smailes Benefit Match', against the full Yorkshire XI, called forth extremely favourable comment from the leading batsmen.

The club, established in 1908, plays its cricket on a delightful 20-acre ground adjoining the factory at Harrow View. It has been in use since 1930, and also has two fine bowling greens, numerous tennis courts, and a pavilion and tea-garden.

Skipper is F. W. Killick, who has Jack Coe as vice-captain. Fred Killick has looked after the side for many years. Jack Coe ('Pudsey' to his pals) comes from Yorkshire, and brought down from the North a characteristic dourness and tactical ability. He is an excellent batsman, and took Rupert Webb's place behind the sticks when Webb left for Sussex.

'Buckie' Harris, the chairman, has guided and shaped the policy of the club for the past twenty years. He does not play now, but, Fred Killick tells me: 'At each successive Annual General Meeting the "Old Rascal" goes through the happy farce of vacating the chair, to be immediately re-elected. When his wicked past eventually catches up with him, it will be an unfortunate day for Kodak cricket.'

Which is yet another proof that officials of any club can do a great deal to promote harmony and enthusiasm, and to bind a club together, by their active interest in the players. How I wish that sort of thing were more general in club cricket.

Len Dolding, another product of the junior XI, is a right-arm spin bowler and brilliant field. He, too, attracted professional attention, and is now on the Lord's ground staff.

Bill Winterbottom joined the Company from Harrow County School, and had a meteoric rise through the junior XI to the first XI. In 1940, he was second in both batting and bowling averages—his first year in senior cricket! He looked like being yet another Kodak player to join the professionals, but he lost his life in 1944 while serving with the Fleet Air Arm. His aggressive fast bowling and stylish batting are still spoken of with pride.

On May 8, 1942, Kodak entertained the Royal Australian Air Force in their first fixture in this country. The Australians had several State players in their side.

The club sponsors a departmental cricket competition in which as many as twenty-five teams compete on a sectional league basis, with the section leaders playing off for the championship. No wonder they're so keen!

Three miles north of Harrow, at Honeypot Lane, Stanmore, is the *North-Western Polytechnic* ground.

A. J. Pond, their secretary, told me that they are not allowed to take any members who are not students or ex-students of the N.-W. Poly, but they can include evening-class students. Every member has to play a fair share of games irrespective of his playing ability. This often has a singular effect on the teams turned out. In 1949, for instance, they had a Nigerian student who had never played cricket before in his life. Now he has become quite enthusiastic about the game.

Reg Hoy, now retired through ill-health, was secretary from 1936 until 1947. He helped to keep the club going throughout the War years. Captain of the club for a season or two during the War was the late Syd Greenaway. A great sportsman and player, he died at Rottingdean in 1948.

A. G. Hoath was the club's most consistent bowler. He is a

'quickie', and in 1945 took 155 wickets. In 1949, he failed by only 2 wickets to secure his '100'. He is a good fielder, and a more than average batsman. He has now joined the L.M.S. Club. Skipper of the side at present is W. Roberts.

The Parochial Board of the Ecclesiastical Commissioners, who hold the freehold of the ground, insist that no Sunday games shall start in the morning and that there shall be no licensed bar on the ground.

Pond told me a story against himself. When fielding in the slips, the ball occasionally rattles off his tin leg. He says the expression of the batsman's face is usually quite remarkable!

Wembley is another London suburb with several cricket clubs. *Wembley Vale Club* has no fewer than four other Wembley teams around it. It was originally called the 'Sudbury Vale Cricket Club', but although it still plays at Vale Farm, it has now assumed the name of Wembley Vale.

L. Relf, their secretary, tells me that E. Cox is their star bowler, having taken more than 100 wickets every year since 1947. In 1949, for instance, he totalled 155. C. J. Dowson is also a magnificent bowler. He, too, has 100 wickets yearly to his credit.

I asked the *Wembley Park* secretary, H. A. Jeffery, to tell me why his small club of only twenty-one playing members did so well. He said: 'Playing as we do, purely for enjoyment, everything is directed with the sole aim of creating and maintaining a successful and happy club. The ability to accept a doubtful decision with no sign of irritation is, in our opinion, as great an achievement as a century or a hat-trick.' L. W. Byerley, as skipper, has had a lot to do with this approach to the game.

One of their wicket-keepers, however, who shall remain nameless, always regarded a cricket match not so much as a game, but rather as a verbal contest. When a batsman approached the wicket, he was greeted in a most encouraging manner, but hope was expressed that his stay would not be too lengthy. The excellent quality of the bowling was usually commented on before the batsman took his first ball. In full hearing of the batsman, first slip would be questioned as to whether he thought: 'John would be bowling his next over as terrifyingly fast as in previous weeks, as he was black and blue from trying to stop his expresses!'

During one match a particular batsman had been subjected

to the full range of the 'keeper's extensive repertoire, and was soon out, bowled. On his way back to the pavilion, as he passed one of the umpires, he was heard to remark that he had been 'talked out'.

A few weeks later, in the return match, the same batsman came in. On taking up his stance our wicket-keeper made an agreeable remark about the weather. Without further ado the batsman swung round to square-leg and in a plaintive voice said, 'Umpire, he's talking again.'

There can't be many clubs in and around London that use their grounds solely for cricket, as *Ealing* does. Many of the finest cricketers in the country have played on the Corfton Road ground: a lovely oasis in a completely built-up area.

The present treasurer, my old friend, Eddie Ingram, needs no introduction to club cricketers. He has been 'spinning 'em' for years, for the Gentlemen of Ireland, Middlesex, the C.C.C., and other well-known clubs.

Secret of Ingram's continued successes has been his beautifully-controlled flight, immaculate length, and change of pace. Often I have been batting against him and thought to myself, 'Eddie isn't bowling so well today,' when up comes an over that stumps me completely.

'Tommy' Thompson is another 'character' in the club. He was skipper until 1950, when F. G. Bull took over. Thompson is still a very fine medium-pace bowler. In his day, he was as quick as most, and got hundreds of wickets with his hostile deliveries.

C. V. G. (Bob) Haines, who used to play for Glamorgan, and Bob Felton, who now leads Brentham, were regular playing members until the War.

Nowadays, the club relies upon such batsmen as W. F. Price, J. E. de W. Denning, G. H. Phillpot, C. R. Matthews, and A. N. Denning for their runs, while it is left to bowlers J. E. de W. Denning, J. Warr, A. F. Taylor, G. H. Phillpot, and Eddie Ingram to dismiss the opposition. In 1949 Ealing had the distinction of Warr's bowling to Brian Boobyer, another member, in the University match at Lord's. As a Middlesex player, Warr toured Australia with the M.C.C. in 1950–51.

One of Ealing's next-door neighbours is the *Shepherd's Bush Club*, which has bowls and tennis sections as well.

However, with fifty to sixty cricketers out of a total membership of 350, the cricket club doesn't do too badly.

Shepherd's Bush first went to its private ground in East Acton Lane—the property of the Goldsmiths' Company—in 1884, the club having been founded two years earlier. Originally, the ground was so small that when a boundary was hit the batsmen changed ends and only three runs were scored! Their first pavilion was built in 1909, but on the enlargement of the ground in 1935, a handsome new brick pavilion was erected.

In 1944, however, a bomb fell just off 'the square', burnt down the old pavilion, and damaged the new one. The Great Western Railway came to the club's rescue and allowed 'home' fixtures to be played on their ground until the Shepherd's Bush ground was restored.

C. T. Burgess, president of the club, is one of the best all-rounders the club has ever had. A brilliant bat, deadly fast-medium bowler, and very safe catch, Charlie first played for the 'Bush' in 1910 and became skipper in 1913. So strong was the 'Bush' batting that year that, in August, H. M. Lemoine, the English amateur international goalkeeper and Hertfordshire wicket-keeper, and D. E. Lewis presented Burgess with a photo of themselves inscribed, 'Nos. 10 and 11, by kind permission of Capt. C. T. Burgess.' Lewis was a slow bowler of immaculate length.

To come more up to date: on the batting strength was S. L. Beton, who for twenty years never failed to get his 'thousand', and played for Middlesex, and Jack Rowley, a splendid 'opener' and most polished bat, both of whom have now retired. P. H. Whyman and D. Capps are leading post-War scorers, with '1,000s' to their credit each season. R. G. Hulbert is a quick-scoring and consistent left-hander, as well as being an acrobatic fielder at short leg, and J. L. Thorne is a steady bat who always seems to get his runs against the 'big names'. For instance, he played a fine not-out innings against the M.C.C. in 1949. D. W. Boatfield is an aggressive bat, and J. Douglas has kept wicket consistently for many seasons.

Then their all-rounders: first and foremost, the skipper— J. Carter—a slow left-hand bowler and hard-hitting bat. For twenty years he has taken 200 wickets regularly, and several times completed the 'double'; R. A. Talbot, originally a fast bowler, was badly wounded in the War, and now spins 'em.

He was told he would have to finish with cricket, but refused to believe it. J. F. Hall, a fast bowler, is also a hard-hitting bat and splendid fielder. For several years, he played for the London Australians.

Early in the thirties, the 'Bush' narrowly won a most exciting but low-scoring match against Slough. It was low-scoring because of Frank Edwards, the Slough and Bucks left-handed bowler, and W. C. Caesar, fast medium for the 'Bush'. Both sides batted twice before time was called. When the 'Bush' batted for the second time, W. J. Munday, going in with 8 wickets down, hit a 4 and doubled the 'Bush' total!

James Payne, who umpired with the club for thirty years, hated frivolous appeals. A new member was put on to bowl at Payne's end, and every time the ball hit the batsman on the leg there was a roar of, 'How's that?' Payne stood it for some time, and was then heard by mid-off, on another appeal, to say, 'Not out, sir, and gentlemen of the Shepherd's Bush Cricket Club do not appeal for things like that!'

A personal performance of which the club is proud occurred in the early thirties. Playing against Finchley, Leslie Bond, a fast bowler, took 6 wickets with successive balls—five clean bowled and the last l.b.w., the batsman being given out by his own father!

Rootes Cricket Club is another in East Acton Lane. More correctly they should be called *Rootes Social and Athletic Club (London Division)*. Their ground is part of the Goldsmiths' East Acton Estate, and how delightfully countrified it looks, too.

In the whole club there are some 2,000 members. Of these, only about thirty play week-end cricket, but more than 100 take part in the inter-house or departmental matches which Rootes arrange among themselves.

Joint-president is Sir Reginald C. Rootes, a keen cricketer who frequently takes part in executive games and invites teams from the organisation to play at his country residence near Maidstone. Chairman of the club is W. M. Rae, who played a lot of cricket in the Midlands in his younger days. He has been associated with the club for many years.

The club began in 1936. First secretary was E. Dewis, who still holds that office, and although over fifty years of age, still enjoys an occasional game. Scorer is the meticulous F. G. Edwards.

Of the players, W. French holds a unique position as he is the only founder-member playing regularly. He has been skipper and vice-skipper of the club, as well as being one of the main-stays in batting and bowling. In 1949, he got over 1,000 runs and took 73 wickets. T. Newlove is one of the most promising youngsters in the team. He was top of the batting averages in 1949 and 1950. G. How took 112 wickets and headed the 1950 bowling averages.

Since 1947, J. Austin has been captain. He has played a lot of good cricket and is a good medium-pace bowler.

Jack Durston, former England and Middlesex player, has an indoor cricket school at Acton, where I have practised on several occasions. He is keenly interested in the Rootes XI, and has given a bat for the best performance each season. It was won in 1949 by R. Breedon, whose consistent bowling was rewarded by 118 wickets, and in 1950 by J. Harman.

The club doesn't go on tour, but has home and away games with associated Rootes clubs at Coventry, Maidstone, Canterbury, etc., and at holiday times attractive matches are always arranged. One of the popular visiting teams is the Ealing Studios side, which usually includes a film personality.

I wonder which Rootes player it was who got married recently? In the dressing-room soon afterwards he was full of the advantages gained through marriage, one of which was that his wife packed his cricket-bag. Comments and observations were unprintable when it was discovered she had forgotten to put in his cricket boots!

Opposite the 'Myllet Arms' on Western Avenue is a sports ground of which many clubs must be envious. It is the home of the *Ealing Dean Club*, now owned and leased from Ealing Borough Council.

Established as long ago as 1846, the club has played through without a break. Among the original founder-members was the famous Tom Hearne, who subsequently played for Middlesex and went to Australia with the first touring side.

Ealing Dean was originally that part of Ealing now known as West Ealing, and the club previously played on Ealing Common, at the back of 'The Green Man', now the site of the Ealing Magistrates' Court.

Early photographs show that players in those days played on

coloured shirts and beaver top-hats. The last game played on 'The Green Man' ground was against an England XI.

In 1947, the club played and *beat* the Middlesex County XI in a match arranged for Jim Sims' benefit. The previous season the club celebrated its centenary and received a special souvenir from the M.C.C. in recognition of its services to cricket.

Total membership of the club today is 275, of whom eighty play cricket as regular members. Since 1934, the club has been fortunate in having C. A. Browne as chairman. L. E. Goble has been honorary secretary since 1940. Skipper since 1940 has been A. P. Pearce.

Large numbers of runs are scored by Ealing Dean regularly— thanks to Pearce himself, Ron Raggett, and George Perham, all of whom I have had the pleasure of entertaining on the BBC ground.

The club's real all-rounder is George Clements, the former Casual-Corinthian footballer and F.A. amateur international. He knocks 'em down, and then proceeds to knock 'em up.

Allan Brazier, who has represented Surrey on several occasions and who broke the Surrey II's aggregate record in 1949, is, and has been, a Dean member for a long time, giving great service to the club before joining the staff at the Oval.

During the 1947 tour, the team was returning from the Dover ground to its Hastings headquarters when the brakes of the coach failed and it careered down a hill out of control. The driver managed to steer it up an incline at the bottom, but being unable to hold the vehicle, it ran back and crashed into a shop window. Fortunately, the players escaped with only a shaking. That sounds like a lively tour!

And now one from the 'home' ground. On two occasions during matches a stoat has invaded the pitch. After chasing the animal away there have usually been several 'ducks' among the subsequent batsmen!

Based in the West Ealing area is the *Great Western Railway Club*, formed way back in 1869, at Green Man Lane. It moved to its present ground at Castle Bar Park in 1900. In 1950, the club celebrated its jubilee.

In pre-War days a 'Week' and tour were always arranged, but these annual events were not revived until 1950, when the club team crossed the water to visit Dublin and district. So here is another club almost back on the pre-1939 path again. To guide it as captain, it has E. A. McDonald.

Before the War, this club was in the top rank of London club cricket, with two well-known players in J. J. Green and C. E. G. Honeyball. It was captained by W. R. S. Morris for some fourteen successful seasons, for most of which he was also chairman. He was succeeded as chairman by George Sturman, a member of the C.C.C. Council for twenty years, and captain of the club's second XI for thirteen years. The present chairman is F. J. Allen, who succeeded G. Sturman last year.

The club's most outstanding player since the War has been R. G. Broadbent, a fine all-rounder who scored over 2,000 runs and took 130 wickets in 1949. In that year he played several games for Middlesex XI, and has now become a Worcester County player.

The secretary is J. B. Morris, fixture secretary is J. C. F. Swallow, and W. R. S. Morris and G. Sturman are still available to give advice to the committee.

The *Polytechnic Cricket Club* has had an interesting history. Under the name of 'Hanover United' (changed to 'Polytechnic' in 1888), the club was started in 1873.

Most of the early matches were played on the public playing-fields of Regent's Park. In 1881, Quintin Hogg, who had then taken over the captaincy, provided the club with its first private ground at Barnes ('The Limes'). Here, members enjoyed playing on a good wicket.

It was in the same year that J. E. K. Studd (Middlesex and Cambridge), C.C.C. president in 1921 and M.C.C. president in 1930, took over from Hogg. Later, J. E. K. became Sir Kynaston.

In 1895, the club had to vacate 'The Limes', which was bought for building purposes, but again Quintin Hogg came to the rescue and secured a ground at Merton Hall, Wimbledon. Then finally, on May 19, 1906, came the club's last move, this time to Chiswick.

George Ogilvie ('Pa') who was secretary and skipper in 1875, died in 1946, while still one of the club's officers. A score-board has been erected in his memory. His son, Percy, was club captain from 1920 to 1934.

Up to 1949, F. L. J. Dolman, a colleague of mine on the Council of the C.C.C. and deputy chairman, was captain of the

E

club. Arthur Bruce is a splendid bat who can keep wicket, field anywhere, and is more than a useful bowler. He scored 900 runs in 1949.

Then there is Pat Bunyan, a left-hand batsman and brilliant cover-point, and another of those who played for London Australians during the War. In 1946, Bunyan played for the C.C.C.

Polytechnic's fast bowler, Albert Cook, took four wickets in four balls *versus* Wembley in 1949. Vic Batchelor bagged 100 wickets in 1947, while all-rounder G. Williams, now captain, took 100 wickets in 1949, and scored nearly 900 runs.

Tommy Futrille has been secretary since 1936, a job which he carries out with enthusiasm. A. C. Lallyette, or 'Lally' as he is known, took over secretarial duties during the War when Futrille was away. Indeed, it was 'Lally' and a few others who kept the club going. 'Poly', by the way, have turned out eleven teams in one day, and regularly field seven.

In 1936 a club called the Chiswick Conservative Imps was formed. This flourished until the War, during which little or no cricket was played.

Immediately afterwards the club was renamed 'The Chiswick Pirates', but even that name was not to last for long. In 1950, when the *Chiswick Cricket Club* ceased to exist, the Chiswick Pirates took their name.

Skipper V. Maynard has behind him such players as A. Morgan, all-rounder G. Burgess, H. Monitz, and D. Streeter. E. Newman was secretary from 1938 until 1949, when he handed over the administration of this fifty-player club to J. Allen. Chiswick play their cricket at Chiswick Homefields Recreation Ground.

No mention of Chiswick would be complete without reference to the club that once played opposite the Chiswick Empire—the *Turnham Green Club*, now at home in Chiswick House grounds.

Since the club was formed in 1853, many famous players have been members and have played on the historic green, from the 'square' of which, it must seem to the casual onlooker, a gentle tap would send the ball straight into the 'Empire'.

In recent years, the best-known Turnham Green players to reach the highest honours have been Patsy Hendren and Jack Robertson.

Originally known as 'Turnham Green Albion' C.C., it later changed its name to the Turnham Green Devonshire C.C., under the presidency of the Duke of Devonshire. In 1882, Turnham Green Colts C.C. came into existence. Two years later the 'Colts' was dropped.

First president was the Middlesex County player, G. H. Jupp, and other noted players were Dr. C. M. Tuke, W. Williams, and George Spillman, all of whom played for Middlesex, as did the Rev. Webber.

L. Pickering, now honorary treasurer and club captain, is interesting when he compares expenditure in 1896 with that of 1949. Total expenses for the club in 1896 was £29 15s. 1d., of which £7 5s. was spent on cricket gear. Recently, total expenses were £550, of which £103 was spent on repairs and equipment!

George Ball and Denis Hendren (Patsy's brother) made their first appearance in 1900. The former, having given the club years of valuable service, is still a keen supporter. Denis Hendren joined the Lord's ground staff five years later.

Coming further up to date, Jack R. Robertson, the Middlesex player's father, is still a very sound opening bat and turns out regularly. Pickering, the other opening bat, never fails to top the '1,000', and D. Marchant, who scores a lot of runs, is one of the club's most stylish batsmen.

S. Sibley and H. Coombe make many runs, and the latter hit the highest individual score—144 against Haywards Heath.

A. Dewey and H. Ventham are bowlers who are always high in the averages. J. Franklin and P. Labbett (bowling), and R. Axworthy, E. Hazell, and R. Walker(batting) are all club 'regulars'.

My contacts with the *Hounslow Cricket Club* are through A. J. Spong, for a long time skipper of the first XI, and 1950 chairman of the C.C.C., and Peter Westerman, one of the club's fast bowlers, who has played many times for Surrey and the C.C.C.

It was Spong who recalled that the club, founded in 1868, has had three club captains whose service totals fifty-seven years. F. Rouse, a founder-member, held office from 1868 to 1888; H. Jackson from 1899 to 1919, and Spong himself from 1934 until 1949. Now H. T. O. Smith, the famous Essex fast bowler, has taken over.

Members of the club who have played on various county grounds are Maurice Read, Harry Jackson, the Rev. Burrows, E. A. Beldham, E. G. Hayes, H. T. O. Smith, Col. H. R. White, and Peter Westerman himself. C.C.C. 'caps' have been won by H. T. O. Smith, C. S. F. Smith, C. K. S. Smith (three brothers), J. G. Heaslip, who also played for the Gentlemen of Ireland and skippered the Civil Service representative XI, A. McLaren, and Peter Westerman.

Every year, under the supervision of the entertainments secretary, Arthur Newman, a cricket 'do' is put on in the pavilion. The stage is rigged up, a play written and acted, and the whole show is put on by the cricket members. The plays, I need hardly say, are always related to cricket.

It was while playing for Essex against Middlesex at Lord's that H. T. O. Smith took three wickets with four balls, breaking a stump in bowling R. W. V. Robins (the Middlesex skipper). In another game, this time for the club against Dulwich Hamlet, who included Laurie Fishlock (Surrey), Smith, in taking 6 for 30 runs, broke four stumps!

Before the War, in a match against Barnet Wanderers, Hounslow declared at 240 for 9 wickets (S. Muntz, 101). When Barnet's fifth wicket fell—Len Newman (Alexandra Park) was fifth out for 143—they were only 7 runs behind with ten minutes to go. A wicket fell to each of the first two balls of the next over and four runs were scored off the remainder. With only one over to go and 3 wickets still standing, 4 runs were needed to win. A run was scored off each of the first three balls of the last over. An attempted run off the fourth ball resulted in a run-out, then H. T. O. Smith took a wicket with each of his last two deliveries. Result—a tie!

In June, 1941, Hounslow played Ealing, at Ealing. After the game had been in progress a short time a Hounslow batsman complained that the pitch was short. A chain was brought out and the pitch found to be only 20 yards. It transpired that all the Ealing wickets had been 2 yards short since the beginning of the season, as the first wicket had been measured out at 20 yards by the chain and the rest marked off the same length! A Hounslow batsman said afterwards: 'I knew the pitch was short. I could see the whites of Tommy's [L. B. Thompson] eyes as he came up to bowl!'

I wonder how many clubs have started with no ground, very little money, but a lot of enthusiasm? *A.E.L.* is one, and to-day, members have a lasting and well-founded organisation.

In 1931, a few employees who were cricket-mad saw the possibilities of starting a club. Year by year, from this modest beginning, A.E.L. added more and more fixtures. Two years after its promising start, A.E.L. thought of acquiring its own ground and pavilion. The spot chosen was at Sutton Minor, in a very pleasant setting near Colnbrook—originally part of a seven-acre poultry farm owned by the chairman of the club, G. B. Fox.

One of the first matches to be played on the new ground was between a Bucks Farmers' XI and the club. It was a great success. In 1936, however, the club had to give up this ground as Chairman Fox gave up his poultry farm. The next site was a field near the laboratory premises. Stout hearts, Admiralty permission, and a small rent got the ground going.

A feature of activities in those days was the lunch-time inter-departmental matches, which often dragged out for three weeks or so, as only half an hour per day could be devoted to the game.

The club has had three Rear-Admirals as presidents—Rear-Admiral the Hon. D. C. Maxwell, Rear-Admiral D. J. Hoare, Rear-Admiral W. G. Cowland. The secretary has usually been the groundsman as well as a playing member, but he has always had great help from other keen volunteers. E. Marsden was the first of the line.

One of the new players in a Colts' match asked the umpire for guard.

'What do you want?' asked the umpire.

'Three legs, please!' replied the Colt.

'You can't have three legs,' retorted the umpire.

'All right, then, give me mid-off,' replied the nervous bats-man!

D. Neighbour, present captain, is one of three brothers. 'L. E.' is the spearhead of the A.E.L. attack, and already has a hat-trick of 100 wickets per season marked up in the club's records. The third brother, Colin, is the club scorer.

J. S. Gardner is vice-captain, R. Mackey, secretary, and the chairman still is G. B. Fox. Fox is very modest about the part he has played, but the club tells me that without him they wouldn't have lasted very long.

Pre-War, five *C.A.V.* club teams were fielded each week-end, but now only two can be raised. A. J. Nevin, the general secretary, told me why: it seems that most of the recognised players retired from the club when the ground was requisitioned, as they refused to play on indifferent public pitches.

Perhaps that is why J. A. Oatway can truly be called the outstanding personality, for besides being a member since 1937, he has been cricket secretary since 1948, was skipper in 1949, and is usually in the first three of the bowling averages. He has remained with the club in an endeavour to see it through its lean period, and still turns out regularly, doing much to encourage the youth of the works to play good cricket.

Before 1947, C.A.V.'s private ground was at Old Oak Road, East Acton. This ground formerly belonged to the Paddenswick C.C., and was used by the club as long ago as 1912. In 1947, however, it was requisitioned for housing, the C.C.C. being unable to do anything to help them. However, there is every hope that, by 1952, the club will be installed at its new ground at Northolt.

Jim Sims was a member of the club before joining the Middlesex side, and is a life member.

Many charity matches were played on the ground against Jack Durston's XI. Most of the Middlesex players took part in them, and in one game, in September, 1938, Joe Hulme and Jim Sims both scored centuries.

Founded in 1896, the *U.C.S. Old Boys' Cricket Club* is the second oldest old boys' club in the country to run a regular side. It ran without a break until World War I. In those days, always two and sometimes three sides were turned out regularly. After 1918, the club was re-formed and now plays in the top grade of London club cricket.

Famous among former U.C.S. Old Boys (old boys of University College School) was G. T. S. Stevens, who played in the England side that regained the Ashes in 1926. From South Africa came M. J. Susskind, who also turned out regularly.

Strangely enough, U.C.S. has never produced a galaxy of international cricketers like other old boys' sides, but the club holds a highly esteemed position in club cricket. Such players as E. S. Westhorpe and A. H. K. Burt—before World War I, without equal as a pair of bowlers—L. Allen, a splendid all-rounder, and J. C. Taylor, an extremely accurate medium-pace bowler, have all been outstanding.

Another present-day personality is a Cambridge Blue, B. M. W. Trapnell, who played for the Gentlemen at Lord's in 1947. E. B. Glanfield, who has been a regular member for more than forty years, is still going strong, and at one time or the other has held every executive post in the club.

The two Allen brothers play a prominent part in U.C.S. Old Boys' cricket today. Bernard is the skipper, wicket-keeper, and opening bat. Brother 'L' is the all-rounder. Both have played for Middlesex II.

Looking after the club's finance is D. J. L. Stevens, while secretarial duties are borne by A. C. Moran, a bowler whose name is seldom out of the Sunday newspapers—in the cricket columns, of course!

The club, with its forty to fifty members, plays 'home' matches on the school ground during the summer holidays. During World War II, the club played twice at Lord's—on both occasions a win against St. Mary's Hospital. It is also Devon's most faithful visiting side. A tour there in 1951 would be its thirtieth.

In 1934, in a game against St. Bart's Hospital, who dismissed the Old Boys' side for 123, the opposition had reached 121 for 4 wickets. Then, the last 6 wickets fell without addition to the score! That year the club had probably its best season, going right through without defeat.

At Finchley in 1928, skipper of the club, J. A. Morley, late-cut a ball and hit his wicket, knocking flat all three stumps. The wicket-keeper caught the ball, and at the same time, the bowler was appealing for l.b.w., as apparently the ball had touched Morley's leg on the way through! The batsman was out all right —but how? Was he l.b.w., 'hit wicket', or caught?

The *Upper Clapton Club* was founded in 1871 by W. Johnson, then a member of the firm of Pinchin, Johnson & Co. He was an enthusiastic cricketer and his residence in Upper Clapton, 'Avenue House', had an extensive field adjoining his garden. Among his friends and neighbours the Upper Clapton Cricket Club was formed.

Johnson engaged a member of the M.C.C. ground staff, a man called Osborne, to be groundsman, and under his supervision, with the assistance of the gardeners, the ground was prepared. One team only was played until after the founder's death and the removal of the club in 1886 to its present nearby ground at Spring Hill, which was taken over from the Upper Clapton Rugby Club. This move marked the beginning of an expansion to, ultimately, three teams.

My old friend F. H. Webster, father of 'Taj' Webster, the former Middlesex player, is still greatly interested in this club. He was president of the C.C.C. in 1938, and is now a live vice-president of that body.

Other members have been S. W. Scott, who played regularly for Middlesex under A. J. Webbe, Sir Arthur Dyke, C.C.C. president in 1933, H. B. and J. H. Hugill, A. L. Evelyn, and, more recently, R. Lister, W. E. Chamberlain, P. M. Undery, C. S. Farnes, and J. W. Luck.

In eighteen-year-old D. Plummer, the club has an all-rounder whom it hopes will develop into a fine player. Jack Atkins has played in several representative North London games and is a very sound and useful bat. D. Ames has proved what a good fast-medium bowler he is, and Billy Brittain, a veteran in his fifty-third year, is still good for some more quick 'fifties'.

We continually hear of tours to places like Germany and Holland, but we seldom hear about the 'return matches'. Upper Clapton were enterprising enough in 1949 to entertain the De Haantjes Club from Holland. T. A. Brittain, the cricket secretary, told me that they all had great fun, and, although Upper Clapton won, the Dutch team showed themselves to be a really first-rate and keen side in the field. Brittain's opposite number in the De Haantjes team wrote to him after his team's return to Holland and said, '*Our players asked me to express specially our gratitude for your cordial reception and great hospitality. We particularly appreciated the hoisting of the Netherlands flag and the big cake at tea with "Welcome Haantjes Cricket Club" written on it.*'

These friendly meetings between ourselves and overseas sporting clubs do far more good than all the peace conferences. What a great pity the Russians never took up cricket!

Perhaps one of the most interesting things about the *North Enfield Club* is that the ground at Clay Hill, Enfield, is the former home of J. T. Bosanquet, England and Middlesex googly bowler. The club still uses the pitch on which he played.

E. J. Cass has been the honorary general secretary since 1935.

F. Barwick, the club fast bowler, apart from topping the club batting averages for the last few years, has had outstanding bowling figures, including 135 wickets in 1949 and 126 in 1948.

Since 1940 the skipper of the first XI has been R. Harrison, who has done so much to build up the club again since the War. G. C. Willis attends to finance and W. Luxton looks after the fixtures.

In the year 1862, the *Potters Bar Club* began, but unfortunately early records are difficult to obtain. Secretary D. G. Strong thinks they are probably locked up in a bank. But H. J. Butcher, club historian, retiring trustee, and former secretary, is well equipped to fill in the gaps.

The club's previous ground was some distance away from its present site, to which it was moved some twenty-one years ago. It was a ploughed field when Potters Bar took it over, but the generosity of some of its pre-War benefactors—few of whom are left now—saw the club through.

Present captain is Arthur Waters, and treasurer, L. H. Mitchell. As for the players, Potters Bar members are modest, and tell me that they 'have had no outstanding player either during the War, or since'.

A match on September 17, 1949, was against a team of six clergymen and five Middlesex County players. They represented the Bishop of London, whose Reconstruction Fund benefited by some £45 as a result. The Bishop's XI won by 57 runs (219 for 9 wickets declared, against 162). The event drew a record crowd.

Kenton Cricket Club started life in 1921 under another name, and has always had a reputation for its hospitality to visitors. Many county and first-class sides play on the ground annually.

Kenton's ground was purchased by the present owner for the use of the club in 1938. It was sub-let during World War II, in view of the shortage of staff, and the club was precluded from using it until the expiry of the lease, following differences of opinion that could not be settled.

But now the club has returned to its home, and is in a more flourishing state than ever before. It is lucky in having concrete wickets for all-weather cricket practice, and every facility for summer and winter social activities.

In the first charity match played in 1944, Jack Durston brought down a side of varying strength to play the club. This was probably the last game in which Jack played, for he gave up active participation on the field soon afterwards. On that occasion the club just lost to the visitors by 4 runs, but over £800 was handed over to the Red Cross Fund.

After that success, games were arranged against the British Empire XI, and a relic of those matches is that Ray Smith's XI still plays the last game of every season against the club.

A. C. Hardyman, the chairman, is a founder-member, and has held every office in turn in the club. Secretary up to 1944 was Walter D. Packwood, another original member, who is still playing at the age of sixty. Organiser up to 1945 was Percy C. Turton (father of Peter Turton), now associated with the Leather-head Club. He helped to raise large sums of money for the Red Cross Fund in the War years.

Terry Nolan, secretary since 1944, has been responsible—with Turton's assistance, he has asked me to say—for raising £2,500 for various charities in three years. One of his latest efforts was to raise £564 10s. for Denis Compton's benefit. Who says money can't be raised by cricket clubs? Only hard work and good organising ability are required. Kenton has both.

W. B. Morris, now with Essex, has been Kenton's outstanding all-rounder in the post-War years. He started with the third XI when he was very young. Alan Bell was the club's outstanding fast bowler. He could be devastating on a fast wicket, but unfortunately, no longer plays regularly.

S. G. Parlett, now with Wembley C.C., has probably been the club's most successful batsman in recent years, rivalled only by A. M. (Fred) Wire, an older member, who was also a more than useful bowler and slip-fielder.

Another Middlesex club my BBC side plays each season is *Hayes Cricket Club*. Hayes played on its own private ground until 1950, when the Council bought it.

Billy Flood, who has played a lot of Conference cricket, is perhaps the outstanding Hayes player nowadays. He has taken almost 2,000 wickets for the club, besides scoring at a high rate. In 1947, for instance, Flood captured 194 wickets, and three years later he took 192, including 'all ten'. And that's a lot of wickets!

Vic Roberts, the club's genial wicket-keeper, has materially helped Flood and the other Hayes' bowlers by missing very few of the chances that come his way. In 1949 he took 74 wickets behind the sticks, and in 1950, 81.

Harold Schofield usually takes his 100 wickets per season, besides making runs when they are wanted. Eric Frewer can also be relied upon to make runs. In 1949, he failed by only a few to top the 1,000 mark. Frank Beakhouse is another stalwart of the club who yearly gets his 100 wickets.

Club history can be traced back to 1850, but reliable records are few and far between. It is sufficient to say that Hayes has gone from strength to strength since the early days, and now plays the best clubs in the London area.

F. C. Hammond, who has been in turn president, club chairman, and is now vice-president, has always been a great help to the club and has done more than his fair share in keeping things going. Vic Roberts, besides being skipper or vice-captain since 1936, was appointed match secretary in 1935. Vic was mainly responsible for keeping Hayes cricket alive during the War. Harold Southcombe was secretary for a number of years, and the chairman of the club is Bernard Greenhead, who has been a member for thirty years. Other stalwarts are Bert Greenhead and Charles Gray.

In 1934 the members built themselves a pavilion; fire razed it to the ground in February, 1950. But by May of that year an even bigger pavilion had been completed and brought into use.

Each year the club plays a game against a county side. On one wartime occasion, Arthur Wellard (Somerset), playing for the London Counties against Hayes, hit Schofield for seven '6's' in nine balls, and scored 52 runs in $8\frac{1}{2}$ minutes. For quick scoring, that must be almost a record.

Hayes's club record is 388 for 8 wickets against South East Ham—the Essex side. Bert Calverley's 172 in 1950 is the highest individual score so far.

In 1948, for Frank Chester's Benefit, the club played the full Middlesex XI. Some 8,000 people were present, and Chester's fund benefited by some £265 in consequence.

Hornsey Cricket Club has a continuous record since 1880, and occasional references to it are made as far back as 1840. The club has always been to the fore in London cricket, and has supplied several players to the counties—especially to Middlesex.

After World War I, when little cricket was played,

tremendous efforts had to be made to get the club going again. H. J. Wenyon, who was capped for Middlesex, was the main-spring of this revival, and the side included such stalwarts as G. W. Hammond, L. T. Weaver, S. L. Clarke, D. L. H. Mercer, and, later on, G. B. Atkinson, J. G. Bott, and F. E. Whitehead.

In 1937 the new pavilion was opened, with two squash courts, facilities for catering, and billiards.

When World War II broke out most of the younger men went into the Forces, but a side was run every Saturday and Sunday with the aid of the Civil Defence, the Home Guard, the Police, and the Forces. Not one match was scratched.

In addition, in 1943, Howard Clark, who was the honorary secretary and captain (1937–46), started the Hornsey C.C. Schools XI, chiefly with a view to giving public school cricketers the opportunity of holiday play. This scheme has now become a permanent feature at Hornsey.

In 1941 the club was invited to play at Lord's as a compliment to George Hammond, a member of Middlesex C.C.C. Committee, who had been elected president of the club in succession to W. F. Harrison. (Its president now is Sir Pelham Warner, who took over in 1944 from Col. H. J. Wenyon, D.S.O.) The match was against Southgate, and was repeated in 1942. In the latter game, when Hornsey's last men—T. Plant and R. W. G. Sommerville— came together, over 120 runs were needed in sixty-five minutes. These two knocked off 80 and played out time.

The 1950 captain was G. L. B. August, the Bedfordshire opening bat. Hornsey's batting is particularly powerful, as there are also R. S. Cooper (Middlesex and C.C.C.), R. L. Clarke, R. Franklin, L. K. Lewis, J. D. Cairns, S. S. Rogers, M. S. Rogers, P. A. C. Kelly, P. F. A. Loffler, and W. Knightley-Smith, a very promising youngster. M. L. Laws (Middlesex) is a very able wicket-keeper, and when he is away, W. Fullwood ('Blossom'), the old Derbyshire wicket-keeper, is there to take his place.

For bowling, Hornsey relies on G. J. F. Williams, F. M. Saunders, S. Feldman, D. H. K. Rata, R. S. Cooper, P. M. C. Whitton, R. L. Clarke, and R. Adams.

Many of these cricketers are of county standard, and, all credit to the club, a considerable number graduated through the Schools XI.

Chapter Four

CLUBS AND THEIR PLAYERS

Histories, outstanding players, and anecdotes of the clubs in Essex.

CRICKET on many of the delightful Essex club and county grounds is always enjoyable, but I retain perhaps more memories of Clacton than of any others. It was at Clacton that I first saw Ken Preston in action. I saw him at close quarters, when batting for Northants, against Essex, and he was bowling fast, I assure you! That Clacton match produced a huge number of runs by both sides. Essex got over 600 in the first innings, and we weren't so many behind at the end.

The *Clacton Club* itself was founded in 1908 by a Sunday-school teacher for the benefit of his youths, and was originally known as the Clacton St. Paul's Cricket Club. By 1914, it had earned the reputation of playing good cricket and had won the Tendring League Cup. After World War I, a ground site on the north fringe of Clacton was purchased, and the members themselves set about the task of laying a good 'square' and building a fine pavilion. A few years later, however, the Clacton Urban District Council opened a recreation ground and part of it was set aside for cricket. (This is now the ground where Essex play their Clacton county matches each year.)

The Clacton Council purchased the club's original ground in North Clacton and granted the club a lease for the use of the recreation ground. It was then that the club changed its name from Clacton St. Paul's C.C. to Clacton-on-Sea.

Since then the club has prospered—producing such players as A. B. Quick, who is now the club captain, and who has scored over a thousand runs each season for a number of years.

Frank Vigar, now a regular member of the Essex side, is also a member. Both these players joined the club as boys. T. H. Leonard, the vice-captain, is another fine player who never fails to score a thousand runs each season. He and Quick usually open for the club, and hold many club records. I well remember their scoring 182 in forty-one minutes for the first wicket in one of their 'needle' matches of 1949.

Including vice-presidents, the total membership is 115, forty-five being playing members, and it is a credit to their organisation that they can turn out three XIs each week. T. A. H. Bond, who has been a member of the club for thirty-two years, has done a fine job of work as honorary secretary for the past eighteen years.

It was Bond who told me about a game against Campsea Ashe in 1949, when Clacton arrived *minus* one player. W. Meacock, who is now eighty-four years old, an ex-player and umpire, filled the breach. Naturally he had to have a runner. After pottering about for a time he made one glorious cover-drive and scampered down the pitch amid tremendous cheers, side by side with his runner!

Residents and visitors alike have come to regard the Clacton Cricket Week as an annual event of great importance. Extremely good fixtures are arranged.

Another club ground in Essex on which the county play is that of *Westcliff-on-Sea*, where the county club has a 'Week'. On this small but delightful cricket arena, it is the ambition of all-comers to hit a ball over the main road and the houses beyond. In consequence, buses, trams, and windows are often imperilled, but fortunately nothing serious has befallen them!

The Westcliff-on-Sea club was established in 1897, and will, therefore, soon be celebrating its diamond jubilee.

In recent years, perhaps the most outstanding Westcliff cricketer has been Harry Crabtree, a great personal friend of mine. Harry played some really great innings for the C.C.C. representative XI and the British Empire XI during the War. For the county, too, he has done yeoman service. It is true to say that he is the club's batting mainstay, and how rarely he lets them down! Now, he is making another reputation for himself at coaching.

L. S. Clarke, who has been given an Essex cap, regularly turns out for the club. He is a brilliant batsman of the sound rather than the adventurous type. Denis Wilcox, former Essex captain and Dulwich College skipper just before I got into the side in 1930, also plays occasionally, but being a schoolmaster, his Saturdays, in particular, are tied up.

The club's president is A. J. Spelling, a former club captain, and for many years the county's treasurer. With J. Allen, honorary secretary, he was responsible for reviving the club's activities after the War. Twenty-five years before joining West-cliff, Spelling was captain of another Essex club, Ilford C.C. Westcliff's present captain is V. J. Thornton, and G. E. McClellan is its treasurer.

Now to another club ground on which the Essex County XI plays regularly—and near London, this time: that of *Romford C.C.* The club had something to celebrate in 1950, when the county held a 'Week' there for the first time.

One player talked about more than anyone else as being the possible saviour of English fast bowling is Kenneth Preston, the Essex professional, who was out of the game in 1949 on account of a leg broken while playing football. He joined Romford in 1943. After 'demobbing' from the Navy in 1947, Ken rejoined the club and started off in the second XI, where in his first match he took 6 wickets for 9 runs. He graduated to the first XI, and soon became outstanding. He was recommended to the county and signed professional forms in 1948.

Also outstanding, but in another capacity, has been R. G. Goodwin, who, as honorary secretary, 'carried' the club throughout the War years. The club's social and press secretary, R. W. Luchford, told me that but for Goodwin's efforts during those hard times, the club would have gone out of existence. He did everything, including carrying the club bag, and—I take it— the cans as well!

At fifty-eight years of age, E. H. Mitchell is the club's oldest playing member. Percy Hodgkinson is another stalwart, a personality on the field, and sets a fine example to the young players, notably by his running between the wickets.

In being since 1872, Romford plays on a ground owned by the Romford Council. It is not a large club, having only forty-five members, but what they lack in numbers they more than make up in keenness and efficiency.

Present chairman is P. A. Myers, and he has C. S. Griffiths to assist him. To arrange the fixtures there is W. H. Read, and finance is looked after by A. R. Warwick.

Gidea Park Cricket Club shares the distinction of having acted as hosts to the county for the first time in 1950. The ground at 'Gallows Corner' was completely relaid in 1948. In spite of the sinister name, there is no 'cut-throat' cricket at 'Gallows Corner' as far as Gidea Park is concerned! On the contrary, typical English club cricket has been played there since 1921.

Most famous of its players was undoubtedly the late Kenneth Farnes, who was a member of the club in the 1920s and 1930s. In recent years, the club has organised a fund for a memorial to his memory.

Several times between 1939 and 1945, I had the opportunity of playing for the British Empire XI on this well-appointed ground. Perhaps what stick in my memory more than anything else are the original and excellent auction sales, conducted after the matches, of various commodities that, at the time, were in short supply. In that way the club was able to raise funds to keep itself solvent during those difficult years.

Apart from Kenneth Farnes, Gidea Park has two other county players on its strength—the brothers Daer—'A. G.' and 'H. B.' The former is well known as a consistently good bat, and an excellent slip-fielder. ' H. B.', besides being a forcing bat with many big scores to his credit, is an accurate and hostile new-ball bowler.

In 1947 a big match was played on the ground for Peter Smith's Benefit. A crowd of some 8,000 saw a most entertaining day's play, and attractive displays by six South African Test players, including vice-captain Dudley Nourse.

E. R. Bailey is the hard-working and enthusiastic secretary, and I wouldn't like to think what the club would do without his advice.

Gidea Park is also fortunate in its choice of match secretary, for L. J. Fletcher has improved the fixture list by personal contact with the bigger clubs. During the close season, J. W. Griffin helps to keep interest in cricket alive among the club's fifty-odd playing members.

Farther east is Colchester, where Essex also plays 'home' matches. The records of the *Colchester and East Essex Cricket Club*—its exact foundation date it not known for certain—go back to about the year 1890.

Through the years the club has been one of the foremost in North Essex. Its ground is at Castle Park, and is considered to be one of the most pleasant in Essex.

A. C. Girling, the chairman, has held office for many years

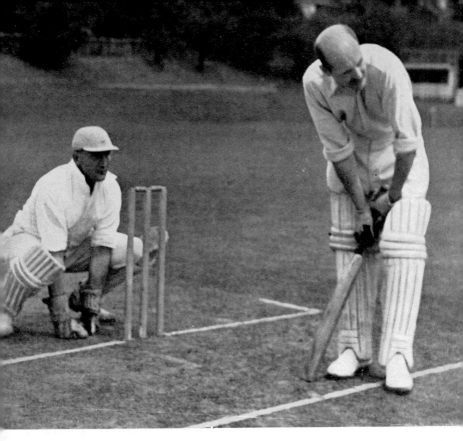

Geoffrey Harrison plays most of his cricket for the Old
Whitgiftians. G. S. A. Parnaby is the wicket-keeper in
this Old Whitgiftian Trial Match

). McDonald-Hobley
(B.B.C.)

C. F. Smith
(Mitcham)

The twelve captains of the Dover Cricket Club shown here cover, in all, forty-three years

Left to right, back row: J. H. Spackman, H. A. Stanway, G. H. Youden, R. J. Briggenshaw, A. J. Took, W. H. Fish

Left to right, front row: L. E. Annand, F. A. Belchamber, H. W. Youden, W. J. Pudney, A. R. Fisher, R. E. Pain

with great success. Russel Wray, who resigned from the secre-
taryship in 1949, served in that office for twenty-five years. His
successor is Alan Everett.

R. B. Hunt (Earls Colne) is the present vice-chairman; he
may be better known to you as an umpire, and a Rugby-football
referee.

The club's two opening bats are schoolmasters—Michael
Rouse and Eric Richards. Both scored more than a thousand runs
in 1949, and it is thanks to them that the opposition usually has
to face a good total. Derek Jackman, a young fast bowler on
whom the club has built high hopes, is a professional footballer
with West Ham, so there's no question about his fitness in the
summer months!

And now back near London to Valentine's Park, where the
Ilford Cricket Club has its home ground, another on the Essex
County list.

The club was established in 1879 and played on the ground
when it was part of a private estate. Then, in the late 'nineties, the
local authority acquired the property, which is now known as
Valentine's Park. Although the cricket ground itself is in a public
park, it is run privately by the Ilford Club. The annual county
festival week, held in May or June, is quite the highlight of
Ilford's summer sporting activities.

President of the C.C.C., in 1949, was George Clatworthy, who
has been secretary of Ilford since 1928. George, on the surface, is
quiet and reserved, but give him something to get his teeth into
and he'll persevere to the bitter end. Ilford is indeed lucky in
having such an enthusiastic, hard-working, and knowledgeable
secretary.

It was largely owing to the fine efforts of E. W. A. Campbell,
treasurer since 1928, that cricket was played on the Ilford
ground during the 1939–45 period. In its president, Ald. A. W.
Green, M.B.E., J.P., the club again has someone who is intensely
interested in the game.

Of the many players 'on the books', there is first B. J. Brooker,
who for sixteen years was skipper of the first XI (1932–47,
inclusive). He was popular and successful both on and off the
field. E. E. Purrier—a C.C.C. cap and a left-hand opening bat—
was vice-captain from 1938 to 1944. Unfortunately, he had to
retire prematurely in 1947 because of injury.

F

From 1948, Ilford has had K. R. Harding as captain, and his able and intelligent leadership has welded a young team into such a powerful and enthusiastic combination that in 1950 the side was unbeaten. His own polished batting earned him a Conference cap a few years ago.

A. E. Evans, yet another C.C.C. cap and opening bat, who did so well in his first county games for Essex, combines a soundness of style with considerable speed in run-getting, and Harold Faragher is an all-rounder who has contributed much to the side's success. He has played for the county team, and has captained the county second XI.

F. E. H. Gibbens, another C.C.C. cap, is a first-class wicketkeeper 'of consistent yet unobtrusive excellence', so George Clatworthy tells me.

Ian Thomson is a right-hand medium-pace bowler with admirable control of the ball; he has been the mainstay of the attack since he joined the club in 1947, straight from school. He should go on improving with experience.

So on to the last of the club grounds on which the county plays that I shall mention here. It belongs to the *Brentwood Club*.

No one who has played on this delightfully situated and pretty ground at Shenfield Road, Brentwood, will argue when I say that it must be one of the loveliest cricket grounds in the country. The county holds a cricket week there annually.

The club was formed in 1881, and famous cricketers who have played for it include C. J. Kortwright, J. J. Reed, and A. F. Lucas. During the War years the first XI skippership was shared between B. W. Vincent and H. G. Waldram. Lewis A. Bayman then became skipper, and both he and Waldram have acted as honorary secretaries. H. L. Dennis and S. A. Parker have also shared the duty.

D. H. Banks, who has been treasurer since 1946, is a big hitter. In a fairly recent match 5 runs were needed, with one ball to go; Banks, who was in at the time, hit a lusty 6 and Brentwood won by 1 run.

The names of W. Goodwin, L. Deasley, E. J. Crook, D. S. Jackson, and J. McIntyre are well known as all-rounders who have been prominent for the club. Major Hill, E. A. Miskin, and R. D. Hunter have all scored more than their share of the runs; L. A. Swain is an outstanding bowler.

Brentwood is a club of some 290 members—which, incidentally, includes 96 tennis players. Fifty-one of the 290 are active cricketers.

The present secretary, S. A. Parker, has reminded me of an incident in a match against Romford during the War in which Brentwood was out for 112. Romford at 108 for 5 had the match well in hand. The sixth wicket fell at 110 and the side was all out at the same total! Four of the last five wickets were taken by the same bowler, and all four were caught by the same fieldsman.

I want to mention some of the Essex county cricketers who have turned their attention to club cricket. The first name to come to mind is Jack Dennis, formerly one of the county's opening batsmen. Jack is a great friend of mine, and now skippers *Loughton Club*, which, incidentally, was founded way back in 1880.

Jack, a charming man with a disarming smile, would not claim now, of course, to be up to county standard, but he still bats well enough to bring him hundreds of runs, and is a perfect example to the youngsters when it comes to stroke play.

Frank S. Foster, C.B.E., J.P., is Loughton's president, and M. C. Symondson does the secretarial duties. John May is an all-rounder on whom Dennis depends a great deal. He was top of the bowling averages in 1948, and has a happy habit of serving up runs when they are most needed. Youngsters N. Madgwick, R. Lord, and P. Shott are 'quite promising', I am told, and should maintain the standard of Loughton cricket.

One of the most famous Essex players to play a lot of club cricket was the late J. W. H. T. Douglas. 'Johnny', with other members of the Douglas family, was a member of the *Harlow Cricket Club*. Naturally enough—he lived there.

Other famous men to represent the club have been W. P. Robertson and Captain Green-Price of Middlesex, Sam Deards, (captain of 'Moon Hall' from 1876 onwards), and the Silcocks. Cricket was played at Moon Hall in 1850.

The St. Mary's Cricket Club, forerunner of present-day Harlow C.C., was founded about 1890. Skipper in those days was the Rev. A. W. Parnell.

Then, in 1900, Marigolds Field became, and still is, the Harlow home.

The club had a very good season in 1948, and was equally successful in 1949, thanks to such players as skipper L. H. J.

Chapman, F. Silcock (top of both batting and bowling averages in recent years), and all-rounders J. Nichol and F. Debnam.

An acute problem that faced the *Epping Cricket Club* in 1948 was that of keeping its ground maintained, when arrangements broke down for the employment of a full-time groundsman. For them, fortunately, this difficulty has now been settled satisfactorily, but this problem has confronted many clubs since the War, and, unhappily, the position is not likely to improve while housing difficulties remain, and suitable men are in 'short supply'.

Epping overcame its trouble by employing part-time labour to carry out evening work on the ground and roping in as many club members as possible to give a hand. Perhaps in compensation, the club won very many more matches that year than it lost.

Another interesting thing about Epping is that it has not been afraid to come into the open about league cricket. At a recent annual meeting, it was agreed that the club would be interested in a cricket league provided it ensured a full fixture list, and travelling facilities were reasonable.

Secretary of Epping for a number of years has been H. J. Mead, with match secretary R. G. Emery to assist him. Skipper is A. Flower, and has all-rounders F. Mansfield, J. Storey, and W. Johnson to help *him*.

At the other end of Epping Forest are a group of well-known clubs—*Buckhurst Hill, Woodford Wells, Woodford Green, South Woodford, and Southbridge Sports*.

First, the *Buckhurst Hill Club*, which the BBC plays regularly. Here chalk up Alec Duff, officially the match secretary, as another of the men who offer unlimited time and enthusiasm.

Its first XI, until recently under the captaincy of Essex cricketer Alan Lavers, has developed into a strong side difficult to beat. Alan himself was the mainstay of both batting and bowling. His off-spin bowling round the wicket, especially on a pitch that is giving him the slightest help, can be devastating. I well remember his playing for the M.C.C. against the C.C.C. at Sevenoaks in 1948, and having all our batsmen in trouble. He has been succeeded by another all-rounder, E. P. Anderton.

R. H. Greensmith, of whom I have a very high opinion, is a young left-hand bat. Since 1948 he has had a high place in the averages. C. J. Lyall is another greatly improved player, and C. J. Williams, besides being a grand fielder, is becoming an excellent batsman.

In 1949, I remember, Buckhurst Hill brought down ex-Somerset player, John H. ('Monkey') Cameron, to Motspur Park. Cameron used to bowl vicious leg-breaks when he was at Cambridge, but has now resorted to slow off-spinners of immaculate length. Anderton, in that game, opened both the batting and the bowling. R. H. Greensmith's brother, W. T., is the leg-spin bowler who has joined Essex as a professional, but the club seems to be luckier than most as it has several other promising youngsters developing steadily.

One of my great regrets is that I haven't yet had an opportunity of playing against the *Woodford Wells Club,* which goes back to 1864. Skipper is E. C. Tedder, aided and abetted by C. D. Walker-Arnott, who does duty as honorary secretary.

It was during the 1947 season that Woodford Wells had such magnificent results from their four Saturday and one Sunday XIs. Of 91 matches arranged, of which 12 were scratched, no fewer than 73 were won.

Another Woodford side against which I have never played, but about which, through the kindness and co-operation of its secretary, Edward Gatcum, I now know a great deal more, is *Woodford Green Club.*

It has been playing cricket at Woodford Green since 1735; and during a long chat with Gatcum he showed me the contents of what will become an interesting history of the club and its ground.

Like so many old-established clubs, it offers so much to interest the reader that it is difficult to know just what to put in and what to leave out. For instance, I was shown an impression of The Green and its environment about the year 1738 from facts supplied by H. H. Stevens, late president of the Woodford Antiquarian Society. Then I was shown some very interesting photographs of teams that have represented the club during the last 200-odd years.

The late Edgar E. Starke held office as president from 1927 until the outbreak of War. Now the president is Sir James Hawkey, with L. Powter as chairman.

Gatcum himself usually bats No. 6 for the club. Dickie

Edwards, now in his thirties, is one of the side's most enthusiastic all-rounders. During the War he contracted infantile paralysis in India, but has successfully thrown off all traces of it, and is the club's reliable No. 4.

Lance Carter, a fast bowler, once took all ten wickets in a match. He usually bags more than 100 wickets a season. The outstanding batsman is undoubtedly Cyril James. He is not the forcing type, but at No. 3 his solidity and reliability usually prove their worth. 'Babs' Sansom, who, incidentally, has been collecting much interesting data about the club, is an all-rounder who has been a member for forty-five years.

If you hear a loud voice calling for a run while you're Woodford Green way, then it's almost sure to be all-rounder 'Spot' Smith. In 1948, for instance, he headed the bowling with the remarkable average of 4·05 runs per wicket, and was third in the batting averages. Other Woodford Green personalities are Allan Sheppard, Don Barber, Joe Root, and P. F. N. Warner.

The match against Woodford Wells on August Bank Holiday has always been a great occasion. It has been played without a break since the formation of the Wells club.

Woodford Wells usually have several county players in their side, but 'The Green' always reckon to put up a good show. In 1948, for instance, they held the Wells XI to a draw, and in 1949, after Wells had scored 200 for 8 wickets, 'The Green' were left to get the runs in 2½ hours. They were out for 160 only ten minutes before time. Club cricket, this, at its best!

It is not generally known that Gilbert Jessop, the famous big-hitter of yesteryear, scored his first century in cricket for *South Woodford Cricket Club*. In more recent years T. G. Grinter has tried to emulate the great man—and how successful he has been!

Grinter, now president of the club, holds a unique place in *Wisden's*. In 1913 he scored six successive hundreds against top-flight clubs. They were: 156 not out against North Middlesex; 188 not out against Malden Wanderers; 107 not out against Edmonton; 184 (for Essex Club and Ground) against Bethnal Green; 168 not out against North Middlesex again, and 130 *versus* Chigwell.

W. L. Heath, a former captain and contemporary of Grinter, has been chairman of committees since 1932.

South Woodford has been in existence since 1884, when it was established behind Churchfields. In 1932 it moved to its present site in Roding Lane, and although in 1940 half the ground was given to allotment holders, it is now back in full use again, so permitting two home fixtures on Saturdays and Sundays.

From 1941 to 1946 the skipper was wicket-keeper A. H. Bassett, perhaps better known as captain of the Freebooters touring side. Since 1947 Jack Glover has taken over the captaincy, and what a grand choice! Besides being a fine bat of the dashing variety, he is a brilliant short-leg fielder, and what I would call an excellent clubman.

Harry T. Ross, treasurer since 1931, is a slow spin bowler with many successes to his credit, and each season Harry's total is always a big one. A namesake of mine, A. W. Bennett, at sixty-five years of age, is still an active member. He bowls for the third XI, and with his medium-pace deliveries of admirable length, proves himself to be more than 'just an old man'. R. George, since 1937, has shown over and over again what a grand all-rounder he is. Others to have done well for the club include batsmen S. Earwacker, J. Rolstone, R. J. Dowsett, R. Byrne, and G. McD. Garland, and bowlers D. Streeton, W. Rowing, and C. Fletcher.

To complete the 'Woodford' group, we have the *Southbridge Sports Club*.

Restarting a club after acquiring a new ground always presents many headaches. In 1948, S. Nash went about the business in such a methodical way that the inevitable upheaval was hardly noticed, and within a very short time the club had settled down—only to move, in 1950, to yet another site.

F. Sawer was for a number of years responsible for the fixtures and was able to arrange an excellent list despite often difficult conditions.

For a club of only twenty-six members to be able to run two regular Saturday matches and one Sunday team is proof of the enthusiasm and drive on the part of all the members.

Originated in 1920 by a group of ex-servicemen, Southbridge has been active ever since. World War II held things up as most of the members went into the Forces, but they are back in strength now. Top players, says P. Marjeram, now cricket secretary, are R. Grove, S. Wright, V. Kilminster, and C. Palmer.

Also in this area is the *Walthamstow Club*.

L. W. Snaith was a member some years back, and when the Essex Club and Ground side, under the late J. W. H. T. Douglas, failed to force a win against the club, the loquacious and youthful Len informed 'Johnny' that his field placings were incorrect!

Snaith was never asked to play for Essex in spite of being such a fine performer. He scored a century for the club when he was only fifteen. A magnificent fielder and spin bowler, he left the club in 1946, when he moved to Leigh-on-Sea.

The club goes back to 1877, but up to 1928, when its present ground was purchased, Walthamstow had to rent one. The purchase money was found by the members, who took all the shares. Six years before that a large pavilion was built by the members and the cost recouped in the following five years, mainly through the untiring efforts of C. Hurst, a former chairman. As the sum involved was £1,200, it was a great effort.

During World War II the club had five bombs on the ground and a buzz bomb within fifty yards. The craters were filled in by members, and the pavilion stayed up by will power! They have high hopes of building another pavilion in the near future, thanks to the efforts of W. E. Black, of the management committee. During the War years club captain Clifford Watkins materially helped to keep the club going.

Now in his eightieth year, H. W. Dongray, the president, is one of the hardest-working members of the club—he is also the treasurer. J. W. Deane keeps all the secretarial matters in good shape. Responsible for fixtures is Reg Rowland, who spent a year with the Essex County Club.

M. R. J. Wood, renowned in Essex for his hard hitting, causes consternation among all ranks of the opposition who meet him for the first time. Often Monty will hit the opening new-ball bowlers for '6' in the first overs of the match! The leading club bat at the time of writing is Ron Houghton, who hit 1,354 runs in 1950.

Sid Couzens is another Walthamstow player. He played his first game for the C.C.C. in 1942 under Kenneth Cranston. Sid joined the club in 1940, and in the next ten years, in spite of the War, took 1,157 wickets, at an average of slightly over 10 runs per wicket. His best season for the club was in 1949 when he took 156 wickets.

Other batting personalities in recent years have been E. H.

Pollard, N. Griffiths, T. Stanley, and R. Webb, and in support of Couzens, J. Deane, H. Silber, who took 128 wickets in 1947, and H. Howorth.

A piece of quick thinking gave victory to the club in 1942 against Chingford. The last two Chingford bats were in. One was a good batsman, the other a 'rabbit'. The last ball of the last over but one was played by the batsman past mid-on for what he had hoped would be one run. Dave Hewson jog-trotted behind the ball for fully twenty-five yards and allowed it to trickle over the boundary. The rabbit was bowled next over!

Another exciting win was against Crofton Park in 1948. Walthamstow won when the last men in ran byes off the last ball of the match. The ball went a few yards past the wicket-keeper, and was fielded by first slip. Sid Couzens, one of the batsmen in, called his partner for a run. He got it, and that made the match a tie, but, in the excitement, slip shied at the wicket and missed. In the scramble that followed the batsmen took another quick single, which gave them victory by one run.

So far I haven't had anything to say about Old Boys' clubs in Essex.

From East Ham Grammar School we get the Old Esthameians; their club, the *Old Esthameians C.C.*

The club itself is a large one, comprising a membership of some 600 members, and covers all forms of social and sporting activities. The cricket section, established in 1925, has about forty-five playing members, and runs two Saturday teams and one on Sundays. Like most clubs, after the War it found itself with a medium-strength fixture list, but thanks to an active committee, and in particular a live honorary secretary and fixture secretary in C. T. Baggott, it now plays some of the strongest clubs in Essex.

Ron Sammon has been its star hitter for some years, and established himself as the highest-scoring batsman of the 1949 season. L. H. West, who has represented the county, is still a fine bat, and G. Nickelson is one of the O.E.'s best all-rounders, having been offered a trial for the county. Like so many others, he had to decline because of business commitments.

'Young' Bill Fearnley, who, cheerfully admitting that he will never see fifty again, keeps going, and in 1949 succeeded in scoring five half centuries. The number of capable batsmen in the side is shown by the fact that, apart from those I have already mentioned, Tangui, Barrett, Coward, Brumwell, and Cox all made '50s' during 1949. Stout, Mills, Deans, plus Tangui, Ron Sammon, and Barrett, do the bowling.

The O.E.'s ground was formerly the grounds of the picturesque 12th century Church of St. Mary, which overlooks the field. After World War II the ground was rented by the Hay's Wharf Club until bought by the East Ham Education Committee in 1923 as a sports ground for the East Ham Grammar School. The old students have the use of the ground and a fully-equipped club-house, which was built as a memorial to the Old Boys who fell in the 1914–18 War.

When Dick Stout, the first XI skipper, was bowling in the first over after tea one day, he obviously had the batsman in difficulties. Expecting a wicket to fall at any moment, the spectators were much amused to hear a small boy turn to one of his pals and say in a loud voice, 'There y'are—'e *does* chuck 'em!'

Another popular Old Boys' side in Essex is the *Old Parkonians Cricket Club*.

Old boys of the Ilford County High School are eligible for membership of this club, which was founded in 1906. About eighty are on the playing strength.

The Old Parkonians play on a public pitch in a pleasant recreation ground, which is in part secluded. Unfortunately, increased housing has caused greater use and wear of the outfield, though the wicket itself is in good condition.

The club's successful efforts to carry on throughout the War years were most praiseworthy, and are reflected in a booklet prepared by Doug Kesby, honorary secretary since 1929.

Ted Willin has been chairman since 1923 and is still in office. Cecil Gray was the first captain of the club (1906–32) with only two short breaks—one in seasons 1913 and 1914, when another captain was in office, and the other for his 1914–18 war service.

After World War I Charles Miller was responsible for restarting the club. He was secretary from 1919 to 1928, and, as the club grew, helped to start a third XI, of which he was captain. From 1932 to 1939 he was first XI skipper. John Stokes was captain of the second XI from 1929 to 1939, and from 1940 took over the first XI.

Ted Drakes, who just failed to get a Blue at Cambridge

University, has played for Lincolnshire. L. Still is an academical batsman of many years' service, and I. W. Robertston just failed to top the 'thousand' in 1949.

Doug Kesby, who left school in 1922, took 105 wickets in his twenty-seventh season. Since he joined the club, he has taken in all 1,835 wickets for the third XI. A. F. Levi is a leg-spin bowler, who took 9 for 36 runs against Ilford on their ground in 1948. Jack Kent is the club's brilliant wicket-keeper—he totalled 35 victims in 1949: 18 caught and 17 stumped.

Kesby told me about a match against Hurst Green during their Sussex—Kent tour in 1949. It was on a Monday—a day on which it is usually difficult to raise a side. Hurst Green batted first and were out for 68. O.P.s had loaned them two of their players to make up their eleven and also a scorer and an umpire. At one period the two O.P. men were batting together for Hurst Green, both umpires and both scorers were O.P.s, and another of the tourists managed the run-by-run score-board. The nine Hurst Green men, meanwhile, sat in a row in front of the pavilion and watched the proceedings. Only member of the tourists not engaged was the father of one of the O.P. players, who sat comfortably in the sun, watching.

Fairlop, where the Old Parkonians has its ground, is also where the *Hale End and South Essex Club* is at home.

Hale End (established in 1919) and South Essex (founded in 1888) amalgamated in 1948, hence the 'double-barrelled' name of the new club.

J. A. Hughes, who got his Essex second XI cap in 1949, completed the double in 1950 for the fifth successive year, and R. Ralph reached his 1,000 runs for the fourth successive year. In scoring 1,986 runs at an average of over 50, Ralph set up a new club record. He also took 53 wickets. J. A. Haynes, as vice-captain, had the worries of captaincy thrust upon him (owing to an injury to E. S. Clark) very early in the season, but in spite of that he topped the 1,000 runs for the first time.

For the second XI, E. Fage was the best batsman, with over 400 runs; he also took 48 wickets. Of the bowlers, N. Patient took 38 wickets for under 10 runs, and H. G. W. Wetton 35 for under 10.

Bearing in mind the facts that the South Essex C.C. did not function after 1939, and that Hale End played right through the War years, it is not surprising that all the names mentioned

above and all the members of the committee played for Hale
End before the amalgamation. H. G. W. Wetton was captain of
the first XI from 1939 to 1947, and E. S. Clark from 1948 to date.
From 1940 to 1946 Wetton was honorary secretary, and is now
back in the job. He also finds time to skipper the second XI.

One of the 'nearest-London' Essex clubs is the *Eton Mission
Club*, which plays on a private ground near Hackney Marshes.
It may sound strange, but it is true, that ever since 1934 I have
never forgotten this club for more than a few minutes at a time.

In the June of that year, Geoffrey Gilbey took me down with
his side to play against the Mission. Geoffrey's XI included
Cutmore and O'Connor of Essex, and several other county
players. In those days I was still at school. The Mission won the
toss and batted first. In spite of our reasonably strong bowling,
the boys batted magnificently and totalled 311. At tea, we were
11 for 3 wickets, and both Cutmore and O'Connor were back in
the pavilion. Before we resumed, Geoffrey Gilbey came over to
Ashley Pilbrow, the Olympic hurdler, who was 3 not out, and
me, and said he would give us both gold watches if we won the
match for him without being separated.

We did win the match, and neither of us was out. Ashley got
159 and I made 124. The watches were presented to us the
following week, and I am wearing mine to this day.

Geoffrey Gilbey, one of the grandest men I have known, was
one of four 'Big White Chiefs' who ran the Mission. His interest
in its welfare was immense and his work on its behalf untiring and
devoted. The cricket section of the club benefited greatly in those
days from the help and advice he gave so freely.

The cricket section was formed in the first year of the club's
formation, in 1881. It then played in various small leagues,
joining the Clapton District Cricket Association in 1904. It
started in the fourth, but by 1929 had reached the premier
division. Eton Mission won the competition that year and again
in 1932, after which it left league cricket for friendly games,
joining the C.C.C. in 1937. Dual job of secretary and treasurer
has been held since 1927 by G. S. Merritt.

Jock Mander has been captain for sixteen years, and does his
job really well. He has the side behind him and his performances
alone give him standing and respect among the younger members.
He has kept wicket for the club for twenty-one years. E. Tinkler,

apart from getting a number of wickets each season, is the club's outstanding batsman. Since 1937 he has been making a regular habit of collecting centuries. Over all these years, his batting average has been just over 64·00.

F. Sumsion joined the side from the Boys' Club in 1937, as a fast bowler. Since the War he has developed into a spin bowler and has taken over 100 wickets regularly. J. MacCartney, with a real cricketing name, joined in 1947, and, from his height of 6 ft. 4 in., he really bangs down the ball. In 1949 he took 184 wickets, and in 1950, 154.

Clayhall Club has its ground at Clayhall Park, Woodford Avenue, Ilford. The Mayor of Ilford opened it in 1935, but from its formation in 1919 until that date the club was known as old Christchurchians.

During the vital 'building-up' period from 1931 to 1946, F. J. Clarke was match secretary, and raised the quality of the fixture list to its present standard. After helping the club with fixtures after the War, Clarke has only just retired.

Clayhall has solved the social problem better than most clubs. Johnnie Sanders and his wife, Doris, work unceasingly to keep this important side of the club's activities running smoothly. During the War they kept all members in touch by a monthly news-letter. Few other clubs can boast of such service.

Present skipper, a fine forcing bat, is F. H. Boyden. He is also an excellent fielder. D. H. Billinghurst is a useful all-rounder, and still holds the club record of 137 not out, made against Cockfosters in 1949. Apart from the War years, captain from 1933 until last season was K. E. Skinner; he was a P.O.W. in Japanese hands from 1942 to 1945.

Like Skinner, an all-rounder, A. R. Kalbraier is a useful opening fast bowler and a big hitter. Southend have good reason to remember him. In 1947 he hit their bowlers all over the field for a speedy century.

Four club members lost their lives when a bomb fell on the 'Prince of Wales' at Chigwell in 1941. They were brothers Harry and Dick Johnson, Jack Kestrell, and Les Wells.

A. V. (Sonny) Avery and Stan Proffitt were members, and played regularly before both joined the county club.

In a village match in 1949 an opponent was hitting out at every ball. After one prodigous straight drive, which went smartly over point's head to the boundary for 6, Clayhall wicket-keeper said to him, 'You didn't mean that to go there, did you?' Whereupon the batsman replied, 'Ah just hits 'em and they goes where they likes!'

From 1922, for the first eight years, *Becontree* played on various pitches in Ilford Council parks, the second XI having a home ground about five miles away from the first XI. In 1930, however, a new extension to Goodmayes Park was opened, and a special pavilion erected by the Council for the use of the club. What a fine example of the help a local council can give when so inclined! In 1940 the ground was taken by the County Agricultural Committee for allotments, but in 1949 the club returned and is now running two elevens again.

President W. Loynds has done a lot for Becontree over the past twenty years. He was secretary from 1932 until 1947.

C. W. Tester was captain from 1935 to 1939 and took over again in 1948. He is an all-rounder and has another all-rounder to help him in F. Shelley. In 1945, Shelley was way up top of the batting averages. In 1948, J. Cavanagh broke one of the club's records by capturing 142 wickets with the low average of 8·23.

But it is E. Oliver who gets most of Becontree's runs. He has been top of the batting averages from 1947 onwards, breaking club records for the number of centuries in a season and for the aggregate number of runs. W. Faulkner, top of the bowling averages several times since 1942, played for the Essex Club and Ground in 1946.

Playing on a short pitch occurs more often than I thought. Becontree's secretary, A. Garrett, recalls how, in a match at Rainham, Becontree's opening fast bowler found difficulty with his length, and the first ball flew over the wicket-keeper's head. All eyes were turned on the bowler as the same thing happened with the next two deliveries. He managed a reasonable length for the remainder of the over.

After consultation with the 'keeper, the bowler complained that the pitch was short. Out came the chain, and the stumps at each end were found to be too near each other by some two yards!

The *Dagenham Club* has been in existence since 1929, and this is another in which the outstanding personality is not a player, but a 'back-room' boy.

G. H. Beale, its honorary secretary, was sixty-one years old before he even considered retiring—after forty-four years on the job. He has served the club for every year of its twenty-one years' existence, and before that served another club for a similar number of years.

Dagenham is now in its fifth year on its present ground, having taken it over after World War II from the agricultural authorities. In this small club of some thirty-five members, perhaps the outstanding playing personality has been G. Pledger, who has taken 100 wickets each season since 1948. L. Page, of the second XI, is also another good bowler who holds several records, among them 'all ten' in an innings on three occasions. In 1949 he took 126 wickets—a club record.

Several years ago at Benfleet (Essex), the club played a match near some tethered horses. Jack Giles, huge and farmer-like, took a huge swipe at a googly, missed it, and was bowled. At that identical moment one of the horses gave out some prolonged neighing, sounding for all the world like hysterical laughter! Now who doesn't believe in the story of the horse who played cricket?

In 1947 the club decided to tour Holland. They were the guests of the Kampong C.C. at Utrecht. I am told the players received a welcome comparable to that of any M.C.C. tourists, and were lavishly entertained. They found the locals very cricket-minded, and had to go all out to beat the Kampong and Utrecht Cricket Clubs. Before the matches, they toured the canals and hide-outs of the wartime resistance movements. This sounds something like a tour.

Near Harlow is the *Bishop's Stortford Club*, which has so much of interest to tell us about the hundreds of famous personalities who have played on its historic and rural ground.

The club is justifiably proud of the fact that it has played on the same ground without a break since it was founded over 125 years ago. F. R. Spofforth, George Parr, Tom Hayward, W. A. Oldfield, A. P. F. Chapman, B. H. Valentine, G. E. C. Wood, Denis Compton, Tom Goddard, Maurice Nichols, Jack O'Connor and the great 'W. G.' himself, are some of the celebrities who have been seen there in action.

In the seventies a team of aboriginals visited the club and one of their members threw a cricket ball over 130 yards! After the match, they entertained spectators with bow-and-arrow shooting and boomerang throwing.

Today there is no boomerang throwing, but some very fine cricket every week-end.

The ground itself belongs to the town, having been given by the late Tresham Gilbey, conditional upon its being used for the playing of cricket. Recently an adjoining field has been purchased for a third XI ground. In the 1860s, William Clarke's All-England XI played a series of annual matches against Bishop's Stortford XXII. Yes, twenty-two.

The year 1947, perhaps, was the most successful in the club's long history. The Saturday side suffered only three defeats in twenty-four matches, and it was in this season that the Rev. E. T. Killick, late of England and Middlesex, and now Vicar of St. Michael's, Bishop's Stortford, first played. In 1949 he scored 1,018 runs in fifteen innings, including four centuries.

Captain of the club is D. F. Cock, who won his Essex cap before the War, and other notable present-day batsmen are H. W. F. Taylor (Cambs.) and F. W. Binks, who seems to score over 1,000 runs season by season.

Consistently among the wickets is A. Thurley. One hundred per season is a target he not only sets himself, but achieved in 1946 and 1947. A. N. Gardiner, L. Reeve, and K. D. Spivey support Thurley in the bowling department.

The club's president is C. H. Edwards, who was captain of the club in the 1920s and has played for Herts. He took over from H. Stanley Tee in 1948. Tee, who resigned in 1950, had followed the late Tresham Gilbey after the latter had held office for thirty years. Chairman is the Rev. E. T. Killick.

Here's an achievement from a financial point of view: the social committee, under the chairmanship of T. G. Saul, raised £750 for the club in the first three post-war years.

J. K. Tee, now club secretary, reminded me that, on August Bank Holiday in 1949, against J. Deyong's XI, the club scored 400 for 6 wickets declared (Killick 117), the highest score on the ground since 1901, when the innings of 402 for 1 wicket was made against Saffron Walden.

In Chelmsford is the ground of *Crompton Parkinson's Club*. I have always been greatly impressed by this ground—it always looks in such very fine condition.

Stinchcombe Stragglers playing a Combined Services side at Stinchcombe, Gloucestershire—one of the prettiest grounds in the country. Walter Hammond, now back in club cricket, and C. S. Dempster, the New Zealand Test player, are batting; Horace Hazell (Somerset) is bowling

Bowling machines, old and new. Compare this first machine of pre-war days (*above*) with its all-electric counterpart (*below*), perfected in 1949

No doubt you remember the name of George Parkinson, who tried to form a group of Essex clubs into a league to play competitive cricket. George was the secretary of the club, and still has an occasional game with the club XI.

T. H. Windibank, managing director of the firm, has been president for many years, and does a lot of entertaining in the cricket world.

The ground is reputed to have one of the best 'squares' in the county, and has facilities for almost every other sport. The club itself was founded in 1889 by the late Colonel R. E. Crompton, founder of the Company.

Present captain is Lloyd Reeve, a brilliant all-rounder and probably the most outstanding cricketer turned out by the club. Like so many other fine club players, he could have had, I am sure, a regular place in the County XI, had he had more time at his disposal. W. J. Dines, who went to Essex, was another of the club's all-rounders.

George Parkinson recalls how Alf Gover (Surrey), after a day of fast bowling which resulted in 0 for 98, asked what was in the wicket. On being told cow manure in plenty, he said. 'I reckon you've got the cow herself underneath as well!'

To continue on through Chelmsford down the main road to the coast would take you near Wickford, some ten miles from Southend, where flourishes the *Wickford Club*, established in 1887 at the Castle Hotel by six founder-members, one of whom, R. True, is alive today.

R. W. Patmore, another founder-member, died in October, 1949, at the age of eighty. For many years Mr. Patmore was president of the club, and how he loved cricket! It was truly his life's interest.

Originally, Wickford's ground was situated behind the Castle Hotel, but in 1898 a fresh ground was obtained in Southend Road—now Mr. Seth Franklin's meadow—where the jubilee celebrations were held and where the club remained until 1908. In the early days only eight or so matches were played, but as Wickford developed so did the cricket club, and now some eighty games are played annually. Since 1908 Wickford has remained on its Runwell Road ground, with its beautiful surroundings.

Patmore himself was a fine batsman and wicket-keeper, and

G

was one of the captains of the Essex Club and Ground sides for over twenty years. Other outstanding players in those days were: G. Winmill, a great all-rounder, Mr. Nichols, senior, and Maurice (M. S.) Nichols (England and Essex). Maurice, or Stan as he was known to his friends, quite naturally brought fame to Wickford.

Present chairman is S. Mapleson, and the captain, S. Coates, with another member of the Mapleson family—J. Mapleson—as vice-captain. A. J. Mayes leads the Sunday XI.

In the early days of the club, R. W. Patmore captained the side in a match in which a certain player thought he should have been playing. This player was asked to act as one of the umpires, and consented. He then gave the captain out l.b.w., which appeared a very wrong decision. After the match the umpire said to the captain, 'You didn't like my decision?' 'No,' said the skipper, 'it was quite wrong.' 'I know it was,' said the unrepentant umpire. 'Now perhaps you will have me as a player in the next match, and not an umpire!'

F. E. Wallace, efficient secretary of the club, tells of a match when the club was on tour in 1934. Against Greylingwell Mental Hospital (Chichester), one of the Wickford players had bowled extremely well to take 5 or 6 wickets. One of the inmates of the hospital went up to him after the match and said, 'Weren't you the man bowling from the pavilion end who bowled our men out?' 'Yes,' said the bowler. 'Well,' retorted the spectator, 'I've not see such b——y tripe for years!'

Wallace re-emphasised to me how hard it is these days for a club to pay its way. In the old days £150 would cover all expenses, including a groundsman. Today it costs £250–£300 per season without a groundsman, whose work has to be carried out voluntarily by members.

West Essex Club, too, is finding that costs of a ground are increasing to what is becoming an almost prohibitive rate. It says it is paying 400 per cent. more rental now than in 1947. If this percentage is right, then it costs the club just about a tenner for every home match played. There is no doubt that something must be done to stop this upward trend of rates and rents, otherwise clubs will very soon find it impossible to carry on.

Founded in 1913, West Essex has been fortunate in having its present ground at Higham's Park for over twenty-five years. W. E. Harriss, the general secretary for many years, has been largely responsible for the expansion of the club, which now includes tennis, hockey, and table tennis. Arthur Speakman is the cricket secretary, and held office during the War years. In 1943, he organised the record-breaking Red Cross match against the Chinghoppers. Arthur also arranges the very popular Kent tour and a fixture list that includes a visit from a West Indies XI during July each year.

Bill Horsey, medium fast bowler, once took 10 Walthamstow wickets for only 8 runs. In 1944—against the same team—he took 8 for 17. In ten successive seasons, he never failed to take 100 wickets.

On the batting side J. Impey is a consistently sound opener; skipper W. D. McDowall also opens, and R. S. Spelling, the wicket-keeper, F. Mixter, and J. Treble usually score freely.

As far as tours are concerned, the club seems to have created a precedent in club cricket, as it has made its headquarters three years running at three different holiday camps. These experiments have been highly successful, from both a playing and a social point of view. It certainly is an idea for other clubs to consider.

Although about fifty cricketers are on the playing strength, the club, with its large tennis and hockey sections, finds that when the annual dinner comes round they can't find a hall in West Essex with enough accommodation.

I must confess to my shame that I first heard of the *Aveley Cricket Club* when George Pullinger (Essex), their match secretary, played for the C.C.C. against the New Zealanders at Guildford in 1949.

The oldest records of the club go back to 1815, when on Thursday, June 22, Eleven Gentlemen of Aveley played Eleven of the Liberty Club for one hundred guineas. The bill advertising this match is still in existence. This game was played on the same ground as the club now occupies.

Before 1939, stalwarts of the club were: F. Pavitt, A. Chisnell, W. Lowe, J. Blows, J. Downes, and S. Pavitt, the latter being chairman of the club for approximately thirty years.

In 1943 the ground was requisitioned by the War Office. Throughout the War years, and for several years after, all matches were of necessity played away from home. Now, however, Aveley are back home again and have settled down.

It is a small club with a mere twenty-one members, but what they have lost in numbers they certainly make up for in keenness. Present chairman is L. Martin, who is one of the Minor Counties umpires, and vice-chairman of Thurrock District Cricket Association. J. D. Watt, a member of the executive committee of the Essex County C.C.. is the financial secretary.

Of the players, George Pullinger is perhaps the most outstanding. He represented Thurrock and District Cricket Association against the County XI and the Bristol Cricket Association, and was awarded his Minor County cap in 1948. The following year he got his county and C.C.C. caps. He is a fine, opening, new-ball bowler, with a disconcerting change of pace and swing. H. Marshall has also represented Thurrock and District C.A., and headed the club bowling averages in 1945, 1946, and 1947. One of his best performances was against Claybury in August, 1948, when he took 9 for 27. H. Revell, a grand all-rounder, was killed at work during the summer of 1949.

Another good club man is Yorkshireman E. Scorah, who, besides being a useful spin bowler, can be a dour, stolid batsman.

Skipper of the club is H. Carter, who also played for Thurrock and District C.A. in 1947 and 1948. He is an excellent 'keeper and an aggressive batsman. L. Eaton, apart from being an opening bat and useful spin bowler, has also kept wicket for Thurrock and District.

In the summer of 1858, a match between 'Married and Single' inaugurated the *Upminster Cricket Club*.

In those days it was common practice to arrange fixtures by sending challenges to neighbouring clubs. T. L. Wilson, who was a founder-member, recalled these interesting facts at a dinner given at the Bell Hotel, on November 27, 1897. Apparently the Married *v.* Single match in 1858 was the only game the club had that year. But as members continued to pay their 2*d.* per week subscription throughout the winter, the club had accumulated a small fund ready to begin operations in earnest in 1859. Soon after, the club played fourteen matches in one season and won them all —among those beaten were East Ham, West Ham, Stratford, Walthamstow, Chigwell, Ilford, and Romford.

H. W. Oscroft, the present secretary, told me that, on the occasion of a youth's match in 1889, it was resolved that a ham weighing 14 lb. and a piece of beef for roasting of about 18 lb.

(or about three ribs) should be provided. The chairman promised a subscription of 5*s.* towards the extra expense. How we could do with 'light' refreshment like that after our matches these days!

Match balls cost only 5*s.* then, and bats 15*s.* For cutting the outfield, which usually took some three hours, they paid a man 1*s.* 7*d.*, while a certain Mr. T. Elliott was paid 4*s.* 2*d.* per day, for five days, for repairing one of the club's tents!

In recent years Upminster's outstanding batsman has been Stanley Eve. In 1943 he played for the A.T.C. at Lord's against the Royal Naval College, Dartmouth, making 91 in this, his first big match. In 1949, at the age of twenty-three, he played regularly for Essex, and in the Warwickshire match scored 120. I was playing for Northants against Essex at Northampton in 1949, and although Stanley did not make a huge score, I was greatly impressed by his fine fielding.

Captain of Upminster is B. Carter, while Jack Smye shoulders the responsibilities of match secretary.

Chapter Five

CLUBS AND THEIR PLAYERS

Histories, outstanding players, and anecdotes of the clubs in Kent.

K ENT has an association of clubs now, but I doubt whether the Club Cricket Conference, of which most of the Kent clubs are members, will be altogether enthusiastic. The association has pledged support to the county, and the project has the strong support of the former Kent captain, Brian Valentine, who has accepted the association 'chair'.

It is surprising that *Wilmington* is not better known outside the county. The club celebrated its jubilee the year War broke out—just in time—and in December, 1949, its diamond jubilee, at which Douglas Wright of England and Kent was the guest of honour.

A fine record here. Of sixty-two members, fifty are on the playing strength, including groundsman Harry Bennett, who has been keeping wicket for the club for twenty-nine years.

Like so many of the Kentish village clubs, it was helped considerably by the patronage of the Lord of the Manor—Lord Tredegar in those days—who allowed a part of Dartford Heath to be cleared. This corner of the heath then cost the club 1s. per annum. Now they pay £52. In 1934 the local council bought part of the estate, so Wilmington now play on what is classed as—but looks nothing like—a public ground.

Club president D. C. Wallis once took 'all 10' for the club, and his predecessor, A. E. Martin, was famous for his under-arm bowling—which takes one back quite a way!

In contrast to Wilmington's 50 of 62 playing members, *C.I.A.* (Chief Inspector of Armaments), a Kentish works club, has well over 1,000 members, but only 45 are active. Their top player is Brigadier K. S. Mackenzie (Free Foresters and Band of Brothers) who not only invariably heads their batting averages, but shared the record first-wicket stand for the club—161 with W. Lover in 1948.

C.I.A. was one of the few clubs to play throughout the War.

A. Hiscock, the captain and a consistent medium-pace bowler, once took the team to a village in Berkshire. When placing his field for the first over, he kept moving one player deeper and deeper. Suddenly, the fielder disappeared. This was obviously one of the occasions when it was *not* profitable to keep one's eye on the skipper. The player was discovered lying at the bottom of the local refuse-pit.

Hayes (Kent) is known to have been in existence since 1834, but two of its more recent activities deserve special mention. In the first place, its private ground has been purchased so that it may be retained for ever as a sports ground. Secondly, its honorary members have their own honorary secretary, P. Jenkins. Jenkins took this new office in 1948, and other clubs would do well to consider a similar appointment. He does everything to ensure patrons 'keep in touch', even down to the publication of a regular news-letter.

Hayes have another of these 'indispensables' in J. Dance, who has voluntarily looked after the square for thirty years. Still bowling left-hand slows is Billy Dance. He and D. J. Spelman (once 10 for 33) are the stock bowlers, and Dance has hit three consecutive centuries. Roger Grandfield skippers the side. Veteran Sid Foster has played for the club since 1930, and now his son shows great promise at wicket-keeping.

Outstanding for *Old Elthamians*, who play on the College ground at Mottingham, is T. G. Light, who in 1949 took 110 wickets for an average of 6·98 and scored 665 runs.

So far the Old Boys have had to play their home games during the school holidays, but now they have bought their own ground; it will be ready in 1951. Their most exciting game? When they wanted two runs to beat Blackheath Wanderers, with their last man in. The wicket-keeper conceded four byes—much to the relief of No. 11.

I like *Bexley*—I used to play against the club for the Old Alleynians before the War—but not just for its cricket (which is good). I like Bexley because the whole town seems to have a personal interest in the club. And, of course, its 'Weeks', when everybody joins in, are famous.

The 1949 festival, in July, was augmented by an 'Old English' game in August. Quite rightly, because there are few clubs more entitled to represent the past. Although established a long time previously, Bexley have proof that in 1805 they beat Kent by an innings and 70, with a team that included Lord Frederick Beauclerk.

Bexley's all-time 'classic' is the match against Emeriti in 1884, when the opening pair, John Shuter, afterwards Surrey captain, and Tom Ashdown, also of Surrey, were unbeaten for 402. Emeriti were out for 131 (W. E. Fennessey, 74 not out), and L. A. Shuter, John's brother, did the hat-trick. Details of this match, printed on silk, are displayed in the club-house.

Bexley had a shock in 1889. They played Lord Harris, the two Shuter brothers, W. B. Friend, W. Rashleigh, W. H. Spottiswood, G. Bird, and W. C. Jackson, but were out for 38 against Bickley Park, who made 138.

More recently Bexley had 'ground trouble', but were saved by J. A. Potter, who bought the ground and charged only a nominal rent. After J. A.'s death, Alistair Potter, J.P., now life president, gave the club a ninety-nine-year lease. His son Jeremy is a regular member of the club side.

Big hitters who played regularly for the club are Arthur Wellard, of Somerset, and F. T. C. ('Hacker') Johnson, now vice-captain of the second XI. Once, at the 'Bat and Ball' ground, Gravesend, 'Hacker' hit 119 in 55 minutes, including eight 6s right out of the ground.

The War put the club out of action, but it was swift to restore the Bexley tradition. Some of the men who have helped it to do so are George Lovegrove, now captain, J. W. Jeffery, who played in a Conference trial in 1949 and scored 1,000 for three successive seasons, and slow-bowler Cyril Hoare. On the organising side, W. S. ('Gimps') Gimber is outstanding. He was chiefly responsible for restarting the 'Week' in 1948. Its remarkable success is a good augury for the club's continued prosperity.

And now to the coast, where one of the most prosperous clubs is *Dover*, which does so much to ensure the success of the county week, first held on its ground in 1906. W. H. Fish (previously captain and now chairman), A. C. Lemey (president, with seventy years of unbroken service to the club), and H. W. Youden (a vice-president) were chiefly responsible for bringing the county side to the ground.

The ground at Crabble, once owned privately, and now belonging to the Corporation, is hewn out of the hillside, and its popularity is so great that Dover never goes on tour. The club prefers to entertain touring sides. But I hear a trip to Paris is contemplated. To get the excursion really organised for first-team members, it is proposed to take the second XI along to play the cricket.

Similarly, there is no official cricket week, but Dover has so many visiting sides in June and July that several weeks in these months are akin to a normal club's 'Week'.

One of the main attractions after the game is 'The Mortuary', a new name for the bar, because of the innumerable inquests held there.

I feel I must pay tribute here to W. T. Moore, honorary secretary and publicity secretary. I wonder whether Dover realises that in Moore it has a publicity secretary who really lives up to his title—quite apart from his executive duties? Moore, his father, and his grandfather have all played for Dover. His son, at five years of age, is the youngest-ever member.

Only one 'local' has ever played for the county. He is E. Crush, a fast-medium bowler and aggressive bat, who won his county cap in 1949 after two seasons of more or less regular county play. One of five cricketing brothers, he learnt the game at Dover County School, and was club secretary from the end of the War until 1949. In the Royal Engineers during the War, he became a captain and won the M.C.

B. H. Lock, capped for Devon in 1935, joined Dover in 1948 and played regularly for Kent II in 1949, gaining his second XI cap after scoring 144 and 127 against his old county in one day.

Two younger men who did well for Dover in 1949 were D. S. Sheppard, who made such a great start in county cricket when chosen for Sussex—and now plays for England—and Worcester reserve wicket-keeper, P. J. Whitcombe, who was in the Army in the Dover area.

Wartime cricket in Dover was rather tricky—to say the least of it. Once W. T. Moore, playing against a Navy XI, hit one through the covers for four. At the identical moment of his stroke, a German long-range shell fell on the hill opposite the ground. The Navy wicket-keeper's only comment was, 'I think you've cracked your bat, chum.'

I like the one about A. J. ('Sam') Took, who has done so much good work for cricket in the South-East, and who, though over fifty years of age, is still playing as well as ever. Apparently, on an off day, he put two 'sitters' off Crush on to the floor. After the second miss, Crush stopped his next run to the wicket, put his hands on his hips and said, 'Now before we go any further, Sam, shall I go and get you a b—— alarm clock?'

Near neighbours, *Folkestone* are great Dover rivals. The two sides share in the great story of a game on May 25, 1872, when only six Folkestone men turned up. The local paper's comments were pithy and to the point. About Folkestone, it said: 'The club must be weak if it cannot draw up an XI for a home match, and in spite of the exertions of the honorary secretary, only five players appeared on time. A sixth arrived at two o'clock.

'To save a total breakdown the first five, by courtesy of their opponents, were put in twice—a state of things most discreditable. In future we trust the Folkestone members will make a better appearance . . . these shortcomings are becoming notorious.'

Folkestone plays its cricket on a public ground now, constructed in 1927 by the Corporation. The club has about 200 members (forty-five are players).

L. W. Godden has been skipper since 1937, and, like Dover, a 'Moore' is honorary secretary—S. A. Moore, who has held the office since 1939 and who, until that date, was honorary treasurer for three years. A. J. S. Clark was 1950's chairman, and F. Brooks Hill, honorary treasurer.

Of the post-War players J. A. Gordon is outstanding, and he completed the double in 1949—a year in which no fewer than seven players scored 1,000 runs each. Not many clubs can boast of such a fine record.

Besides Gordon and skipper Godden, Folkestone has often seen W. C. Blacklocks, B. Goodsell, and Brooks Hill in devastating form with the bat, and the opposition bowled out repeatedly by friend Gordon and S. G. Burden. In 1950, Goodsell completed 'the double' and also took all 10 wickets in an innings—a feat not performed by a Folkestone player since 1931.

Folkestone runs two Saturday sides and one on Sundays, and resumed its annual cricket 'Week' in June of 1950. Like most other clubs on the coast, it does not tour.

Don't be misled by the name *West Kent Wanderers*. It has its home ground in Greenwich Park, and although classed as 'public', only the Wanderers and the R.N. College (Greenwich) are allowed to use it. From its foundation in 1856 up to the outbreak of the Second World War, the club played on some part of Blackheath.

When all but six of the playing members were called up in 1939, ex-match secretary W. J. Nelan had a terrific job to keep a side in the field throughout the War. But he did it. W. A. H. Shaw, honorary secretary and treasurer, 1932–39, could not resume his dual post in 1945, but in 1946 he became chairman, and in his new office has been just as beneficial to the club. He has been greatly helped by R. E. Chipperfield, who assumed the Shaw mantle as secretary and treasurer.

The Christopherson family has been associated with the club for many, many years, and Nevill Christopherson, now Kent's secretary, is an ex-president.

Through all its ups and downs, the club has had no greater supporter than George Barker, over seventy now and still playing. Indeed, for 1950 George bought a new bat—he thought his other was beginning to weaken!

West Kent's top player has been John Bell, captain from 1932, who played minor counties cricket for Suffolk before the War. He has completed the double six times, and in 1939 hit five 6s and a 4 in one over.

R. J. Wood, vice-captain, joined as a schoolboy in 1937 after an unsuccessful trial for the county. In 1947 he scored 2,600 in fewer than forty innings, and over 1,600 runs in both 1948 and 1949. In 1948 he played in a C.C.C. trial at Finchley, and is still club individual-record holder, with 209 not out against Gravesend.

And here's a man for opponents to watch—A. Bishop. He joined in 1948, and in that season and 1949 took 119 wickets for averages of 6·94 and 6·73 respectively.

What a game is cricket! And what a day for the Allsopp brothers when they arrived at the wicket together with 6 out for 33. Their partnership lasted only forty minutes, but in that time Doug hit his first hundred (116), the younger, Norman, his first 50 (53 not out), and together they put on 174.

Wanderers still like to wander—occasionally. So every year they tour East Anglia, just to remind each other how nice it is to

have their own ground. And, back in the 1920s, they visited
Belgium.

How much some people do for cricket—and how few hear
about it! Not many know, for instance, that Captain, then
Commander, C. B. Fry, was responsible for the lay-out of the
Central Y.M.C.A. ground at Mottingham.

C. B. Fry, of course, needs no introduction. The club, perhaps,
does. It is the cricket section of seventy—all players—of the
Y.M.C.A.'s total of over 2,000 members. The ground of twenty
acres was given, free of all cost, by the late Edwin Harrop,
and pre-War contained four squares. One has been sacrificed to
enlarge the boundaries for the remaining three.

Like so many others, Centyma, as the club is known, had the
ground commandeered during the War, and when it was handed
back in 1946 it was practically unplayable. And there were only
two pre-War members—H. G. Pooler and George Hodgson—to
re-establish both club and ground.

They managed it, and in 1950 had a minimum of four elevens.
Their best player, batsman Arthur Corbishley, was captain in
1947 and 1948. Centyma teams have included men from India,
Australia, West Indies, East Africa, and Ceylon. The pleasure
they get can be no more than that of the men who have done
the 'impossible' to provide it.

Blackheath has the distinction of having Nevill Christopherson
—nephew of Stanley Christopherson, late president of the
M.C.C.—as a member (Nevill's earlier association with West
Kent is mentioned above).

It was he who 'resurrected' the Blackheath club after it had
been out of action during the War. Its first post-War season was
1946, and Christopherson was honorary secretary and honorary
treasurer until 1949, when he took on his present job with Kent.

Blackheath, of course, draws on the rugby club for quite a few
cricketers. Latest captain (1949–50) is Howard Taylor, a
good bat and useful medium-paced bowler who has played for
Kent. Top all-rounder is J. G. W. Davis, but the club doesn't see
as much of him as it would like because business frequently takes
him abroad.

One of the most consistent all-rounders and captain of the
Sunday side is R. C. ('Bill') Williams. C. G. ('Tim') Toppin, a

brilliant field, at times demoralises the opposition with some very hard hitting.

The ground had a varied career during the War, receiving five direct hits by bombs—it was a balloon site—but sport continued almost uninterrupted because Greenwich A.T.C. units and Civil Defence teams played football and cricket all the time.

Blackheath is another club that took a long time to 'branch out', as 1950 was the year of its first home 'Week'. It had taken the club from 1885 to decide to hold one!

Elmers End, with only fifty-five playing members, manages to run three Saturday and two Sunday sides, so it is no surprise to find that the executive was keen enough to keep the club going through the War. This was owing, in the main, to the president, Hubert Ashton, Cambridge Blue; J. G. Semple, honorary general secretary and captain, and the honorary treasurer, M. G. White.

Albert and Fred Dawes, the Crystal Palace footballers, have both done well for the club, and although Albert has left the district, Fred, injured in 1949, returned to the side the following year. Alan Patterson played for London Counties during the War and completed the double for the club in 1944. So did M. B. Watts, who has been so successful since War ended—he did it in 1947.

Elmers End was formed in 1884, but it was not until 1920 that it purchased its present ground in Croydon Road, Beckenham. It was prevented by the War from building the brick pavilion on which members had set their hearts. Nevertheless, a 'running' score-box was installed in 1949, and they were hoping for permission to add the pavilion very shortly afterwards. If their record is any criterion, they'll manage it somehow.

In contrast to Elmers End, *The Times Cricket Club*, whose ground is at Ravensbourne, was fortunate in completing its pavilion just *before* the War.

The Times Club goes back nearly seventy years, and is certainly the oldest club of the London daily newspapers. Matches among the morning newspapers have taken place these many years, but there are far fewer clubs to play them today. The London Daily Newspaper League was suspended at the outbreak of war and has not yet been restarted, but before that the John Walter Presentation Cup was keenly contested and was won many times by *The Times* Club. Country-house matches were arranged yearly at Bear Wood, Berkshire, cricket weeks were a regular feature, and the strongest Conference sides were entertained.

The Rajputana touring team visited the club in 1936. The result was an exciting match which the visitors won. The Lords and Commons Cricket Club were regular visitors. Cambridge University sent sides, and Andy Sandham brought along a mixed XI of amateurs and professionals each season.

One regular Sunday XI and one Saturday side have entertained regularly at Ravensbourne since 1918, under the late Fred Spackman's enthusiastic captaincy.

Perhaps one of the best-known names in *Times* cricket is that of Dick Nash, secretary many years before the War and now fixture secretary. He did much to ensure that Saturday and Sunday games were resumed from 1945 onwards. A. S. Horry is now honorary secretary.

Not far away from the *Times* ground, we meet a club that was founded back in 1890. The origin of the *Cyphers Cricket Club* is associated with a club called Brixton Amateurs, which was formed by Charles Adye and his brothers. After a successful eleven years, it left its ground at Dulwich and migrated to Kingshall Road, Beckenham. A few members from the Brixton Wanderers C.C. decided to join the new club, which first played under the name of 'Cyphers' in 1903.

The present spacious and well-planned pavilion was opened in 1936. In 1944, however, it suffered some superficial damage from a German rocket. Two teams were kept going throughout the 1939–45 War, but by 1947 the fixture list was restored to four regular teams, with an occasional fifth.

Members are frequently asked whence the club derives its name. It appears that when the Adye brothers moved from Dulwich, members could not agree on a suitable name. After much discussion a certain member suggested that, as they were all worthy cricketers and had, no doubt, made a 'duck', they should call themselves the 'Cyphers'.

One of the earliest games played on the Kingshall Road ground was against a team captained by W. G. Grace, and on many other occasions he came to play with his inseparable friend,

Murdoch. In its time the club has entertained many famous cricketers, among them Archie McLaren, the Ashton brothers, the Bryan brothers, Arthur Day, Ernest Beldam, H. J. Enthoven, C. T. A. Wilkinson, G. J. V. Weigall, Rev. F. H. Gillingham, and R. W. V. Robins.

Among the names of well-known club cricketers, we find that those who have done a great deal for the Cyphers are: L. W. Simmons, who was captain for twenty years, and father of 'Simbo' Simmons, the present secretary of the Old Alleynians C.C., P. B. Wise, A. W. R. Matthews, and N. P. Andrews, who also played for my county—Northamptonshire.

I am sure few clubs have been represented by so many family cricketers as the Cyphers have been. Over the years there have been the Adye brothers—C. W., E., F. J., E. H.; the Wardle brothers—F. J., P., W. A., also D. J. (son of W. A.); the Gale brothers—E. T., L. H., R. D.; the Beardwell brothers—W. R., A. E., A. R., also H. A. (son of A. R.); and the Duncan family—W., and his sons, J. W., R. A., and P. R.

R. Holloway, who was skipper from 1936 to 1949, is now president of the club. B. W. Newton has been general secretary since 1938, and T. Andrews, treasurer for a number of years. The cricket secretaries recently have been: R. J. S. Booty, who did duty from 1938 to 1940 and took on again in 1946, and M. G. R. Booty, who carried on during the War years from 1940 to 1945.

E. M. Wisdom has been skipper since 1949. He consistently scores a lot of runs, and with T. H. Jenner, who has been very prominent in the batting line since 1934, appears regularly in the club cricket columns in the Sunday papers. A. E. Beardwell, from 1920 to 1948, was another backbone of the side when it came to getting runs; J. A. Bills, L. W. Black, and E. G. Purnell are others who have never let the side down.

In W. A. Wardle, now sixty-six years of age, the Cyphers have their oldest playing member. He has been turning out regularly for the club since 1919. Other bowlers to cause consternation among the ranks of the opposition are C. H. Tinsley (from 1928 to 1948), F. W. Parker, F. J. Kelsh, J. A. F. Crawford, and W. A. Dorset. Kelsh, by the way, holds the record for the club for the greatest number of wickets in a season—148 in 1949. However, 'Griff' (E. A. Griffiths) must have taken more wickets for the club than any other member, as he is still bowling after taking his 1,000th wicket in 1936!

With a large squad of younger members, the Cyphers can look forward to many years of successful club cricket.

One of the most famous of the Kent clubs is *Beckenham*, which can trace its history back to 1866. If all its more celebrated members could turn out together, not only would the club beat practically any other club in the country, but it would give several of the counties a run for their money.

What a side! A. W. H. Mallett (Oxford and Kent); W. Murray-Wood (Oxford and Kent); R. J. Morris, O. J. Wait (both of Cambridge University); the Bryan brothers—G. J., and my great friend, R. T.; C. T. A. Wilkinson (Surrey); B. C. Phillips (squash rackets international and big-cricket hitter); and captain of the full-day side, T. D. Mitchell. E. W. S. Boult is skipper of the half-day XI, and C. H. Miller captains the Wizards.

Beckenham has a magnificent score-board, erected many years ago by the late Colonel Bryan, father of G. J., R. T., and J. L. This board shows everything, including the wicket-keeper's name, bowling analyses, and the essentials such as the individual batsmen's totals and which bowlers are performing at any particular moment.

Beckenham ground is at Foxgrove Road. Quiet and secluded, it must be one of the most beautiful in the county.

K. Burgess Smith became general secretary in 1946. Cricket secretaries have been R. Curwen (up to 1944), A. Cecil Pearce (1945), W. H. Mallett (Tony's father) (1946–49), and W. G. Edmonds (1950). In charge of fixtures is P. Shervington.

Unlike so many others, the club has been most diligent about keeping records, and in the pavilion are framed averages of all players since the club was founded, excepting for the years of World War I.

There's one 'must' for all visitors. They must bring their club flag to hang on the score-board opposite the Beckenham flag, while the match is in progress.

Right next to Beckenham is *Bickley Park*, another club of long-standing. Since its foundation in 1868 it has always played on its ground at Foxgrove Avenue, Beckenham. Naturally, Beckenham are traditional rivals, and others in the same category are Bromley and West Kent, the games against these three opponents being practically unbroken in the eighty-odd years of the club's existence. Bickley's ground, by the way, was formerly part of a deer park. A. S. Rogers, captain and secretary, has done a lot to keep Bickley 'on the map'.

Still in Beckenham, we come now to the *Lloyds Bank Club*. Banks cricket flourishes as much as ever, and perhaps the three cricketers who have helped to establish and keep Lloyds Bank in the very top flight are Frank Crang, chairman and skipper, 1929–39, Ronnie Bryan, ex-skipper of Kent and Beckenham, captain, 1926–39, and Freddie Stiff, skipper, 1946–48.

These three are still active first XI players, although Crang and Stiff have been with the club for the last twenty-five years. For twenty of them they have batted Nos. 1 and 2 for the Bank, and had a reputation of being the best opening pair of London club cricketers. I don't like to think of the number of times the two together have hit 50 and then the 100 in games in which I have been playing.

Freddie Stiff, born within a stone's-throw of Lord's, must be one of the most outstanding club cricketers never to have represented his County. He scores far in excess of a thousand runs every season, and has hit more than seventy-five centuries.

Ronnie Bryan rejoined the Bank club when it restarted after the War in 1946. He has a formidable record. Now in his fifty-second year, his one remaining ambition is to complete 50,000 runs before he retires. Judging by his magnificent form in 1949 and 1950, he will reach that figure soon. So far he has scored more than 80 centuries in club cricket. And apart from his batting, he is an excellent slow bowler, with an average of more than 70 wickets per season.

Frank Penn is now the skipper and assistant secretary. I first met Frank in Italy during the War, when he was based in the Naval Fort at Naples. I saw quite a lot of him then, especially at some of the naval concerts in the Fort. Together we used to join Philip Slessor, the announcer, and Con Mahoney, BBC confederates of mine.

Frank told me about his tour in 1949. They were playing on the pretty Ross-on-Wye ground for the first time, and a very keen youngster in the XI, who was doing well with the ball, was enthusing on the wonderful setting of the ground with the River Wye running behind the sight-screen. Ronnie Bryan, who was standing down, warned him that he might be knocked out of the

H

ground into the river. 'That's all right—I'd have a fielder deep midstream,' was the reply.

Pre-War, Lloyds Bank toured Kent and then East Anglia. Since the War they have been going to the West Country. Their own ground in Coper's Cope Road, Beckenham, has some magnificent wickets and a fine pavilion. Like many other Bank teams, six sides are put into the field on Saturdays, though out of an overall figure of 1,000 members of the sports club, only ninety-six are active cricketers.

Still at Beckenham and still with the Banks we find the *Forbanks Club*, established in 1922. Members are the non-clerical staff of four banks—Bank of England, Midland, National Provincial, and Westminster—hence the name. Their ground is a private one at Beckenham Hill. Forbanks has 1,200 members, of whom approximately seventy are playing cricketers.

Skipper is R. Knight, who, apart from captaining the side, is a very effective bowler. Against a Westminster Bank XI in 1947 Knight took all 10 wickets for 47 runs, and in 1949 took 13 wickets for a 7·4 analysis.

To support him he has C. Beagley (vice-captain), R. Pettit (honorary secretary), L. Brain, S. Smith, E. King, A. Baker, H. Hutton, F. Bull, F. Jacobs, R. Duly, W. Holman, D. Penn, L. Lee, and W. Kimble.

One of the biggest private grounds in the country is the twenty-nine acres—opened in 1921—of the *Midland Bank* adjoining New Beckenham station. The club itself was established about 1873. E. C. Long is captain of the first team, but there are six other Saturday XIs and a Sunday side as well.

Having come across so many Banks clubs at Beckenham, this seems an opportune moment to mention the *United Banks*. As the name implies, this is a representative Banks club, and it can field a very useful side indeed. Their top match, perhaps, is against *United Insurances*—a similar organisation. F. E. Crang, of Lloyds, is to the fore again here—as chairman.

From the Banks—and back to school. R. S. Morriss was in charge of cricket at Sir Joseph Williamson's School, Rochester, for thirty-five years. And now he is still chairman of the *Old*

Williamsonians, the old boys' club he founded in 1912. He had to 'found' it twice, the second time being after World War I in 1919.

Old Williamsonians, indeed, have had the worst of both world wars. Their original ground on Rochester Esplanade was lost in World War II when it was requisitioned. The ground was neglected and the pavilion destroyed by enemy action, so the school sold it to the local Corporation. The destruction of the pavilion was indeed a body blow. It was the reward of ten years of effort to raise the funds, and was opened in 1930 by Lord Harris. Now the old boys, by the courtesy of the governors, play on the school ground. J. A. Brooks is captain.

A great day in the club's history was when they played a Maidstone church side and were put out for 84. Maidstone had made 80 for 4 when G. L. Martin announced he would do the hat-trick. And he did—with the last three balls of his over.

Not to be outdone, G. L. Morriss proclaimed that he would do likewise. Lo! and behold—as the church team might have put it—he took a wicket with each of his next three balls. That made six out in six successive balls, and the old boys had won by 4 runs. No writer of cricket fiction would dare to suggest such a possibility—let alone have his bowlers announce their intentions beforehand.

There are four 'Bromley' teams in Kent—*Bromley* itself, *Bromley Common*, *Bromley Parish Church Club*, and *Bromley Town*. The first named is the best known, having been established since 1820 and having a close association with Beckenham, Blackheath, and the other big local clubs. H. S. Greensted is captain. It has one thing, at least, in common with the church team—no Sunday play.

Bromley Common has existed officially for only sixty years, but a cricket club has been on the Common since 1812, when the Princes Plain Club was formed. The present club, which sprang from Princes Plain, owes its ground to the Norman family. Mr. Charles Norman granted it to them in 1889, in which year his son, Mr. A. C. Norman, J.P., became president, remaining in office until his death in 1948. He, in turn, was succeeded by his son—Major-General C. W. Norman, C.B.E. The year 1948 was a sad one for the club because it was then also that R. S. Jackson, twenty-five years a player, retired. During those twenty-five years he was treasurer for fifteen, and honorary secretary and treasurer for the other ten. Present honorary secretary is H. Veness, and D. Pearson is treasurer.

Of their players, D. Bunting, a brilliant left-hand bat and spin bowler, scored 4,487 runs in the first five seasons after the War and took 480 wickets. He completed the double in 1944. H. Venn, opening batsman, is also a medium-fast bowler. He scored 5,896 runs from 1945 to 1950 and took over 300 wickets. Bunting and Venn both scored over 1,000 runs in 1950. And for captain there is a choice of three: W. Squire or E. Mills for Saturday matches, and G. L. West for Sundays.

Interesting, that, and by no means uncommon. But I've never quite got used to the idea myself, and although I realise a job shared is a job halved, I doubt whether the benefit outweighs the very decided advantage of a team's having the same 'handling' for every game.

Eltham Cricket Club, founded about 1863, was re-formed in 1944 chiefly by the present president, A. de Winter, and secretary, Vic Knight. But Eltham has great claim to fame. Dr. W. G. Grace used to captain the club, and he last appeared for it about 1912. The late Sir C. Aubrey Smith was a leading vice-president in his time and did a lot for the club. Two other vice-presidents are Canadians, H. J. Knight and R. Jeffreys.

Outstanding on the field in more recent years has been E. Sherwood, who has taken more than 100 wickets in each season since World War II. Secretary Knight is known better for his big hitting, and Arthur Dann has had considerable success as captain.

Knight, as I say, has achieved fame as a hitter. Against the Old Colfeians at Lee towards the end of the War, Knight was going for some quick runs when, during the bowler's run up to the wicket, he dropped his bat and ran straight for the boundary and into a W.A.A.F.'s dug-out. When the doodle-bug he had seen approaching had passed over the ground, he resumed his innings, but his fame as a hitter was surpassed for ever. He was club sprint champion from that day.

Swanscombe and Greenhithe Club has a promising county teenager in Alan Dixon, who played his first match for Kent—against Essex—in 1950. Swanscombe, seventy years old this year, has a good reputation locally as 'progressives'.

It is certainly catholic in its touring: Devon, Cornwall, Somerset, Norfolk, and the Isle of Wight. Home 'Weeks' are few, but there was a special jubilee week in 1930.

Shipowner W. J. Everard, a member of Lloyds and formerly a Kent county councillor, is club president, and it was mainly owing to him and secretaries C. W. Gooderham and R. Petheram (match secretary), and I. Borland (treasurer), that the club has regained its status since the War. While their hopes for the future rest on young members, players who have 'carried' the club for so long include K. Atkinson, H. Croucher, K. Webb, R. Petheram, E. and R. Hills, and A. Hand.

One of Swanscombe's touring games in the Isle of Wight gave their opening pair 117. Just before they were parted an old gentleman wanted to know whence this pair came. On being told Kent, he promptly replied that that couldn't be true. If it was, he added, there was no earthly reason why Kent should be in the bottom half of the championship table.

Cricket was played on the common land at Sevenoaks early in the 18th century and the records go back to 1734. So *Sevenoaks Vine* is justly entitled to consider itself one of the oldest clubs in the country. It still plays on the common land given to the town by the 3rd Duke of Dorset in 1773, and has exclusive use of it for cricket. Curiously, the ground caused the only break in over 200 years' cricket at the club: when it was levelled—and consequently became unplayable—for a couple of seasons in the 1890s.

E. A. Tootal saved another stoppage during the World War II when, as honorary treasurer, he ran the club practically single-handed. But Vine has survived the bad times, and in 1950 had one of the strongest and most successful teams in southern club cricket.

M. Begent is a fine opening bat. When with Orpington, he scored 1,000 runs when sixteen and 2,000 when seventeen years of age, refusing offers to turn professional. Captain and wicket-keeper from 1937 to 1949, D. C. G. Raikes won his Oxford Blue and played as an amateur for Gloucester and Kent. Now he is club chairman.

Norman Golds, the captain, is a good partner for Begent, and to bowl there are all-rounder Ken Smart (from Centymca), J. G. Sagar, and Norman Gavin. Gavin joined from Catford Wanderers in 1949, and made up the side's one real deficiency—a slow left-

arm spinner. Another addition was wicket-keeper G. Downton
and he, like Gavin, Smart, and Begent, has won a C.C.C. cap.

All-rounder S. G. Smith, who played many times for th
Conference, left some time ago and now plays for Westcliff-on
Sea. A measure of the support given to chairman Raike
and the club is shown by the 358 members, of whom sixty
six play.

Like the Vine, there was cricket at *Tunbridge Wells* long befor
the official founding date of the club, but the earliest reference i
to a game on the common in 1782 when Groombridge bea
Tunbridge Wells by four notches.

Play continued there until 1898, when the Nevill Ground, i
Warwick Park, was laid out so that county cricket could b
brought back to the town. Tunbridge Wells, of course, classe
itself with other fortunates like Horsham, Brighton, Worthing
Gravesend, Romford, Hastings, and Eastbourne, all of which pla
on grounds considered by the counties to be up to first-clas
professional standards.

Captain since 1948 has been W. Isard, who once moved t
and played for Croydon, and then returned to take over th
captaincy. He is a Conference 'cap', while pace bowler, Desmon
Hall, had a C.C.C. game against the Universities Athletic Unio
in 1949.

Peter Hearn, who plays regularly for the county now, is th
grandson of a previous Nevill groundsman and son of an ol
playing member and ex-secretary of Tunbridge Wells. On th
executive side, treasurer P. G. Hamlin has been a vice-presiden
of the C.C.C. since 1925. The president is the Marquess c
Abergavenny.

Clubs in Middlesex talk fondly of the Walkers of Southgate
but *Cobham*, Kent, also has its Walker family.

Present Cobham chairman, Jack Walker, is, I am told, th
local sub-postmaster. He played for Kent against Essex a
Gravesend in 1948 and his father captained Cobham for twenty
five years. So Jack was in the chair for the club centenary celebra
tions in 1950; and his grandfather played in the Golden Jubile
match between the village and Cobham Hall in 1900.

Cobham, of course, is the club that produced The Ashe
Cobham Park was the home of the Earls of Darnley until 193

and the Honourable Ivor Bligh played there regularly. When he captained the English team that went to Australia and won the 1883 Test series, the stumps were burnt at the end of the last game and Bligh brought the ashes back to Cobham Hall where they were kept until 1929. Then they were presented to the cricket museum at Lord's.

Some say that Charles Dickens himself used to watch cricket at Cobham, but it is certain that George Bennett, who played for Kent, and was in the first team that went to Australia in 1862, played cricket on this village green.

More recently we have C. S. Marriott, one of the best leg-break bowlers Kent ever had—incidentally, he taught me cricket at Dulwich College, where he was cricket master—George Collins, and R. D. Browne.

Another Kent club holding what it claims is a unique record, is *Chislehurst*, which plays on the West Kent ground. This, I am told, is the only cricket ground in England protected by Act of Parliament. That may be so, but I know quite a lot of other clubs with almost as good an insurance. Their grounds are available 'in perpetuity' for cricket.

Chislehurst membership includes Douglas Wright. President is Colonel F. J. F. Edlmann, and D. Kearns is both captain and secretary.

One of the many *Metropolitan Police* sides is based at The Warren, Hayes, where the club-house and grounds were opened in 1935, chiefly as a result of the efforts of Lord Trenchard (then the Commissioner of Police) and a number of his friends. No. 4 District plays there.

The mansion club-house, delightful in every aspect, was once lived in by the son of Hall Caine. There is always a magnificent show of rhododendrons during the season, a lovely setting for the club, which, as well as cricket, offers members lawn tennis, soccer, rugby, and athletics.

During World War II, No. 4 District kept its cricket going chiefly with games against Services sides.

When Alf Tootell and brothers Albert and Fred Dawes—the Crystal Palace footballers—joined the police, they played fairly regularly for the club. Albert Dawes and F. Ruddy, indeed, played in police representative matches and also turned out occasionally for the British Empire XI. Ruddy was an all-rounder who completed the double on numerous occasions, but I am assured that his habit of chewing a daisy in every match had nothing to do with his success.

Club fast bowler is Stan Hardes, known locally as 'Knees and Elbows'. The chairman is Chief Superintendent B. J. Hefford, while Deputy Commander R. E. Franklin, o.b.e., is the treasurer.

During an attack by the *Luftwaffe* on Biggin Hill airfield one glorious summer afternoon, a stray German pilot came down low and sprayed the square and players with machine-gun fire. Best comment on this incident when the players had regained their breath was, 'Obviously not a cricketer!'

From 10s. a year subscription in 1877 and a subsequent loss on the year, to a large combined and progressive sports club is *Sidcup's* contribution to cricket in the county.

When the local football club applied to use the ground in the winter of 1884, the rent was £4. Now a similar facility would probably cost hundreds. However, the £4 rent then must have meant a lot to the club, for the following season the cricketers started a second XI on the strength of it.

A great occasion in the early days was when, in 1913, F. H. Huish brought a side down to play the club. He had R. R. Relf, K. L. Hutchings, E. G. Hayes, E. Hendren, H. R. Murrell, and V. C. W. Jupp in his side!

Long-service men on the committee include W. S. Harvey, the secretary. He joined the club in 1920. F. M. Turnbull played for the C.C.C. in the thirties, and Ken Poulter, captain since 1946, has had a committee job since 1934, two years after joining the club. Ken, now a Conference councillor, does not play so much cricket these days, and it is seldom that he turns out on Sundays, preferring to give the younger men a chance.

The six years (1939–45) during which the club was closed made little difference to its prosperity—in fact, it is since the War that Sidcup has grown really strong again.

The club reopened with three XIs in 1946, added a Sunday XI the following season, and in that year amalgamated to form the Sidcup Sports Club, comprising the local cricket, football, and tennis clubs. This, indeed, has proved the financial answer to the problem of increasing costs in a number of places. It is seldom one finds these days clubs devoted exclusively to cricket. More's the pity.

J. L. Bryan, Cambridge, Kent, and England cricketing brother of Ronnie Bryan wrote an article in May, 1935, for one of our daily newspapers on club cricket, under the heading of 'Cricket starts—and stops—on the village green'.

He may well have had in mind the village green of *Meopham*, where under the shadow of the famous windmill, they have been playing cricket since 1778.

In every bit of publicity about the club—the material was shown to me by the present secretary, F. C. Taylor, who has been in office since 1928—emphasis has been laid on the sporting way in which its games have been played and the excellent team spirit throughout the club.

It seems that ghosts of old-time cricketers were seen by the villagers in 1933—ghosts of well-known players of a hundred years before. All this was very much in everyone's mind when, at that year's Annual General Meeting, a little wooden box, with the name of a certain cocoa manufacturer on it, was placed on the chairman's table. This box had been discovered in Meopham Mill by a certain Dave Norton, who found it contained papers and documents appertaining to cricket played by the club.

Among these papers was a set of rules of the club drawn up in 1881. One of them read: 'If the secretary was found guilty of any neglect, he shall be fined one shilling.' Another laid down a fine of 6*d*. should be imposed on any player who swore persistently or smoked during a match. A third demanded a fine of 1*d*. for a dropped catch. For failing to attend a meeting, the penalty was 6*d*.

I wonder how much better we should fare with a few similar rules in operation today? Perhaps we should see less of that infernal disease, apathy!

For many years, Major R. A. Arnold, a life-president, was captain and chairman. He has done much for the club, and still attends matches regularly, despite his age.

Since World War II, the club owes much to Derek Baker, the treasurer, for putting it in such good financial shape, and to Garry Grugeon, the chairman, J. Nixon (landlord of the Cricketer's Inn), the entertainment secretary, and Jack Harvey, the team secretary. They have done much to revive post-War Meopham cricket.

The club is greatly indebted to Captain T. M. Barrett, R.N., for the notes he has compiled on Meopham cricket, and for its historical records.

Of the performers, P. B. Dunthorne, one of the club's most consistent bats, had an extremely good season in 1949, when he scored four centuries in his 'thousand'. Len Preston, their best bowler, took 94 wickets in the same year—nineteen more than the year before. Len also scores runs. In 1948, in one of his bright centuries, he made 136 in seventy minutes. That in itself is a creditable performance, but more important was that of his 136 —104 came from boundaries, with twelve 6s and eight 4s!

John French is another, almost regular, centurion. Like Preston he is also a big hitter. His 121 on a Whit Monday against the Nore officers included five 6s and thirteen 4s. John Newcombe is another fine bat, and has headed the batting averages.

Bill Russell, the present skipper, is an all-rounder who keeps the side together well. That is why Meopham produces some of the brightest cricket for miles around. Russell bowls medium right-hand swingers, and comes from a Meopham family who have played cricket on the village green for generations.

Syd Bishop, the wicket-keeper, has such a fine record that he has done a lot to improve the bowling averages. The club is rightly proud of its final match of the 1929 season, when they played against a team under the captaincy of Charlie Wright, the Kent fast bowler. Meopham beat their opponents, who also included J. Hubble, another county performer, by 6 runs. Meopham scored 115, of which A. Stevens got 23. Wright's XI was dismissed for 109 with only five minutes to spare.

Chapter Six

CLUBS AND THEIR PLAYERS

Histories, outstanding players, and anecdotes of the clubs in Surrey.

ANY account of Surrey club cricket can begin very appropriately with mention of the *Mitcham Club*, where cricket has been played on the famous 'Green' since 1720. Indeed, I believe that Mitcham Green is the only ground in England on which cricket has been played regularly for nearly 250 years: certainly, we read about a Great Cricket Match in 1730 played between the Gentlemen of London and Mecham.

The Green, a public ground right in the centre of the town, is kept magnificently. The wicket is one of the best in London, and the outfield is perfect. In the 1880s the Australians used to go to Mitcham to have a knock before their tour began. Later Jack Hobbs and Andy Sandham, the great England and Surrey pair, used to play there regularly.

E. J. Ide is the skipper of the first XI now, and has had a string of batting and bowling performances to his credit. He has played for Surrey second XI and the C.C.C. He usually tops the club's batting averages, and has once been at the head of the bowling figures.

Fred Smith is another great Mitcham all-rounder. He has often played for the C.C.C. XI. One of his best feats was in 1948 when he took all 10 wickets against Banstead and then only failed by 2 runs to score a century!

Jack Miell is another Mitcham member who has played for the C.C.C., and for Surrey second XI. He scores at a high rate and is very nippy in the field.

R. S. Culmer is another grand all-rounder, having headed the batting and bowling averages on many occasions. He has represented the C.C.C. and the Young Amateurs of Surrey, and in 1946 skippered the United Services (Egypt) XI in three unofficial 'Tests' against United Services (Palestine).

Other notable club personalities are S. L. Smith, who has scored more than sixty centuries and more than 25,000 runs, and has played for the C.C.C., and the Young Players of Surrey;

R. Parker, a forcing bat, who was top of the batting averages in 1947, and W. Stockbridge, an all-rounder who has done extremely well for the second XI. His father was a Mitcham player in the days of T. P. Harvey, J. Keen, A. F. Clarke, and T. Richardson.

Before the War I used to play regularly on The Green for the BBC side against Mitcham, but since 1946, with the great juggle that fixtures secretaries had to effect, Mitcham unfortunately dropped out. Only temporarily, I hope.

Unlike old-established Mitcham, the *BBC Club* was not formed until 1925, but in twenty-five years it has become one of the strongest sides in London club cricket, with such fine players as the West Indian quartet—Allan Rae, the Test opening batsman; all-rounder Dr. C. B. ('Bertie') Clarke, Ken Ablack, and Ernest Eytle. Then there is Len Phillips, who was skipper in 1946 and 1947. He is our oldest playing member.

Len, now vice-captain, is one of the biggest hitters—in spite of some unorthodox strokes and no batting gloves—in the club game. One of the best hits I ever saw anywhere was in a game on our Motspur Park ground. The ball cleared the pavilion by some thirty feet and landed in the tennis courts. All who know the size of our ground will appreciate the length of this straight drive. Len also takes over as wicket-keeper when Max Robertson, the commentator, is not available.

The club, started by the late Sir Dan Godfrey's son and Raymond Newton, began slowly with such personalities as Pat Beckett—a wild Irishman, if there ever was one—and Arthur Sellick, the popular 'little man' from the Wiltshire and Gloucestershire county sides, and who today, at the age of seventy-four, is still getting wickets and scoring runs. Sellick used to look after our wicket at Motspur Park, and what a magnificent job he made of it. Then we had the late 'Bandy' O'Donnell, a left-hander whom you may remember as conductor of the BBC Military Band in those days.

Laurence Gilliam, now head of BBC Features, and Michael Standing, head of Variety, are others. Michael skippered the side immediately after the War, when he was a very fine medium-pace bowler who could go on all day—and usually did! Illness, unfortunately, has stopped his playing and what a loss he has been to the side.

In its early days the club probably owed more to George

Dailey, who died some years ago, than to any other person. His untiring efforts to bring in—and on—the youngsters did much to encourage interest in cricket within the Corporation.

Bowker Andrews, former Blackheath rugger forward, is another who more than played his part in helping to establish the club. Bowker, at sixteen-odd-stone, kept wicket and, in spite of his weight, over short distances he was very fast. Never shall I forget his race over 100 yards with Len Phillips, even then a little portly, during one 'Week' before World War II. He was leading with ten yards to go, but down came his trousers and he couldn't finish! He is now in Manchester, and it is one of our greatest regrets that we no longer have him in the side.

Another pre-War supporter was former Deputy Director-General Sir Cecil Graves, a member of the M.C.C. His batting on more than one occasion got us out of a nasty hole. Other personalities of a few years back included Stephen Fry, son of the great 'C. B.', who inherited some of his father's magnificent strokes; G. S. Strode, who in the early 'thirties was secretary, and is now head of BBC Publications; former captain of the second XI and now Cricket Secretary, Jim Titshall; Teddy French, who took over secretarial duties from Strode, and is still our fixture secretary, in spite of his having turned to golf for his main pastime; 'Ajax' Farrar—'Uncle Ajax' of the Children's Hour, who set such a fine example as second XI skipper for so many years, and R. Wade, until recently chairman of the BBC Club, who played regularly up to a few years ago.

Other playing members now are 'Mac' Hobley, the television announcer, who is a more than useful all-rounder; Philip Thompson, a left-handed opening bat; George Hillier, our popular and cheery fast bowler; Frank East, a new left-hand slow bowler, who only came into the first XI in 1949; Jack Rich, who also plays for Beckenham; Colin Barker, a young and promising batsman; and 'Old Nick' (H. H. Nicholson), who in 1950 led the second XI with marked success.

From 1925 until the ground was opened at Motspur Park, the BBC played on a ground in Streatham Vale. On July 4, 1929, we played our opening match on our new ground, but it was three years later that our 'square' was laid, under the guiding hand of 'Bosser' Martin, then head-groundsman at the Oval. Now there are three well laid-out cricket grounds, with excellent 'squares' and outfields that could be worse, considering the amount of football and hockey played on them throughout the winter. Their consistent quality is a credit to the secretary of the BBC club, 'Nobby' Clarke.

The BBC has a very strong fixture list, but possibly one of the best games we have is against *The Old Alleynians C.C.* during the August Bank-holiday week-end. Few can argue that they are not one of the strongest old boys' sides in the country. They can pick this XI: H. T. Bartlett, S. C. Griffith, T. E. Bailey, A. W. Mallett, A. C. Shirreff, D. R. Wilcox, A. H. H. Gilligan, O. J. Wait, J. H. Lockton, F. King—with myself to make up the number. Indeed, it *has* been picked. We played on April 23, 1950, to celebrate the opening of the Old Alleynians' new ground.

Since its foundation in 1928, the club has been a 'semi-wanderer'. Away matches were arranged at the beginning of the season and home matches towards the end, the latter being played on the Dulwich College School ground when the boys are on holiday. Recently, however, the headmaster, C. H. Gilkes, whose father was one of the most brilliant headmasters the College has ever had, informed the Old Boys that he was unwilling to extend the facilities for playing home matches on the school ground. Accordingly an appeal for £2,000 was launched. Old Alleynians responded with a quick £1,500 and a new ground was acquired on Dulwich Common, the home of the Old Alleynian's Rugby Football Club.

Lieutenant-Colonel Geoffrey Rimbault was the first O.A. captain, and, apart from duty overseas, has played regularly. He is still the club's best batsman. I well remember his brilliant 154 against the BBC on our ground in 1948. It was a gem.

Johnny Lockton, former Surrey player, took over the captaincy in 1929, during one of Rimbault's absences. Johnny was skipper when I first played for the Old Boys in 1930, while still at school. And what a good skipper he was! At that time he had support from such fine all-rounders as Jimmy Perts, a colleague of my father's in the Bank of England, F. G. ('Bertie') Mabbott, and P. E. Musgrave. Together they so built the club that it soon took its place in the top-flight of London club cricket.

Another all-rounder, now honorary secretary, is 'Simbo' Simmons, who has worked very hard indeed to keep the Old

Alleynian flag flying. 'Simbo's' father did a lot for the Cyphers during his cricketing days.

W. M. Collinson, now treasurer, is a fine forcing bat, who played several times with me in the British Empire XI at the beginning of the War.

Kenneth Seale is the present skipper. Other prominent members are: W. Darby; M. H. Bushby, school captain in 1949; Alan Frankford (brother of Denis Frankford, who would undoubtedly have played rugger for England if a severe illness had not cut short his playing days soon after leaving school) and Johnny's son, Leslie Lockton, a good left-arm spin bowler.

One of the BBC's next-door neighbours, and one against whom we play an annual 'derby' match, is the *Malden Wanderers Club*, founded in 1879.

Now a club with sixty playing members, Malden's greatest 'character' for many years has been Jim Walker, now president of the club, in 1950 president of the C.C.C., and formerly chairman of its selection and match committee. Jim is one of the most cheery people you could meet. His glowing countenance itself dispels gloom. He captained the Malden first XI from 1919 to 1935, and was a fine forcing bat, besides being a very useful fast bowler.

Arthur Hulland, with his well-known moustache, was another 'character'. He died in the late 'forties. Arthur was a county hockey player in his time, and an impartial and fearless chairman of the cricket club.

C. M. Tredwell is now skipper, having taken over from Jack Seward in 1949. 'Treddy', of Parson's Green before World War II, used to play regularly for Middlesex II. Otherwise known as the 'maestro', Treddy is a more than useful off-break bowler and a fine opening bat.

Alf Gadsby was captain from 1936 until his retirement in 1947. An astute and popular captain, Alf was originally a fast 'slinger', but profitably changed to slow 'tweakers'. Vic Elworthy, after many years with the club, still takes his 100 wickets each season with his beautifully-controlled, easy action. Billy Field is another grand club man. He took 10 wickets in a match in 1948 with his medium-fast deliveries, and has been a member of the club since 1929, when he left school.

'Pa' Dawes, the G.O.M. of the club, still plays occasionally for the third XI at the wonderful age of eighty-two! He is a slow left-arm spinner, and one of Jim Walker's band of helpers on the ground in the club's early days.

Leslie Murray, probably Malden's outstanding bat, is a left-hander. He can also be a quite devastating new-ball bowler. He has made many fine knocks for the representative C.C.C. XI.

Jack Seward, skipper in 1948, is a fine forcing bat, and is known as one of the best cover-points in club cricket. Vic Ransom, Hants fast bowler, is also a member and plays frequently.

Keith Walker, Jim's son, plays for Barclays Bank on Saturdays, and Malden Wanderers on Sundays. With vicious leg-spinners, he can, on his day, go right through any side. His action is peculiar and certainly unique—he seems to bowl from behind his right ear. His performances for the C.C.C. against the M.C.C. and the Navy have been first class.

Tubby Creed, an opening pace bowler, was a popular member of this all-round side, and another very useful bat is Doug Fleming.

Against Herne Hill, some years before the War, Malden needed six to win at the beginning of the last over. Alf Gadsby was at one end; Vic Ransom at the other. Vic played the first three balls straight back to the bowler, and cheerfully reassured his captain that everything was under control. Then came more inaction, with the next two balls being played carefully for no runs. Off the last ball of the match, with everyone looking hard the other way, Vic lunged out, and the ball soared merrily out of the ground for six!

It was people like Jim Walker and 'Pa' Dawes who were mainly responsible for converting the present ground in Cambridge Avenue, New Malden, from rough pasture land. Now the Wanderers own the freehold, and with a golf course along one end of the ground and back gardens on two other sides, the club is not likely to find buildings around them for years to come.

Another delightful Surrey ground in the heart of the town, and only ten minutes from Sandown Racecourse, is the *Esher Club*.

The club met many difficulties from its foundation in 1864 until the early 1900s, but somehow it was kept in existence, and during the last half-century has reached a membership of 250.

Before World War I the Australians played on the ground.

I used to play regularly on the ground in the early 'thirties, for a side called the Onions (of all names!) that was organised by the Saunders brothers, Jarchow and C. R. Maxwell from Brighton College, Billy Griffith, Hugh Bartlett, and myself.

Ebby Gerrish—skipper from 1927 to 1947—is now president, and there is no question but that a substantial part of the club's success is owing to him. During many of these years, R. Eglington —whom many will remember as skipper of Surrey II when they won the Minor Counties Championship in 1939—has been vice-captain. Today, H. R. Crouch is the captain of the club, with B. J. A. Lowe—well known as a rugger player—as deputy. L. E. Langley is the honorary secretary, and R. E. Goldsmith the treasurer. Goldsmith took over from T. A. Ryder, who held office for twenty years.

R. D. Jupp has been the star bat recently. In 1949 he had an average of 54·89 for 1,592 runs.

An Esher all-rounder who has done particularly well is B. N. S. Kidson, and as Crouch and R. C. Eglington, 1950 vice-captain, both enjoy success with bat and ball, and the club can call on J. C. Hubbard, England rugby full-back, Esher can truly be called a team of 'all-rounders'.

J. A. Harrison, former Haileybury School captain, has settled at Esher and plays for the club regularly. A. J. W. Blair is the 'stock' bowler, but is compensated by the number of wickets he takes. In 1950, W. R. Hammond, former England captain, who now lives at Esher, played six innings for the club, averaging 81·25.

In a charity match on the ground in 1948, the club batted first and declared with quite a number of runs on the board. Things were not going too well for the visitors. Charlie Barnett (England and Gloucestershire) was out in the first over. Then Learie Constantine, the West Indian Test player, who is a life member of Esher, came in to bat. Constantine was about to be caught off his wrist by the wicket-keeper, when a loud shout was heard from the first-slip saying, 'For Heaven's sake drop it!' The catch was duly missed and was followed by a beautiful 70 from Constantine—much to the crowd's delight. Connie will remember that match!

Some 166 years before the foundation of Esher, they were playing cricket at *East Molesey*, or Moulsey Hurst as it was called in those days.

'This is the stuff cricket is made of,' said H.R.H. the Duke of

I

Edinburgh, when he visited this historic ground one Sunday in June of 1949 (the club were playing the New Zealand tourists). 'It is ideal for cricket here,' he added.

And ideal it is, with the River Thames running lazily along the pavilion end of the ground and the picturesque Hurst Park Racecourse not very far away. The club claims the ground as one of the oldest cricket grounds still in existence, and has records to show that cricket was played there over 250 years ago.

A newspaper report in the year 1731 says: 'A great cricket match was played at Moulsey Hurst, in Surrey, between the Kingston men and the County of Surrey for 25 gns. a side, which was won by the latter. Some thousands of persons of both sexes were present.' Apart from anything else, one very important point arises here: it seems clear that the ladies of those days were more interested in the game than those of the present day!

For the next thirty years or so, many interesting matches were played, and visiting sides included the Prince of Wales' XI, Surrey, London, Middlesex, and Kent.

From 1786 to 1791, Surrey used to play their matches there and on The Holt, near Farnham, according to cricketing authority James Pycroft. The pitch then was part of the grassland that we now know as Hurst Park. Of the many personalities who have played on this ground, perhaps the greatest batsman Molesey ever saw was William Beldham, born near Farnham in 1766.

The famous old Dr. 'W. G.' played there and made his usual 'stack' of runs, while Jack Hobbs and Andy Sandham batted there as recently as 1939.

But perhaps the greatest array of all time was seen at that match in June, 1949. All the New Zealand Test players were in action, and opposing them were: Walter Robins (skipper), Laurie Fishlock (Surrey), George Tribe (Australia), W. Alley (New South Wales), and B. Constable (Surrey).

The Robins family have long been associated with the club. Colonel V. I., in particular, did a tremendous amount 'behind the scenes', as did W. T. Graburn, ex-Surrey amateur, who was secretary for fifty years. The road past the ground—Graburn Way—commemorates him.

East Molesey has purchased the freehold of the ground as a memorial to players who fell in the last war, and when £2,026 was raised in 1943 the ground was free of debt. The New Zealand Government contributed £100, and the Surrey County

Council and Esher U.D.C. £250 each. A new brick pavilion is to be erected at a cost of £3,500.

Frederick Edward Smith, a New Zealander, will be remembered as one of the most promising young players the club has known—his fame rivalling even the great Beldham. He scored 1,000 runs in three of the four seasons he was with the club, and took more than 100 wickets. In one match he took all 10 wickets, including a hat-trick, the last 4 wickets falling without a run being scored. A New Zealand Army captain, he was killed at El Alamein.

Australian-born M. Parker, in January, 1948, was appointed equerry to the Duke of Edinburgh. He sometimes keeps wicket for Molesey. Eric Edwards, a first-class all-rounder, started with Molesey as a boy scorer; in 1948 he took over 100 wickets. J. Thompson, the present thirty-eight-year-old captain, has played a lot of cricket in Ireland, where he was born. A. Swift, a comparative newcomer to the club, is a batsman and a good fielder, while R. J. Attawell, a forcing bat, is really outstanding at cover.

Youngest member of the side is J. Goddard, only sixteen years of age. He is a promising bat and wicket-keeper, and I think we shall be hearing a great deal more about this youngster later on. Fast-medium bowler K. Cracknell promises to become a useful all-rounder.

President of the club is B. M. Turner, who did so much to raise money to save the ground, and vice-presidents include: the Rt. Hon. E. J. Harrison, Resident Minister for the Commonwealth of Australia; Field-Marshal Lord Birdwood, and the Earl of Ypres. The Rt. Hon. W. J. Jordan, Resident Minister for New Zealand, has been made an honorary life member of the club.

I played on the ground several times before the War. Once, with Hugh Bartlett and Billy Griffith, I turned out for the Old Alleynians. None of us should have been playing, as we were all at school at the time, but took a chance, as we didn't see how the news would leak out. Little publicity was given to Sunday games then.

However, Hugh Bartlett made a beast of himself and scored something like 239, including thirteen 6s, most of them into the river, but not one on to the famous Taggs Island. He got a great deal of publicity from local newspapers, with the result that all three of us were up in front of the headmaster the next day. Hit for 6 was right!

Like East Molesey, *Teddington* is a Thames-side club.

Stan Squires, Surrey all-rounder, who died early in 1950, learned his cricket with Teddington, which began some time before 1833, although there are no records to show the actual year of foundation. A. Slade-Lucas used to play for the club, and more recently John Armitage, the present president and one of the biggest hitters in the game, also turned out regularly.

The club played little cricket during the 1939–45 period. Losing its pavilion was a very great blow indeed, but, like other clubs faced with similar difficulties, it has pulled through.

Skipper J. S. Pearsall sets a fine example to the young players. The steady and consistent Flight-Lieutenant G. K. Senior can always be relied upon to get runs, and wicket-keeper is L. J. E. Saunders, the club secretary. Fast bowler J. N. Chilcott took 83 wickets in 1949, and against a strong Wimbledon XI took all 10 wickets for 53 runs—7 of them clean bowled.

Secretary Saunders reminded me of another incident in which the Wimbledon club was involved. In 1948 Teddington batted first and got a reasonable score. Wimbledon, after batting fairly steadily, wanted five runs to win, with three wickets in hand when the last over was called. The captain did what few of us would do in similar circumstances. He changed the bowling, putting himself on for the last over. He captured the last three wickets with the last three balls of the match and Teddington won. But what a chance to take!

The 1950 season was one of the best in the club's history, the first XI losing only twice.

Another Surrey 'club-on-the-Thames' is *Chertsey*.

For a long time no records of the early history of Chertsey could be traced, but cricket has certainly been played there almost continuously since 1775. And there is proof that a game between Chertsey and Moulsey Hurst was played as early as 1755. Another big match early in Chertsey history took place on the Burway ground in 1778, when Surrey challenged and beat Hampshire for 100 guineas a side.

The present ground was opened in May, 1922, by Sir Edward Stein, Bt., then president of the club, who gave the greater part of the purchase money. Another well-known figure whose name appears on the subscription list is Lord Camrose, who became president on the death of Sir Edward Stein.

H. Wicks, chairman for the past twenty-five years and a trustee of the ground, has the records of the club from 1755 to date. He was a playing member for over forty years, and captain when the ground opened in 1921. President now is S. A. Wylde. Skipper in recent years has been E. J. Sheffield.

Of the players, K. J. Stiles tells me that L. Dodd must be considered the best all-rounder. Moreover, he is a great club worker—a born cricket enthusiast, in fact.

The *Spencer Club*, Wandsworth, is typical of these 'built-up-all-round' sport clubs. I know it well because I used to play a lot of cricket there in the 'thirties.

They were playing cricket at Wandsworth in 1872, when Earl Spencer, the Lord of the Manor, permitted the founders to drain and enclose, by means of posts and chains, a portion of the common. H. G. Latham, now president, was one of the early pioneers and is often on the ground.

C. E. Nicol, captain from 1940 to 1945 and chairman from 1940 to 1950, has scored a lot of runs, including many centuries. W. G. ('Guy') Tarrant, is another player well known to me. He has been skipper since 1946, and in the last ten years has scored more than 15,000 runs including twenty-five centuries. In view of the intervening War years, that is really going some.

E. J. Caeser, who for those ten years has opened with Guy, has scored only slightly fewer runs—and has taken over 500 wickets as well. D. E. Plim started in the second XI in 1945, but quickly graduated to the first, and in the same year headed the batting averages.

F. W. Chinnyah, now secretary, told me that before World War I, F. M. Barton began a game as wicket-keeper *versus* Surrey Club and Ground and secured two or three stumpings and catches. Then followed a Surrey stand. Barton took off his pads, went on to bowl left arm, then changed to right arm, secured several wickets and afterwards scored 70 runs!

In 1941, three bombs were dropped by the *Luftwaffe* on the ground (one wrecking a sight-screen) on the Sunday preceding the cricket week. Thanks to the voluntary efforts of the members, the Tuesday's game was played as arranged, though

Monday's game had to be transferred to a neighbouring ground. Spirit like that will keep any cricket club going.

Adjoining Wandsworth Common we find the *Old Grammarians Club*.

To D. J. Morrow, its match secretary, must go full credit for the progress made by this Battersea Grammar School Old Boys' side. Morrow has been in office since 1926, when the club was founded. In those early days only a few games were played, but now the club plays two games on Saturdays and Sundays, and runs a Devon tour every year.

The Old Grammarians took over the ground which formerly belonged to the Heathfield Cricket Club—a club where the South Africans played the C.C.C. in the early 1920s.

L. G. Merrett, who has captained the side for a number of years, got a Conference cap in the early 1930s, and is the only O.G. player ever to have taken ten wickets in an innings.

J. W. Durham secured 100 wickets in 1947 and George Simkins scored 1,000 runs in 1948. C. W. L'Archer, 1949 honorary secretary, also has some fine bowling performances. Every year since 1947 he has taken 100 wickets, and in 1949 his 'bag' went up to 149. He also scored 1,400 runs. These performances earned him a C.C.C. trial. Very few bowlers can boast of five hat-tricks, but L'Archer managed this in 1949.

The O.G.s played a match in Oxted's cricket week in 1949, and during the game everyone was amazed to see the fielders suddenly throw themselves flat on the ground one by one. It looked like cricket in an air-raid again, but this time it was an enormous swarm of bees buzzing across the pitch about three feet from the ground. I am told there were no casualties!

Something very similar occurred in 1947 when I was playing for Northants against Worcestershire at Wellingborough. The swarm that day took a great liking to Bertie Clarke, and followed him about all over the outfield!

Down the line from Wandsworth Common is the *Streatham Club*.

Although I have lived most of my life in Streatham, I must admit that until recently I knew little about this old-established club. Founded in 1805, the club first played on Streatham Common.

The founder-members drew up seventeen rules—which, incidentally, were formed at the 'Horse and Groom' on Monday May 5, 1806, and revised at the London Tavern on Tuesday, January 27, 1807.

One rule states: 'Any gentleman playing in Jackets, Breeches, or Pantaloons, shall be fined half a crown; Nankeen or white may be worn at pleasure.' Another reads: 'That every member coming at half past three o'clock by the President's watch, shall forfeit half a crown.' Perhaps the most illuminating of all is No. 5, which says: 'That the subscription for each member be *Five Guineas*, which must be paid into the hands of the president, vice-president or secretary, on or before the second meeting of the club (in every season) under the forfeiture of *One Guinea*'!

That rule is interesting. It shows that they paid dearly for the game they loved in those days. I wonder how much quicker subscriptions would come rolling in nowadays if a large fine were imposed for non-payment by a certain date?

Between 1939 and 1945 the burden of running the club and keeping things together fell almost entirely upon A. S. Turney, who, when he resigned the captaincy in 1948, had skippered the club for eleven years. Neville Miller is the president, as he has been for a great number of years. He played for the club from 1893 until 1934, and in the 35 playing sessions scored 36,382 runs (average 48·7) including 88 centuries. In 1906 and 1911 he did the 'double'. In the only county match in which he played, in 1899, he scored a century for Surrey against Sussex. He still turns out regularly for committee meetings and is also the club treasurer. No wonder Streatham is proud of him.

One of the club's best all-rounders of modern times is Geoffrey Smith. He was a member from 1946 to 1948, when he moved to Canterbury. Nowadays he plays mainly for the Old Blues. Smith is one of the best attacking fast bowlers I know, and I shall never forget his sustained bowling against the Royal Navy for the C.C.C. at Hastings in 1949. He bowled accurately and hostilely for hours on end and came out of the match with really magnificent figures. Against the New Zealanders at Guildford later on in the season he did it again, and if I could have my way, Smith is one player I should never be without. He played for Surrey II in the Minor Counties Championship in 1948 and 1949.

Laurence Williams is another who has played for the C.C.C.

He and his twin brother, Roy, are indistinguishable when batting together, and both have also played their part in helping the club, as has W. G. Chapman, the secretary.

Further down Streatham High Road towards Croydon we come to Norbury, where we find the *Barclays Bank Club*.

The names of Barclays and 'Nobby' Hunt are almost synonymous. For a long time, Nobby has been a tremendously important factor, not only in Barclays Bank cricket, but in every sphere of club cricket. He has skippered the representative C.C.C. XIs on numerous occasions, and can truly be said to be not only the complete cricketer, but perhaps the best-equipped captain I have ever met. He plays the game seriously—as it should be—but never loses sight of the fact that in club cricket there is only one afternoon in which twenty-two players are trying to get enjoyment. Personal records mean nothing to him—although he holds masses of them—and on more than one occasion I have known him declare an innings closed even though one more over would have given him the chance of a century.

Another person who has done a great deal for the club, both as player and executive, is Jack Cooper, who became president of the C.C.C. in 1950. He was secretary of Barclays from 1921 to 1938, when E. J. Western took over. During some of the War years Jack Cooper took on these duties again and helped to keep the club alive.

Barclays has two private grounds—the one at Norbury and the other at Ealing. Norbury is the main one, and what a delightful ground it is, in its rural setting just a stone's-throw off the main road. Originally the ground belonged to Norbury Park C.C., but in 1911 it was secured by the London South-Western Bank, and when, in 1918, Barclays, the London and Provincial, and the London and South-Western Banks amalgamated, the present club took over.

Like other big sports organisations, the cricket section is part of the sports club. Six sides play on Saturdays and one on Sundays, at both Ealing and Norbury. In the provinces almost every Barclays area has its own sports club, but none comes in any way under the jurisdiction of the London club.

Apart from Hunt and Cooper, who as batsmen scored far too many runs from a bowler's point of view, there is Keith Walker —son of Jimmy Walker, whom I have mentioned when writing of his own club, Malden Wanderers. If Keith only had more time, many county sides would like him to play for them.

L. G. Bamidge, T. R. Liddle, D. J. Smith, P. F. Lettington, and R. Frith get most of Barclays runs. John Marriott, though not bowling as fast as in the years gone by, is still decidedly hostile for a few overs with the new ball. Medium-paced D. J. Smith is an all-rounder, and E. R. Bedford another steady bowler.

One of the best stories Nobby Hunt tells concerns a game in which he played for the British Empire XI at Coventry, towards the end of the War. Ray Smith (Essex) and Nobby were batting at the tea interval—Ray having just started while Nobby was 38 not out. During the interval, there was great excitement as it had been announced that Japan had surrendered unconditionally. The news was announced to the crowd followed by the playing of the National Anthem. This done, Nobby proceeded to take first ball after the interval which he played carefully to mid-off. A 'leather lung' on the terraces roared out, 'Come on, Hunt—it's post-War cricket now—get a move on!'

Dodds, Essex opening batsman, was a member of the Bank in 1938 and 1939. In his first match Nobby Hunt took him into the slips with him to make him feel at home. In the first over a snick off the fast bowler flew about a foot outside Nobby's right foot. A few years before he might have caught it. There was a sudden flash and young Dodds took a marvellous catch at full length about three inches off the ground. Nobby was obviously delighted and said so, but Dodds replied: 'Sorry I left it a bit late. I thought it was your catch, skipper!'

Another 'Bank' club with its ground in Surrey is the *Bank of England*, whose 'best-ever' player was undoubtedly H. M. Bannister ('Stairs' to his friends). He played from 1909 to 1939 and from 1919 to 1930 was club captain. Before and after World War II Bannister played for Leicester, and in his first match for the county took 4 for 23 and 3 for 24 against the South Africans. During his career with the Bank he must have taken well over 2,000 wickets and scored at least 10,000 runs.

H. F. Gilbert, who took over from Bannister in 1931, remained in office until 1939. A. T. Pitman has been joint secretary since 1927. M. T. D. Wyatt shared the job with him from 1934 to 1948.

The Bank lost one of London's leading club cricketers when S. M. H. (Maurice) Spearing was killed in the War. He had played for Cheshire before joining the Bank in London in 1928, after which he had frequent games for C.C.C. XIs, many of which he captained.

After the War, J. F. Gilbert was succeeded by N. R. Gillett (1946–49), and he, in turn, handed over to R. T. Somerville. These last two, like C. C. Lockitt, R. B. A. Smith, and J. A. Hopwood, are prolific run-getters. Hopwood made a club record of over 2,000 runs in 1948.

All-rounders who are extremely well known are D. P. Henry and E. J. L. Poole, who share the bowling with G. A. Mill, W. O. Lane, and P. R. Fraser.

Bank of England sides from 1870 used to 'wander' until the ground at Roehampton was acquired in 1908. They have not lost the old habit either—a fortnight's tour of Kent and Sussex is a feature of each season.

From Roehampton let us cross over to Croydon, where we find a great number of cricket grounds within a few miles of one another. In the Croham Road, South Croydon, are the *Old Whitgiftians*.

This old boys' side was once mistaken for a side of Devonshire convicts during one of the Old Whitgiftian tours of Sussex. Presumably, 'Whitgiftian' and 'Widdecombe' sounded similar to a Sussex yokel!

Originally known as Whitgift Wanderers, the club changed to Old Whitgiftians C.C. in 1909, but had to continue as a wandering club until very much later. In 1930, however, the club secured its present ground, with enough room for two 'tables'. In the twenty years since it settled down there, the club has gone steadily ahead and now manages to turn out five XIs, which, as most old boys' clubs know, is really something. In addition, it runs the tour and a home 'Week'.

H. T. Groom, now the club's president, was previously secretary for twenty-three years. P. G. Markham was captain of the club from 1927 to 1947, and is proud of the fact that he made his maiden century when turned fifty years of age. He has now retired.

Geoffrey Harrison is now secretary, and keeps everyone in order, especially his brother, J. W. 'J. W.' is a fine forcing bat and leg-spin bowler, while 'G. T.' is another all-rounder on whom the club depends a great deal. Both Harrisons were in the Whitgift

School XI together in 1922, and have continued to play together ever since.

Martin Turner is now captain and is a very big hitter, as one would rather expect from a rugby international. G. S. A. Parnaby is the wicket-keeper and returned to the side in 1950.

Next, down the main Brighton road, is Purley, and near Purley is Kenley. In the early days of the *Kenley Club*, founded as long ago as 1880, the Crawford family used to turn out regularly and were members for years. The Tufnell family were also members; the late Carleton Tufnell was a great cricket legislator, and his son kept wicket for England in South Africa in the 1909–10 tour.

Not a member, but a visitor to the ground on several occasions, was W. G. Grace. I wonder how many of these well-established clubs have *not* had the pleasure of entertaining the Doctor on some occasion or the other? Very few, I'm sure. If nothing else, 'W. G.' was a traveller, and made a habit of playing on as many pitches and against as many different types of bowling as he could.

H. E. Monger was about Kenley's 'best ever' club bat. In 1925 he scored six consecutive centuries—all against strong opponents, one being Surrey Club and Ground. In another game, with his brother, the pair put on 256 in 110 minutes to win an important match.

Since 1940, J. L. Wild, chairman of a large firm of public works contractors, has been the club's president, and it has been extremely fortunate to have as its secretary W. Graham, c.b., m.b.e., who has been a member of the club since 1920 and honorary secretary since 1928. Graham is still an active playing member. From its forty members, Kenley fields two XIs every Saturday, with occasional Sunday matches, played on its lovely ground under the shadow of Riddlesdown.

The *Old Coulsdon Club* has to thank the workers on the estate and the Lord of the Manor for its foundation in 1870.

Apart from one or two short spells—especially during the Wars—they have played cricket continuously in Grange Park, Old Coulsdon, which was originally owned by the local squire. He lived in the Grange just behind the ground. It was bought by the local council in the 1920s.

The club is very proud that it still has two members, both umpiring, who joined well over fifty years ago. 'Without Albie Beadle and Mo Yemm the club wouldn't be the same,' says G. T. Hoskins, the club's secretary.

In the days before the ground became public, and the village consisted of a mere handful of houses and cottages, there was no 'local'. A club, 'The Cherry Tree', was formed and met behind the general stores under the management of one Charlie Hollands, in a room about 9 ft. square. Membership of the Old Coulsdon C.C. was conditional on membership of 'The Cherry Tree', and on a Saturday evening the club was slightly over-crowded! That 'The Cherry Tree' is no longer in existence is a source of great sorrow to the members.

President is Vernon Harbord, and the vice-presidents are J. S. Cooper, L. H. Neal, G. L. Smith, A. E. Beadle, and F. O. Watts. Treasurer is G. Palmer. Skippers of the two sides are W. F. Palmer (first XI) and J. Gilson, with L. K. Brooks and C. Hover as the respective vice-captains.

Brooks is an all-rounder, being a slow bowler and good bat; P. L. Smith and W. A. Pattison shoulder the responsibility of opening, and the stock bowler is G. Blamey.

Near Croydon aerodrome is the *Wallington Club*. There have been many stories told about a 'club-bag's' going astray, but A. W. Y. Speller tells one of the best. He loaded his car with seven of his team's cricket-bags, plus the club-bag, only to find, on arriving at the opponents' ground, that he had left his own behind!

Formed in 1921, the club acquired a ground a year later in Sandy Lane, Wallington. Of the founder-members, G. W. Dewey, A. W. Y. Speller, A. Wadley, senior, and A. T. Wadey are still with the club. The club survived the War years in spite of the absence of ground staff, and from 1940 to 1945 an average of three teams every week-end was put into the field, despite the close attention of enemy aircraft and consequent bomb damage.

Perhaps present chairman Speller, and C. H. A. Goddard, secretary since 1935, were chiefly responsible for such a fine record. Another long-standing member is H. E. L. Piercy, in his day one of the best 'keepers in club cricket.

In the club itself, which caters for all sport, there are some 400 members. Among the sixty-six active cricketers A. T. Wadey and A. Ready are useful all-rounders, although Ready is a better bowler than bat. One of his best performances was 9 for 60 against East Molesey.

F. W. Clark, a left-hand 'opener', has been consistent for years, and shares the club's first-wicket record by making 272 in 1932. K. King, who has played for Surrey, is a stylish and forcing batsman. J. S. Venn scored over a thousand runs and took 100 wickets in 1944. K. H. Baker, a useful all-rounder, topped the batting averages in 1950.

R. E. L. Ellingham has skippered several of the XIs from time to time. A top-line bowler is L. Blundell (medium-pace). Goddard, the secretary, reminds me of a hurricane century by the late Major R. J. Walker: in 1944 he scored 113 in forty minutes, the last 50, which included four 6s in one over, being obtained in ten minutes.

Although *Beddington* doesn't know it, I think I owe my keen interest in club cricket more to one of their old members than to anyone else. During my school holidays I used to go to Sheringham, near Cromer, in Norfolk. Very early in my 'teens I met a Beddington player, by the name of Clark, who always organised the big cricket matches on the sands. And how important we used to think those matches were! It was this 'sand' cricket that first stimulated my interest in the game.

The club was founded in Beddington Park as early as 1863, and one of its earliest members was Robert Henderson, who played for Surrey from 1881 to 1895 and scored seventy centuries during that period. Surrey held the county championship for seven consecutive seasons in those days.

Perhaps an even more famous club member was G. M. Reay, who joined in 1905 and retired in 1940. He played for Surrey from 1913 to 1914 and from 1920 to 1923. Had he had the time, Gilly Reay would have played more regularly for the county. He, along with Robert Henderson and R. A. Sheppard, hold places of honour in Beddington history.

Not many southern clubs can boast of a thousand spectators at week-ends, but this number often watch Beddington players in action. S. H. Cooper, since joining in 1926, is generally regarded as one of the best club wicket-keepers. He 'kept' for Surrey on several occasions before the War, and is a fine forcing batsman. R. W. Bulfield has been a member since 1919 and treasurer since 1940. In the years between he was a regular playing member.

Another player and member of the committee who gave invaluable assistance in re-establishing the club after World War II is J. K. Gass. He is the bar secretary, which, as we all know, involves a great deal of hard work. Mrs. V. Gass, so secretary A. D. Hampson tells me, deserves as much credit for the efficient running of the club as anyone else. She often serves as many as 140 teas on a Saturday afternoon.

M. Murray is perhaps Beddington's most promising young batsman. In 1949 he played for the R.A.F., and opened the innings for the Combined Services XI.

Hampson recalls a quaint umpiring decision in a match against Cheam in 1899. One of the opposing batsmen was obviously out to a simple catch. As the batsman didn't move towards the pavilion the side appealed. But the umpire wasn't having that. His response: 'Not out. You were too slow in appealing!'

In 1901 the London County C.C. paid their first visit to Beddington under W. G.'s captaincy. The doctor and some of his side apparently booked their fares to Beddington Lane station—a long way from the ground. It was hot and the bags heavy, and after covering some of the distance W. G. hailed a passing cattle truck to take them on to the ground. On that occasion he made 51, but on another scored a characteristic 147.

The following year, in another match for London County, the doctor was batting, and early in his innings was caught in the slips by the Rector, who stood with the ball in his hand. The batsman made no attempt to leave the wicket, and the umpire, to whom the side appealed, said 'Not out'. Apparently he was a great admirer of W. G. W. G. himself turned to the fieldsman and said, 'Well, Rector, I shall not give you *another* chance.' The very next ball was touched in the same way, but the Rector apparently had not recovered from the shock and let the ball drop!

To give up playing at seventeen years of age and then to return to the game at the age of forty-four is no mean feat. But, having made a 'come-back', to open the innings for your club successfully and at the age of fifty-six to score your first century *and* knock up your first '1,000' in a season is quite amazing. Yet all this happened to Dr. G. E. Foxwell, chairman of the *Epsom Sports Club*.

There is no question but that Epsom cricket has a rich history and tradition behind it. The Epsom Cricket Club only recently amalgamated with the local hockey and tennis clubs to form the Epsom Sports Club.

The club is believed to have been established at least 150 years ago, and Epsom often played at Lord's in and about 1800. First it played on Epsom Downs, possibly on the race-course, but round about 1880 obtained the present ground in Woodcote Road, Epsom.

Some fifteen years ago, Captain E. E. Schnadhorst, president of the club, purchased the cricket ground from General Sir Edward Northey and set up a trust for 500 years, whereby it became known as the Schnadhorst Memorial Ground. By the terms of the trust, it is dedicated to open-air sport for all time.

I have always been very much impressed by the fact that club cricket a hundred years or so ago was stronger than county cricket—a fact unfortunately reversed today. In 1815, for instance, Epsom C.C. beat all-Middlesex in a game in which a host of famous cricketers appeared.

A year later Epsom beat Sussex at Lord's by two wickets, in spite of the fact that Epsom loaned William Lambert to Sussex for the match—Lambert being considered at the time to be the greatest all-rounder of his day! In the Epsom side in that game was William Ward—a name not so well known as 'Lord', but nevertheless a man to whom cricketers all over the world owe a very great debt of gratitude. It was Ward who saved Lord's from the builders by buying out Tom Lord's interest in the ground.

Round about that time Epsom also played some interesting matches with Kent, Gloucestershire, Surrey (who were beaten at the Oval in 1867 by a mere seven runs), and several of the more famous 'wandering' clubs.

During the War of 1939–45 the Epsom club played continously—no match being scratched because of air raids or flying bombs—and many famous cricketers of England and Australia played in Service XIs against it.

I remember playing for the British Empire XI at Epsom in 1941. After a most enjoyable day's cricket, Mick Bebbington, our wicket-keeper, found an old cart-horse in a nearby field. My most vivid memory is of Bertie Clarke riding the animal bareback and hanging on like grim death while the horse, flat out, galloped the length of the field.

Skipper since 1947 has been P. J. Howell. Wilfred Waters, a colleague of mine on the C.C.C. council, was captain for years up to 1947, and has been the club's outstanding batsman. Stanley Oxley, whom Malden Wanderers were sorry to see go, has always been a magnificent fast bowler. David Fletcher, now with Surrey, used to play for the club during the War years, but has returned for his club games to his first side—Banstead.

Jim Harold, former Essex wicket-keeper and until his recent death landlord of the 'Red Lion', Epsom, was another regular player. Epsom's most prolific opening pair in recent years, W. F. Waters and R. G. Foxwell (the latter now with Sutton C.C.), shared in many big stands, their record—probably also a record for the club—being 221 against Roehampton C.C., each scoring a century.

To encourage young players, the club runs a colts' side for boys up to eighteen years of age, under the direction of F. Simpson. An annual colts' cricket week is a feature of the summer holidays.

In one wartime match, Epsom's opponents wanted 4 runs to win, with 6 wickets to go. F. Simpson completely upset the apple-cart by taking all 6 wickets without another run on the scoreboard! In another match round about the same time, Epsom's visitors dismissed the club for 32. Confident of victory, they turned their batting order upside down—and duly won, *but* by only 1 wicket! Which goes to prove the old adage—never play about until the game is won.

Ewell is not far from Epsom, but in this short journey we go from one extreme to another—from a club of long standing to a relatively new side. It was in 1938 that the *Ewell Court Club* introduced cricket into a new district. All its members were previously unknown to each other.

After only one season came the War, but the club had its own ground—on the Gibraltar Recreation Ground, West Ewell, and members played fairly regularly.

The present secretary, R. J. Bell, tells me that one of the original members who did much to build up the club's reputation was Arthur Judge—he has now retired, to the club's very real regret.

Victor Kerridge, the captain, although now fifty-six years o

G. Wreford (Brondesbury) brilliantly caught by D. B. Carr (former Oxford captain) in the C.C.C. *v.* M.C.C. match at Lord's on August 17, 1950

H. L. ('Bill') Palfrey, the Dulwich C.C. captain

(*Top*) Tommy Evans (Harefield) had an excellent season in 1950 with his left-arm spinners

(*Bottom left*) Oliver Battcock (Bucks. and Datchet)

(*Bottom right*) Arthur Dann (Eltham)

age, is still a useful wicket-keeper, and assists greatly both on and off the field.

One of the club's favourite stories concerns a local team, who, with half an hour to go, had 8 wickets down and 60 runs to make. The batsmen carefully played each ball back to the bowler. A local farmer suddenly shouted, 'It gets dark about eight o'clock in these parts—same as anywhere else!'

Back at Coulsdon there is the *Cane Hill Hospital Club*, a comparatively small organisation of only twenty members. But it is vigorously active.

Not long ago such well-known cricketers as the brothers J. C., F., and V. Crawford, as well as Dr. Littlejohn of Middlesex, all played here. The Crawfords' father was the first resident chaplain of the hospital.

R. Stone is now secretary, and captain is F. Cottam, who in 1947 scored well over a thousand runs. G. Gallup is the all-rounder of the team. He took all 10 wickets against Ravensbourne in 1948. Both G. Dover and J. Willis are bowlers who regularly take over 100 wickets a season.

Another small but sporting body is the *Whiteley Village Club*, at Walton-on-Thames. The village itself owes its existence to the late Sir William Whiteley, and is one of the most attractive you will find anywhere.

The club was formed in 1919. Its present president is Colonel G. B. Chetwynd Stapylton. Ron Fuller is the captain and honorary treasurer. In 1948 he took thirty-eight catches, and in the same year A. Kerr, one of their most reliable batsmen, scored 500 runs in the first two months of the season. J. Cole headed the batting averages for 1947 and 1948.

Since the early days of the club, J. Anstead has been in the team, but he recently retired. Loath to give up his association with the game, he is now umpire, and the club has made him a life member.

In 1949, when the club was playing at Barnes Green, Sussex, Whiteley Village batted first, and the opening pair made a century stand, while the rest of the side had a most enjoyable time in the bar overlooking the ground. They all failed miserably to support their opening batsmen when it came to their turn, but I am assured the game turned out all right in the end.

K

In 1947, against Caneswood Hill, Whiteley wanted one run to win off the last ball of the match. Number 11 batsman hit it straight to a fielder and ran. The fieldsman threw the wicket down and the umpire gave the batsman out, telling him that he was very unlucky as he was only half an inch out of his crease. The decision here seemed to be as close as the result of the match!

There must be many motorists who, while crossing Wimbledon Common near the 'Telegraph Inn' on their way to the Kingston by-pass, have said, 'There's a typical village green for you!' And you could never wish to see a more pleasant sight on a hot Saturday afternoon than the ground on Putney Heath where the *Roehampton Club* plays its cricket.

It is both public and private. Given to the club by the Lord of the Manor, Earl Spencer, in 1842, it remained in sole use by the club until 1871, when Parliament passed the Wimbledon and Putney Commons Act. It is not enclosed and the public is welcomed, but organised games other than those of the club are not permitted.

First intended for 'villagers', 'outsiders' from the City were eventually allowed to join, and from 1900 onwards such figures as the Hugh Smith family (Lord Bicester is one of the sons), the Charrington family, the Earl of Leven, and the cricketing family of Browns—Freddie (skipper of England and Northants), Freddie's brother 'A. M.', and their father have all played for the club at some time or the other.

Even now the club has many links with 'the good old days'. Ernest W. Powley, the general secretary, for instance: he has links with the club, through his family, that go back to 1859. Ernest himself has just completed fifty-two years of service with the club, and was skipper from 1920 to 1933.

Chairman of the general committee and a member since 1922, Frank Covey was skipper in the difficult post-War season of 1946 after being vice-captain from 1934 to 1939. D. W. Denman, who has been a member since 1916 and is a contemporary of Ernest Powley, holds the job of treasurer. John R. Butterworth, who serves on the C.C.C. Council and who has been a member since 1929, has kept up the standard of fixtures.

Wilfred Martin, another hard worker, has been a member since 1932, is secretary of the appeals committee, and is responsible for raising the sum of £2,000 for a new pavilion.

Behind the scenes is Lieut.-Col. H. M. Lambert, O.B.E., who bears the attractive title of Ranger of Wimbledon Common. His son, Paul, also a Roehampton member, was in the 1942 Dulwich College XI with Trevor Bailey, England and Essex all-rounder, and Tony Mallett, for a while in charge of cricket at the school.

E. J. Adams, besides being an opening bat and useful change bowler, is also a wicket-keeper. What an all-rounder to have in any side! He has played for Somerset and never fails to get his 1,000 runs every season.

F. H. Chalk, who became captain in 1948, got a lot of runs and took 100 wickets in 1947–1948–1949. Former captain W. Scott joined the club in 1927. In 1946 Scott and Chalk toured Holland with a team from Wandsworth.

Scott, whose 111 not out against Cranleigh in 1949 was one of the highlights of the club season, went in when the score was 9 for 3 wickets. Half the side was out for 52 by lunch. After Scott's effort, Roehampton declared at 197 for 7 wickets.

The ninth wicket club record was broken in 1949 by D. Pulleyn and Scott in an away game against Haywards Heath. They put on 100 runs after the side had been 32 for 8 wickets.

F. W. Simpson, a former captain and a member since 1926, is now cricket and soccer coach to the R.A.F. College at Cranwell.

Opposite the Star Hotel, Felbridge, near East Grinstead, is the *North End and Felbridge Club*, which has been in existence since 1893, though the present ground was not opened until 1928.

'Behind the scenes' officials are H. W. Brooker, the secretary; I. D. Margary, the president, and F. M. Henn. Skipper J. C. Holmes got things going again after the War, and John Allison has carried on since 1949.

H. Pope, an all-rounder, usually manages to get more than 100 wickets a year. W. Smith is another all-rounder, and ex-skipper Holmes had his best season in 1948.

In 1949, after they had dismissed their opponents for 130, North End and Felbridge collapsed and were 31 for 6 wickets. Then R. Jones, who scored 50, and Pope pulled the game out of the fire, and the club won handsomely by 2 wickets.

The *Farncombe Club* now play at Broadwater, which is the name by which the club was known in 1874. The owner of the ground then was a Mr. A. Marshall who, having been away on holiday, returned to find his beautiful barley field turned into a cricket ground.

The ground soon became famous because eight years later Surrey C.C.C., having had a spot of trouble about the lease on its own Kennington ground, went to Broadwater to play Notts. Incidentally Mr. Marshall, the original owner, was the first of many generations of Marshalls to be associated with the club. Two of them, S. F.—who, I believe, was a General—and Henry, were presidents between the years 1856 and 1878.

In 1947, to mark the centenary of the ground, E. R. T. Holmes, former Surrey skipper, took a strong side down to play the club. Alan Melville, the South African captain, Brian Castor, present secretary of Surrey C.C.C., the Bedser twins, Laurie Fishlock, Eddie Watts, Bob Gregory, the late Stan Squires, and several other Surrey county cricketers helped to celebrate a really great day in style.

W. Duncan Wright, the present secretary, has been in office since 1939. He has done a lot to assist the twenty-over mid-week cricket played in this part of Surrey and in which Farncombe takes part.

Like most large sports clubs with hundreds of members, only a fraction of whom belong to the cricket section, *Pearl Assurance* cricketers number only forty out of approximately 1,000.

The ground, with its fine pavilion, was opened in 1934. It is now, without doubt, one of the finest 'squares' in the London area. It was on the Pearl ground that the Publishers *versus* Authors matches of 1947 and 1948 were played.

E. A. Haynes is their star player. He always scores freely and has twice been 'capped' for the C.C.C.

A. T. Smalley, the secretary, tells me that most of the club records were destroyed during the War, but he well remembers the club's Isle of Wight tour in 1934. Frank Astill, the skipper, was on his honeymoon at the same time, but was persuaded to turn out for 'just one match'. He did, and celebrated it by scoring a century!

Anyone who has played on the N.A.A.F.I. sports ground at Morden will know the ground almost 'next door' in Bishopsford Road, where *Carshalton* first played over a hundred years ago.

The club is lucky to have J. Tavares, a West Indian, who, like many of his countrymen, is a useful all-rounder. A. Herring is an opening bat and reliable wicket-keeper, and W. Mummery more often than not manages to score his 50 runs a match.

Carshalton is one of the clubs who have a Saturday and a Sunday captain. Saturday is duty day for H. Berrett, and F. Baker takes over on Sundays.

Richmond Athletic ground usually means rugby, but it is there that the *St. Luke's Club* plays its home games. Founded in 1889, it shares the ground with the Richmond Town and Sheen Clubs.

Before 1932, when it moved to the Athletic ground, the club used to play on lively wickets and rough outfields in a local park. Fortunately, that's all over now.

Secretary since 1946 and a past captain, R. S. Williams is one of three sons of the late A. G. Williams, who did more than anyone else to keep the club going in its early days.

The club depends to a very large extent on J. Freeman and G. Young, a fast bowler, who took 118 wickets in 1949, and on R. Gardner and all-rounder A. Major to score the runs.

To support St. Luke's Church, after which the club is named, a match was arranged in 1949 to be played in old-time flannels and beards. It was a windy day, and all the beards were blown off!

One of St. Luke's greatest and most exciting wins was in 1948, when Shepperton dismissed the club for 32. St. Luke's won —by 2 runs.

One of the greatest tributes to cricket organisation must go to the *R.N.V.R. Club*, formed only in 1946, yet now playing sides such as Dartford, Wimbledon, Nomads, Richmond, Alexandra Park, Beckenham, and East Molesey, and a two-day game against the Royal Navy as well.

The first—and present—secretary, R. L. Bristowe, and L. C. Asser, captain 1946–48, decided over a glass of beer in 1946 to found the club, and managed to arrange six matches that year, the side of six or seven regulars being made up to strength 'by fair means or foul'.

These founders are now life members. Loughton cricketers will remember Asser—he formerly played with them, and for Old

Ardinians. Present president, Dr. A. J. Lewis, used to play rugby for Guy's.

Joint captain in 1948 was J. A. Arnott, from Cheltenham College XI. He was succeeded by B. A. Crabb, of Old Citizens and Epsom, who still holds the job. Vice-captains in 1949 were D. St. C. Stannard, who has played for the Navy in Malta, and C. H. Cane, who has turned out for Old Ardinians, Broxbourne, and Barclays Bank. W. S. Harris took over from Stannard in 1950.

They have a great variety of men in R.N.V.R.: batsman R. F. Hazell comes from Lancing Rovers and Incogniti, Harris has played for Cambridge Crusaders and M.C.C., and left-hander P. J. Sergeant has played for the Royal Navy. Bowler J. D. McGregor, now abroad, has played for the Navy, and V. F. F. Feeny, the slow stock bowler, was at one time a Surrey 'colt'.

The private ground at Cobham is rented from Old Surbitonians and shared with the R.N.V.R. rugby club, but this is a recent innovation. From 1946 until 1948 they were 'wanderers'.

That first post-War summer must certainly have been a bit tricky. Against R.N. Barracks (Chatham) the club lost 5 for 22 while Asser and four of his team were 'racing' from London in a 1926 car, which had four punctures on the way. But they just made it in time to take the total to 130.

Against Byfleet in 1948, the home side was out for 130. R.N.V.R. had reached 126 for 6 when Byfleet gave the ball to off-spinner G. Connelly—kindly loaned to Byfleet for the occasion by the V.R. He promptly took the last four wickets to give Byfleet a win.

To their great credit, the club has also managed a regular tour of Sussex in the first week of August, and plays, among others, Lancing Rovers, Burgess Hill, Southwick, Middleton, and Cuckfield.

H. A. Denney, of *Hook and Southborough*, played his first game for the club in 1914—and is still playing. He has scored centuries many times, and on three occasions has taken all 10 wickets in an innings. J. M. Jennings is a useful all-rounder, and more than useful as the captain. He has done a great deal for the club. Hook and Southborough, founded about 1880, was 'out of action' during the 1914–18 War. W. Aggas, who died only recently, was captain then, and helped S. B. Lawless, of Thames Ditton, H. C. Wilkins, and T. E. Newman to get the club going again. Newman, who has played for the club for forty years, is now president.

Some years before World War II a 'big' London club fixed a visit in late September and put Hook out for under the 100. At tea the visiting skipper was heard to say, 'We'll knock those off for the first wicket.' Lawless rallied his boys to such purpose that the Londoners were out for 37. Who says the best players leave the villages?

The West Indians, on tour here in 1950, have this much in common with *Dulwich*—R. K. Nunes, their skipper in 1928 and now chairman of West Indies Board, is an old boy of Dulwich College and a member of the Dulwich Club.

From 1867 there was a cricket club in Camberwell which, until 1888, was known as the Aeolian C.C. Some of its matches each year were played in conjunction with the Lennox C.C., the joint combination being known as Dulwich C.C. In 1888 there was a complete amalgamation, and since then the club has been known as Dulwich.

There was, however, an earlier Dulwich club, as two of its representatives were present at the foundation meeting of the Surrey County C.C. in 1845. An even earlier reference is to a player who was professional to the Dulwich and Streatham clubs in 1833. Apparently this earlier club must have become defunct before 1867.

Dulwich bowlers, I believe, can claim an all-time record. Four of them have taken all 10 wickets in an innings: W. J. Baker *versus* Mitcham in 1920; W. K. Yonge *versus* Sutton in 1925; Len Summers *versus* Epsom in 1932 and The Wanderers in 1927, and J. W. Meekins *versus* Purley in 1949.

From forty-nine games played by the club immediately after World War II to 159 arranged nowadays is a big hop, but hard-working match secretary H. D. Curran has managed it.

F. Huntley, who joined the club in 1897, was largely responsible for the club's survival during wartime. H. A. Robertson, the present president, was an active playing member until 1948 and still turns out occasionally, and L. S. Humphries, the post-War honorary secretary, has recently been elected a vice-president for his services to the club.

Of the players, A. C. Shirreff, another pal of mine from

Dulwich College, who has played for Cambridge University, Kent, Hampshire, R.A.F., and the United Services, headed the batting averages in 1948 and 1949; in '49 he averaged 98·66! W. D. Finch, an all-rounder—left-handed bat and slow bowler— has taken over 400 wickets and made more than 7,000 runs since the War. He has played for me in the C.C.C. XI and for the representative Surrey Association of Cricket Clubs XI.

In 1944, the United States Army Air Force played a match on this ground, after which an American flag was presented to the club; it is flown on Independence Day each year. The club has also been presented with a New Zealand flag, in recognition of the hospitality extended to New Zealand servicemen during the War.

H. L. Palfrey (Bill) is the present skipper; J. E. Manning, D. F. R. Emus, with whom I opened the batting at school, and Tony Fairbairns, with whom I was brought up as a child, have done more than their share in maintaining the prestige of the Dulwich C.C.

From time to time light-fingered persons have visited the dressing-rooms while play has been in progress, and all escaped detection until one Sunday in August, 1949. On that day the club was playing two games against Alleyn Old Boys, whose ground adjoins the Dulwich ground. Dulwich was batting, and one of the batsmen waiting to go in saw a man in the visitors' dressing-room with one hand in a coat pocket. The hue and cry was raised at once, and the culprit ran down a lane beside the Alleyn Old Boys' ground. Here, the other Dulwich XI was in the field, and immediately it was realised what was on, the game was abandoned.

A chase ensued over gardens and in and out of houses until the thief was caught in the kitchen of one of Dulwich's honorary members, who came in expecting to find that his new refrigerator was being stolen! Instead, he found his kitchen full of cricketers overpowering the thief.

The thief subsequently proved to be a deserter from the Army, and was promptly handed over to the military authorities.

Sutton Cricket Club played matches on Sutton Green between 1840 and 1850, and in the 'fifties moved to the present ground in Cheam Road. The field, part of Lower Cheam House Estate, was first lent by Sir E. Antrobus and later by Mr. H. L. Antrobus.

No rent was charged, but it was the custom to give the keeper a gallon of whisky at Christmas. In those days 10s. equalled about £11 today. Subsequently a small rent was charged, and in 1902 a company was formed by members and the ground bought. In 1865, the club acquired from the L.B. & S.C. Railway the waiting-room at Sutton Station for use as a pavilion, and it is still on the ground. In 1906 a new pavilion was built, the donor being the president, Sir Ralph C. Forster. This building was destroyed in 1940 by an incendiary bomb, and a number of old records and photographs were lost.

In 1872, Akroyd Hyslop became captain and raised the status of the club during his reign of twenty-two years. Matches were played with M.C.C., Surrey Club and Ground, and In-cogniti. After several captaincy changes from 1894 to 1898, G. R. Blades was elected in 1899 with V. R. Bromage as honor-ary secretary. The former, now Lord Ebbisham, has been president for twenty years, and was captain until 1906. R. M. Bell was captain 1907-14, and in a long membership has the astonishing record of 2,000 wickets with his slow off-breaks. Of many fine all-rounders up to that time, the best among the regular players were probably R. A. Shepperd and G. H. Hadfield.

During the difficult times after the War, D. D. Napper, another all-rounder, was captain, 1919-24 (his son, B. D., had the same post in 1946). He was succeeded by J. D. Crosthwaite, 1925-26, and E. J. Henderson, 1927-37, and again from 1947 to 1950. C. Thain, another all-round player, was captain 1938-39.

W. G. Grace, who captained his club, London County, in a regular fixture with Sutton, made many appearances and always drew a big crowd. On one occasion, having been given out before he had scored, he insisted he had not hit the ball, and that the spectators had all come to see him bat, which was probably true. It was the umpire, Lockwood, who then went off the field.

The club's record score is 225, made against Horton Asylum in 1910 in very quick time by J. E. Jewell, who hit four sixes in one over. Two of his brothers also played for Sutton: A. N., who appeared for the Gentlemen at Lord's, and M. F. S., who later captained Worcestershire. D. J. Knight, of England and Oxford, and the late F. G. H. Chalk, who captained Kent and won the D.F.C., were members from their school days, and the former, who made a century for the club at the age of fourteen, still

delights us with his effortless stroke play. Another member from
his school days is R. W. Skene, the Oxford Blue, but he seldom
plays now. R. H. Williamson, a fine batsman, left-arm bowler,
and brilliant fielder, lost his life as a Mosquito pilot in 1942, and
B. Stevens, a dashing bat, and J. H. Norman, D.S.C., a useful all-
rounder, also gave their lives.

Touring sides from overseas have often visited Sutton. Before
1914 the Merion Club from Philadelphia came several times, and
in the past twenty years De Flamingos from Holland have paid
half a dozen visits. And the club itself has visited Kent, Sussex,
and Devon.

Normally, there is one whole-day XI and three half-day, but
it is often difficult to arrange suitable games for four sides with
only one ground. Of the regular players in the whole-day XI,
Laurie Henwood is outstanding as a batsman and is a useful
slow bowler and fine field. In the holidays, B. R. J. Walker and
R. J. Knight strengthen the side in all departments. Very useful
all-rounders are H. N. Bligh, B. Sukias, D. B. Vale, and F. L.
Hollingbery—the last-named a fierce and unconventional hitter.
K. L. Robinson is a fine defensive bat, and E. White has played
many useful innings. Since the War, the most successful player in
the half-day elevens, as an all-rounder, has been C. A. Boxall.
Other leading bowlers are J. M. and J. W. Hitchen and D. R. C.
Philip.

There is a flourishing schoolboy section under veterans
T. J. Wheeler and C. A. Oakey, and last year a dozen matches
were played against other teams—apart from practice games. In
1950, John Walter hit over 1,000 runs for the club—it was his
first season since leaving school.

Sutton has an extraordinary record in one respect—it has had
only two groundsmen since 1898: A. Coleman from then until
1934, when K. A. Harman took over at the age of twenty after
two years as assistant.

L. V. Straker, treasurer from 1919 to 1927, recently resigned
from the committee after fifty years' service. His son, J. L. E. S.,
has been honorary secretary since the War. W. J. Read is
honorary treasurer. Stanley Lewis ('Grandpa') was secretary,
1928–39, and is still doing sterling work for the youngsters.

Chapter Seven

CLUBS AND THEIR PLAYERS

Histories, outstanding players, and anecdotes of clubs in other counties.

PERHAPS the best known of all Sussex cricket grounds is the Central at Hastings: the town first had a 'festival' week there in 1886.

Hastings lost that distinction in 1924 to Folkestone, but has regained it since the War.

It was on this ground that Jessop scored his 191 of 234 in ninety minutes, hitting 6 after 6 into the South Terrace. And here Dr. Grace, after an unfortunate first innings, was presented with a pair of pheasants just before his second knock. The diplomatic choice of bird will be noted!

In 1938, a committee consisting of J. M. Swattand (South Saxons), Reg. Robotham (Hastings and St. Leonards), A. E. Chambers (Ramblers), and L. A. J. Glyde (Municipal) formed a club to play cricket on the Central Ground—on Sundays. Many objections were raised, but it was proved that the trust deed did not prohibit Sunday play, and that the intepretation of the deed from 1872 until that date whereby Sunday games were banned was wrong.

So the *Hastings Priory Club*, despite many lamentations locally, began its career in 1939. And throughout the War, with most matches arranged on a week-to-week basis, the Priory played every Sunday except one—May 23, 1943, when the Nazis dropped twenty-five H.E. bombs on the town.

With its wartime achievements a by-word, Priory's post-War success was assured. In 1945–46 members numbered about 400, and a Sunday outing to play cricket against them at Hastings is a very popular week-end with London clubs like Ealing Dean, Gravesend, Barclays Bank, Malden Wanderers, Law Society, and Middlesex Wanderers.

V. J. Pain is captain, and Priory's outstanding bat is Reg Robotham who also keeps wicket and is equally good at cover point. A county second XI player, he has also played four times for the C.C.C. and for Sussex against the M.C.C. in the 1946 local festival. In four pre-War seasons, 1935–38, he scored over 2,000 runs, and holds or shares more Priory records than any other player.

Frank Watson, veteran of many seasons, still gets more than his share of wickets with his off-breaks. In his thirties he was a good hitter and once scored 105 in thirty-three minutes for South Saxons against Old Whitgiftians. Watson was nearer fifty than forty years old when he got his first C.C.C. cap—against the Royal Navy in the two-day match at Hastings in 1949. His best performance? Ten for 22 against West Surrey, captained by George Potter, who were all out for 49, in 1947. They had an 'illuminated' score-card made for Frank to commemorate the great day.

Another very useful all-rounder is Hilary Abeyaratne, from Ceylon, who joined the club while studying in England, and equalled Watson's club record of 50 wickets in the season in 1949. He played cricket, rugby, and tennis for Kandy University, Ceylon. Pace bowler John Farrar has yet to equal his school performance for Dover College, when he took all 10 King's College, Taunton, wickets for 21 runs, but he has had considerable success for Priory.

Priory, like so many other clubs these days, fulfils what it considers to be an obligation by encouraging coaching, and runs a special scheme for juniors. Local cricket is showing the benefit already.

St. Andrew's (Burgess Hill), in East Sussex, prides itself on its family atmosphere. And why not? All these men are, or have been, playing members:

The brothers E. and C. Cheesman;

The brothers R. E. and A. E. Betts, whose late father was a founder-member, and umpire for ten years;

The brothers T. H., G. W. J., and R. F. Avery;

T. Sayers and his two sons, E. J. and D. W;

W. J. Monnery and his two sons, W. J. and J. A;

S. King, senior and junior (father and son);

F. E. and E. Sellwood (father—secretary since 1921—and son).

And if that's not a record it deserves to be. Each of these families has at least one member on the club committee, which is headed by the Rev. G. Tindal-Atkinson, president since the club's formation in 1920. Of the 115 members (forty-eight playing) no fewer than forty are vice-presidents, which probably accounts for the happy financial state of the club.

Members of the side for many years are R. E. Betts (captain), G. W. Avery, S. King, W. J. Monnery (junior), C. Parks (brother of Jim and Harry Parks), G. B. Tate (brother of Maurice), and C. C. Clarke (Derbyshire). Clarke has also played for Sussex, and Avery and Betts for the county Club and Ground side. Avery, indeed, picked as a wicket-keeper, hit a century in his first Club and Ground game.

Meanwhile his brother, R. F. Avery, captains the second XI. St. Andrew's claim to its 'family' title can hardly be challenged— certainly, *I* know of no club that can do so.

Quite a thing, as they say down Brighton way, was the resignation in 1949 of the *Brighton, Hove, and District Club Cricket Association* from the Club Cricket Conference. The club prefers to rely on the Sussex Cricket Association, which, by supporting a form of league cricket, found itself out of favour with the Conference.

How unfortunate! The Conference is prepared to face the possibility of losing members, it seems, in preference to winking the official eye at competitive cricket. Yet the eye winks very effectively at the Flora Doris competition held every year in the Guildford district of Surrey. The only difference, as far as I can see, is that the Sussex clubs play at week-ends, but the Surrey competition is in mid-week. Surely a very fine distinction!

Meanwhile Brighton's Association continues in strength, and has representatives on the Brighton Parks Committee and the Sussex Association. Eighteen of Brighton's selected youngsters have professional coaching in the winter, and there is constant liaison with the county and the Young Amateurs. Many similar small associations co-operate like this, but Brighton's district organisation gives a fine example of what such co-operation can mean to cricket in general.

A prominent member of the Association is, as one would assume, the *Brighton and Hove Club*, founded as recently as 1945 by an amalgamation of the Hove C.C. and the Brighton Non-descripts. H. W. Sayers, of the old Hove club, is present chairman, and the president is Sussex cricketer Sir Alan Saunders.

S. H. Baker (Hove) and A. C. Cruttenden (Nondescripts)

did most towards the amalgamation, and were the first secretary and chairman respectively of the new club. The old Steyning player, E. W. Mitchell, is team secretary. Vice-presidents include S. C. Griffith, of England and Sussex (and a writer on the game for the *Sunday Times*), and Patsy Hendren (Middlesex and England), now the county coach.

The club plays on the county ground at Eaton Road, Hove, and former Streatham player J. L. D. Robertson has proved an outstanding all-rounder. One of his 'off' days, though, was against Lewes Priory in 1949. He broke his bat on the second ball and rejected a substitute bat at the end of the over as being too heavy. Having obtained another, he was promptly caught without scoring. It was a little hard, therefore, when he overheard a local supporter comment to a friend, 'I've seen all the best batsmen get "ducks" but they didn't have to have three bats to do it.'

Peter Beechens, top of the club bowling in 1949, joined only that season, and in the second game played against the club for Noel Bennett's XI. Bent on making a good impression, eighteen-year-old Peter relied on no half-measures. He bowled out the whole of the Brighton side, his analysis showing only 8 runs in 13.3 overs, 7 of which were maidens. Brighton was out for 41, the lowest total of the season.

Robertson and A. A. Ansell (another from Steyning) have played for the county Club and Ground side, and H. M. Rimmer and Peter Wales for the county second XI. B. H. G. Kent, left-hand opening bat and captain, holds the record aggregate for one season, and another 'opener', Brian Miller, former club captain, was also captain of Blundell's School. Oxford soccer Blue, L. W. A. Raven, of Oxford Authentics, plays when on leave from India, and second XI captain Ken Gilkes is now on the Sussex C.C.C. Committee.

J. H. C. Marshall, now chairman, has been an official of the *Littlehampton Club* for over forty years. He recalls A. W. F. Somerset, who led the first M.C.C. side to the West Indies, and his son, A. C. Somerset. Both captained the club for a period of years.

Sir Arthur Conan-Doyle, J. W. A. Stephenson, R. C. Mordaunt, and D. N. Moore all played for Littlehampton. While, perhaps, there is no outstanding member of the present first XI, the all-round standard has produced some very satisfactory results. V. C. Geason, first post-War captain, who still holds the job, was chiefly responsible for matches during the War years, and the story of Littlehampton is incomplete without mention of their scorer and fixture secretary since 1920, J. A. Jesse.

The club has played at The Sports Field since 1897, when the ground was presented to the town by the late Duke of Norfolk, but was first in existence in 1872.

Some years ago A. C. Somerset hit 32 in an over, and in 1948 B. G. Carver and R. Sims, still one of the best batsmen, hit 120 in fifty-nine minutes in an opening partnership. R. Vincent keeps on bowling. He has taken his 100 a season for years past.

Just about a mile north of Worthing Central station lies *Broadwater Green*—a large pear-shaped area of grassland. It is thought that cricket was played there, under the shadow of the beautiful twelfth-century church, as early as 1771. In the British Museum, among the Harleian Charters, is an attested document whereby William de Offenton, then Lord of the Manor, granted 'an area of land for the people's pleasure'. It has, so I gather, always been accepted that this part of the green should be kept for cricket.

The late William Greenyer, and later his son, Charles, voluntarily undertook the maintenance and laying out of the square and outfield. Bowlers like Horace Mitchell, Leonard Mainwaring and Walter C. Blaker, and county bats like A. F. Somerset and Frank Gresson have played there.

In recent years the club has encouraged the youngsters by forming teams of 'under fourteens' and 'under eighteens', which perhaps accounts for the present club membership of well over 200.

Abe Duffield has been captain of the first XI for a number of years. Kenneth Suttle, originally a junior, played for Sussex in 1949. Denis Greenfield has been given a trial with the county team. Vince Taylor, a useful batsman, is also a brilliant wicketkeeper.

Walter Blaker tells me that T. R. H. McDonnell is one of their youngsters who played for the Sussex Amateurs, and another, Billy Greenyer, for the Sussex Colts, both doing quite creditably, but perhaps wicket-keeper-batsman John Moore, once captain of the 'under fourteens', is the boy the club relies upon most to prove the value of the help it gives the youngsters.

A Sussex club and ground of which I am extremely fond is *Middleton-on-Sea*. Back in the early 'thirties Hugh Bartlett, Billy Griffith, and I—all three of us still at Dulwich—used to spend most of our summer holidays on the ground. Often Billy and I would get up to the ground at 7 a.m. and prepare the wicket for the day's match.

Originally, it was the village ground, on which the villagers, including the blacksmith, formed the side. There was no pavilion then, and in those early days it was Colonel Strong, as secretary, who did much to establish the club as one of the best in Sussex.

Nowadays, with a very strong fixture list—which includes matches almost daily throughout August—few clubs can recall a list of players like this: A. G. Doggart, the present skipper E. E. Harrison, Sussex second XI player who, with John Lock, shares the vice-skippership, J. A. Cummings, A. R. Hayman, Nigel Haig, the old Middlesex player, Jack Langmead, first-class at all games, Hubert Doggart, 1950 captain of Cambridge and joint Sussex skipper, his brother, A. P. Doggart, Johnny Kemp, H. D. Nicholson, C. B. Cuthbertson, Norman Fuente, M. D. Neligan, J. Mence, Joe O'Gorman, A. E. R. Gilligan, E. Hendren, J. K. Mathews, D. Sheppard, who went with the M.C.C. to Australia in 1950, G. N. Allen, John Holman, and Terence Bayntun ('Pink Toes' to his friends!). The full Cambridge XI, under Hubert Doggart, played the club in 1950.

Incidentally, Nigel Haig took his first hat-trick in cricket while playing for Middleton, where they are all still convinced that he was bowling as well as ever when he finally decided to give up the game.

It was off G. N. Allen's bowling that the famous swallow was killed, to which I have referred in writing of South Hampstead.

One of the best Middleton stories concerns Jack Williams, the Richmond player, who, playing for Sidmouth when Middleton were touring there, struck the ball firmly and hit a chimney stack of the Belmont Hotel, adjoining the ground. Wade asked facetiously if it was a 'six', and to his amazement a Sidmouth 'local' replied: 'Four for that. For six it has to go right over.'

·   ·   ·   ·   ·

Jack Cooper (Barclays Bank) uses his feet in jumping out to drive. He was elected 1950 President of the C.C.C.

Con Davies (Alexandra Park), another C.C.C. Councillor, also moves out to drive

Alan Lavers (Essex and Buck-hurst Hill) pulls a ball to leg

L. Blundell (Wallington) in action on the Addiscombe ground

The earliest information available about the *Brighton Brunswick Cricket Club* tells of Jack Davey—a relative of one of the present-day playing members, Eric Davey—who was the first professional to the Brunswick. A master carpenter by trade, he was on the ground staff of the M.C.C. at Lord's before coming to Brighton. In 1881 he built the Brunswick Pavilion, which, until it was taken down recently, stood in the ladies' enclosure at the County Ground, Hove.

In 1893 the Brunswick played a two-day game against the Wanderers (Bromley), when the result was a draw. Batting first, the Wanderers scored 169 runs and the Brunswick replied with 281. In their second innings the Wanderers were 172 for 6, and the match was left drawn. In 1949, the Brunswick had more fortune in this match, the first against the Wanderers since that date. The Brunswick declared at 245 for 5 and the Wanderers were all out for 224.

The Wilson family has a prominent place in the club's story —beginning with Alderman E. J. Wilson, J.P., a vice-president, they have done a great deal for the side over many years. 'F. W.', the present president, is an uncle of the present vice-captain, 'N. F. K.', and A. K. is still playing regularly after thirty-eight years with the side: in his first game for the club, in 1911, he took a wicket with the first ball he bowled.

Everyone who frequents the pavilion at Hove will know Barker Smith, now nearly eighty years of age, and always to be found with his Press-cuttings book and full of the stories of the games that were played in the early days of this century.

One of the greatest all-rounders for the Brunswick was the late Arthur Collings, father of Geoffrey, a member of the club and later a professional on the ground staff. Arthur Collings must have held the record for the number of years as a playing member, for he last played in 1939 when he was sixty-seven. Another name to be found in the score book of the Brunswick is that of Percy Fender, the England captain of years ago, who was a vice-president of the club.

Since World War II the Brunswick has entertained many teams from other counties, including the Yorkshire Owls, Chorlton-cum-Hardy, Gloucester C.C., Bristol C.C., West Surrey C.C., the Wanderers, Bromley, Leicester, and Ivanhoe. Its own annual tour is always in Devon.

The club derives its name from the Royal Brunswick ground

at Hove, named after the House of Hanover, of which George IV
was a descendant.

Hampshire, for cricketers at least, includes the Isle of Wight,
and one of the two island clubs in membership with the C.C.C.
is *Ventnor*. And what remarkable success it has achieved! Simply
by satisfying local needs for better-class club cricket, it attracts
crowds averaging 500 every Sunday and, as honorary secretary
J. H. Owen tells me, 'all have deck-chairs'. What a lesson for
many other clubs!

That's why gate receipts—about £80 before 1946—are now
about £500 yearly. All is spent on the ground, including the
employment of a full-time groundsman. All this is the more
remarkable when it is realised that Ventnor has a total membership of only 150 (forty players).

Perhaps the natural surroundings of the amphitheatre
ground, rented from the Royal National Hospital, do a lot to
attract visitors.

Playing star of 1949 was Peter Mabey, with well over 1,000
runs and 100 wickets. In 1948 he took 4 wickets in 4 balls—all
bowled. And they were proud of their wicket-keeper, Kent, too,
but have lost him to the Navy.

In all these endeavours and results, I'm told, president
G. F. Newland has been a prime mover, and his great day each
season, just as it is for the club, is when the county team visits
it for a one-day game.

The other Conference club on the island is *Rookwood C.C.*,
composed of members of the Parkhurst Prison staff. They have a
fine ground and, as their captain, E. C. Wearne, has mentioned,
a real 'sporting' marl wicket, which they have produced over a
period of years.

R. Wright is their secretary and I know Rookwood, who
have a very useful team, are keen to play touring sides, so if any
of the clubs whose 'stamping ground' for tours is in this area,
Rookwood will give you a game—any time.

Now to the other end of the county—*Basingstoke*. Long-
service members here, too: Rex Lamb, now president, was club
captain for twenty-five years and has been secretary since 1943.

E. J. H. Hammond was formerly Catford C.C. president for ten years. Captain now is Howard Lawson, who used to bowl for the county.

'Daddy' of them all—in age and performance—is A. T. Butler, who at seventy still plays. He first turned out for the club in 1897. Two years later he became groundsman—a position he has held ever since. He regularly completed the double in his younger days, and now his three sons all play for the club.

Butler, when sixty-eight, approached secretary Hammond and asked to appear before the committee as he had a serious complaint. He duly appeared and when asked the trouble he replied, 'It's not the club, it's the selection committee. They don't give me the cricket I'm entitled to. I only played three games last month.'

Left-hander 'F.T.' is now best of the Butler family. He opens, and regularly gets his 1,000 a season. Another left-hander and left-arm slow bowler, G. A. F. Jewell, completed the double in 1948 and 1949.

And now back to the seaside. *Bournemouth*, with something like sixty playing members of a total 750 membership, is extremely fortunate. First, in Percy Ford, its president, and a fellow-councillor of the Club Cricket Conference, it has someone who devotes much time and energy to its interests.

It was Percy Ford who put up such a fight, together with the C.C.C., to get petrol during the rationing for country clubs to fulfil fixtures. Then we have the two Hebdens—'G. L.' and his son 'G. G. L.', who have done a great deal to foster Bournemouth cricket.

'G. L.' died in 1946, but Geoffrey is still the star batsman. When skippering the C.C.C. XI against the Royal Navy at Portsmouth in 1948, I had Hebden with me, and I was much impressed by the all-round quality of his play.

Established in 1926, the club acquired its ground in 1929, and opened it on July 5, 1930, with a match between the Gents of Hants and the Gents of Dorset.

Apart from those I have already mentioned, players R. H. Moore, D. F. Walker, and the late General R. M. Poore (president until 1938) have done great things for Bournemouth cricket. General Poore, incidentally, played for Hampshire, and in the golden age of cricket topped the English batting averages with an average of 97. His 304 remained highest for the county until beaten by R. H. Moore in 1937.

Moore often made many runs for the club while still at school. He is a forceful and aggressive player and before his twenty-first birthday scored 1,500 runs in one season of first-class cricket. 'Don' Walker went to Hampshire in 1937. He was a good left-hand bat, first-class wicket-keeper, and magnificent field. He died when with the R.A.F. during the War.

Recent batsmen who have done well include E. C. J. Honey, who, with George Hebden, put on the record-breaking unbroken partnership of 284 for the first wicket against Ealing, C. J. Barnes, and J. V. Summers. For bowling they have C. J. Sanders, H. S. Shaw, both of whom took eighty-seven wickets in 1949, G. Ford, C. G. Ormiston, and C. J. Barnes.

During World War II the Australian and New Zealand Air Forces were strongly represented in Bournemouth. They played an extraordinary 'Test' Match in 1943—*on March 16*, if you please! The weather was fine and warm, and spectators lounged in deck-chairs. The match took place on turf, began at 1.30 p.m. and finished at 4 p.m., the Aussies winning by 76 runs. Playing were K. Carmody and Keith Miller.

But Bournemouth had an even more unusual side on the ground in 1933 against Old Tauntonians. Their side was composed of five fathers with their five sons, plus a wicket-keeper. I am told the 'keeper didn't feel the strain unduly.

Always mention with bated breath—even now—*Portsmouth Alliance* when visiting the *Havant* club. Alliance once put Havant's second XI out for 6 runs, 4 of which were byes. But that was a long time ago—1902.

In Havant Park, Havant has one of the finest club grounds in the south. Approximately six acres in extent, part of it was purchased by public subscription and the rest given by the late General Sir Frederick Fitzwygram, of Leigh Park, Havant. The whole was conveyed in 1887 to the local authorities, in those days the Havant Local Board. The Board promptly raised a loan to returf the ground and build a pavilion, and these had a gala opening in 1890, when a team from Havant Local Board played a Portsmouth Town Council XI.

The Blake family has a long association with Havant. Philip Blake was captain for many years until resigning in 1948, when he was succeeded by J. P. Parker, who has played for the county for several seasons, and toured the West Indies with the M.C.C.

Both Mr. Blake's sons have played for the club. The late J. P. Blake, Cambridge Blue and county player, was killed on active service in Italy in 1944; David Blake, the younger son, now plays for Hampshire as often as possible.

Few Havant cricketers go far afield for their game, but of the top club men since 1939—G. A. Bridger, R. G. Armstrong, J. P. Parker, R. Fletcher, C. A. Joliffe, E. F. Norman, and F. G. Emery—George Emery made a day excursion to Norbury in 1949 when he was invited to play in a Conference trial.

New players include W. E. Latcham, Dr. D. W. T. O'Neill, both Minor County players, and J. Perkins, captain of the Isle of Wight.

Over 100 people belong to Havant, and most important to the club of those who no longer play are E. R. Smith, former honorary secretary, and E. W. Devonshire, the treasurer, both with twenty-eight years' service.

Club cricket in *Aldershot*, quite naturally, has until recently been overshadowed by Army cricket, although the cricket club was first founded in 1873, when its ground at Boxall's Lane was used twice by the county club.

The club went out of existence for thirty-eight years, but was revived again in 1947 at the request of the Hampshire County C.C., who were seeking more support from North Hampshire. The present ground, opened in 1948, is of such size that in future years the county may be able to play there. Leased to the club by the Borough Council, the ground itself is private.

Playing membership (sixty-two) in relation to actual members (120) is good, and one of the committee formed to revive the club in 1947 was George Collins, old Kent and England player, who died in 1949. Captain since 1947 is G. M. Birch, who plays also for The Wanderers, the Sabbatarians, and the Hampshire Hogs.

Team spirit is one of Aldershot's greatest assets, and Birch, who is also honorary secretary, was diffident in giving me individual performance details. However, after some consideration he decided that perhaps T. E. Whittaker and J. Astin are the two who form the backbone of the batting. Derek Bowden and

D. J. Kerr (left-arm spin) are promising young bowlers, and I am told that the county club is interested in them both.

The first match played on Aldershot's new ground must have been a bit tricky. It had been hoped to entertain Basingstoke, but the ground was unfit, so arrangements were made to borrow an Army ground. These broke down at the very last moment, and there was no alternative but to use the new ground for the match. On arrival the players found that only the 'square' was cut and prepared, while the remainder of the outfield was almost ready for the hay harvest!

There are only eighty members (thirty-two players) of *Bude C.C.*, the only Conference club in Cornwall, but between them they raised £600 in three years for improvements to their private ground.

They managed to play sixty matches in 1949 and establish what must be pretty well an all-time club record. L. Cobbledick, D. Abbott, C. Pickard, and L. J. Sweet each took over 100 wickets. Indeed, Sweet, the captain, has taken over 100 wickets and scored nearly 1,000 runs in many seasons.

Doyen of the club and still a member is A. H. Dickinson, who was one of the original members in 1870.

Some of the best Cornish cricket is run on the league basis, and the county is separated, roughly, into 'east' and 'west' sections, all playing all in each.

Old Whitgiftian Geoffrey Harrison, who has played in this competition, tells me that the matches produce good but (for him) rather too keen cricket, and that the final match between the winners of the two sections is so often an anti-climax because the clubs have to wait until September before the finalists are known. So the day's play is curtailed by about an hour, as it is dark by six o'clock in Cornwall at that time of the year, and the percentage of drawn finals is rather too high. Most competing clubs have a professional, who is often the groundsman as well.

Devon, Gloucester, and Somerset, like Cornwall, have few 'Conference' clubs. And why should they, indeed? They have their own more local associations. And what a name they have for hospitality—a bye-word with all clubs who go on summer tours in the west. How easily the names come to mind:

Torquay, Bovey Tracey, Paignton, Exmouth, Newton Abbot, Lynmouth.

South Gloucester Club provided a surprise for Londoners in 1948 when two of its players were invited to play in a special C.C.C. trial at Finchley. Only one could make the journey, but like all the other aspirants, he had the most wretched luck—the game was ruined by rain.

Some of my best and happiest memories of wartime cricket are of games played on the delightful *Stinchcombe Stragglers* ground, near Gloucester, where the club was founded some thirty years ago.

The side then comprised the Gloucestershire Neale family from Berkeley Vale, and the Listers from Stinchcombe and Dursley. Up to 1930 only Saturday matches were played. At this period of the club's history, H. J. H. Alpass, the Old Cliftonian, was a member.

In 1929, Arthur Bennett, not only a namesake of mine but a very good friend, joined. By 1931 he was honorary secretary and treasurer, jobs which he still holds, and 1932 saw ground improvements and the erection of the most magnificent screens I have ever seen.

Many famous players have played on the ground, including Maurice Jewell (Worcestershire), Harry Leaman, now living at Bristol and one of the stalwarts of the Long Ashton club, K. G. Harvey, a brilliant wicket-keeper, P. G. H. Fender, and, of course, Walter Hammond.

Sunday cricket is now a feature of the club's activities, and it annually goes on a Devon tour, to play games against the Royal Navy, Devon Dumplings, and the Royal Naval Barracks (Devonport), among others.

President since 1938 is Dr. T. P. Leighton. Players come from distances of twenty miles or more to play, and it is quite rare to find any of the villagers (population 200) in the side. It is a great achievement to have established and maintained such a wonderful club in the heart of the country.

I suppose I've a soft spot for Stinchcombe and can hardly be blamed for thinking the wicket wonderful, because I broke the ground record with 217 for R. J. Coley's team against the club in 1949. But like so many, many clubs, Stinchcombe is a testi-

monial to the endless work of a handful of men. I mean those
people who, although their playing days may be over—or,
indeed, may never have begun—never cease to work for cricket.
As I've said before, there is always at least one such man in every
club, and I have tried to mention as many of them in this book
as I can. Too seldom does their work receive the recognition
upon which we all—knowingly or not—rely so much. Long may
be their line!

Before the War I used to play regularly at Arlesey against
the *Three Counties Hospital Club*, so named because the hospital
is situated near the boundary line of Bedfordshire, Huntingdon-
shire, and Hertfordshire. I turned out in those days for Old
Alleynians, but the fixture has now been dropped.

Since 1860 this Hospital side has been going without inter-
ruption, and some of the better-known players include P. G.
Robinson, A. Woodhouse, T. W. Saunders, H. B. Goddard,
J. H. Buckley, the brothers E. and C. Albon, I. Ward, and
E. Page.

Ivan Ward, oldest playing member, has been regularly in the
side for twenty-five years. He is also the vice-captain of the team,
which nowadays usually includes E. Page, A. Haywood, G.
Callingham, G. and E. Bircumshaw, T. Short, E. Smart, R. R.
Robinson, R. Haywood, H. Pogmore, and F. Mays.

Ward reminds me that they have as fine a wicket as you'll
find anywhere. As if I didn't know! I've played on it often enough.
For prolific scorer Len Newman (Alexandra Park), though, it has
always been a 'bogey' ground.

The public come in and watch, and on the 'shirt-front' wicket
expect to see 500 runs in the day. In fact, it is almost a rule that
one daren't declare under 250! I believe the North and South
Thames Licensed Victuallers are among the most popular
visitors, from the spectators' point of view. They go round the
ground with packets of cigarettes and I am told that the patients,
having got their gift, hastily change places so as to get another!

While on the subject of cigarettes, there is the story of a
home match in which fags were short. All the blazers hanging
in the pavilion were searched and plenty were found in the pocket
of a blazer believed to belong to one of the men batting. They
were handed round to everyone.

When the batsman was out he put on his blazer and pulled

out an unopened packet of cigarettes. Faces dropped. The cigarettes so liberally distributed had been from the blazer of one of the opponents.

In the 'thirties I made a tour of the *Vauxhall Motor Works* at Luton. I was naturally impressed, but perhaps most of all by their cricket ground. It was bomb-damaged during the War, but they carried on with cricket, chiefly against Service sides.

Vauxhall's is one of the classic examples of what a good factory club can offer its members. Perfect ground, wicket, and surroundings, all for a few pence a week. Yet only sixty belong to the cricket section.

Jim Dransfield—match secretary and general club factotum —was the 1950 chairman. T. H. Clark, the Surrey batsman, was a member, and for five years scored 1,000 runs each season—and all before he came of age. Before joining Surrey he was Bedfordshire's opening bat.

R. L. Hills is truly the all-rounder—wicket-keeper, useful bowler, and batsman. He has kept wicket regularly for Bedfordshire since the War, and on occasions has taken off his pads to bowl for the county. A. Capstick, Vauxhall's regular opening batsman, is also a wicket-keeper. He, too, has played for the county, and is, perhaps, the club's most consistent batsman.

Other county players still active with the club are: J. Nixon, a left-hand batsman and skipper for the past two seasons, and A. Heymeson, slow left-arm bowler; L. Williams, right-arm fast bowler, played for Herts in 1948. H. Hayhurst, another young left-arm fast bowler, took 100 wickets in 1949, and included a hat-trick against Dover.

Star performance for the club, probably unequalled in cricket, was in a match against Leyland Motors, at Luton on June 13, 1948. E. Parkin, Vauxhall's fast bowler, had the first four Leyland men caught by his first slip, A. Nelsey, the last three completing a hat-trick.

The Leyland club, by the way, is now defunct. Since a business merger Hawker's have taken over, although the ground, on which the Kingston festival is played, is still known as Leyland's. It was at this ground that the West Indies tourists of 1950 played their first official match—a one-day game against the Club Cricket Conference.

Vauxhall's had great success in raising funds for the Red Cross during the War, against sides like the British Empire XI. During that time a feature was a two-day game with H.Q., Royal Australian Air Force. In one game, Vauxhall's declared at 412 for 4 (T. Clark 104, R. Hills 113 not, A. Capstick 67, and J. Nixon 54), and the R.A.A.F. replied with 361 for 7 wickets (J. Workman 120 and B. Sheidow 126). In a return game L. Williams took 8 R.A.A.F. wickets for 10 runs in a total of 148!

We all know how extremely helpful a president can be to any club, but without F. E. Spicer, *Dunstable C.C.* would have had no cricket at all from 1940 to 1949. Its president gave it the use of his own private ground at no rent, and also provided the groundsman.

In May, 1950, Dunstable opened its new private ground with a game against Bedfordshire. Its treasurer must have done a great job in raising £1,000 in twelve months towards the cost of developing this ground, but the club has still to find a further £1,000 to get on a sound financial basis.

This is another club that has supplied players liberally to the county. M. L. Kilby is not only Bedfordshire's fast bowler, but their No. 3 bat, with the excellent average of fifty or more during recent seasons.

C. E. Bourne joined Dunstable straight from school and topped the club batting averages in his third season with an average of over fifty, and scored several not-out centuries.

Louis Palmer, honorary secretary for seventeen consecutive years and skipper in 1948 and 1949, is always well up in the batting averages. He told me the story of how, on one occasion, T. G. Payton was bowling at A. B. Poole (the Bedfordshire captain). Poole jumped out to a half-volley and drove it hard straight back to the bowler. The ball struck Payton on the forehead and was caught by cover-point at least thirty yards from the wicket. In the excitement Poole helped to escort Payton from the field. He then took his stance again at the wicket, quite unaware of the fact that he was out until an appeal was made.

Payton still averages three centuries a season, although well over fifty years of age. He is a brother of the late Wilfred Payton, of Notts.

Dunstable's 'week', always a regular annual event, was

discontinued when War began, but once the new ground is well established there is little doubt it will be resumed.

To mention bowling in Buckinghamshire automatically introduces the *Slough Club* pair, Vic Lund and Frank Edwards. Against the London Counties XI during the War, in one of the Red Cross matches organised by Slough, this pair put a side of first-class batsmen out for under ninety on a good wicket. Slough won, and the ball was engraved and is now one of the club 'relics'.

Victor Lund has taken more wickets year by year than any other bowler I know. His immaculate length, combined with swing and a devastating off-spin, have made him a bowler to be feared. He topped the Minor Counties bowling averages while playing for Bucks and has won a C.C.C. cap.

Frank Edwards, the Bucks professional, plays often as an amateur in the school holidays, and always enjoys his game.

And there are plenty of other very useful cricketers at Slough. That excellent fielder, Hubert Wilmot, is also a forcing bat with a powerful off-drive; Tom Lawford has been described to me as 'one of the best wicket-keepers in Bucks who has never played for the county'. Peter Isherwood, an old Berkhamsted schoolboy, was elected captain for 1951. An excellent all-rounder, he topped both batting and bowling averages for Bucks in 1949. He is quite an outstanding personality and a ready-made successor to Doug Stott, captain for so many years.

Another all-rounder is Jim Hastie, a forcing left-handed batsman and useful left-hand bowler. He excels in the field and, already holding a C.C.C. cap, won his county cap in 1949. Oldest member still playing is Bill Southall, still a good, forcing No. 1.

We have to go back to 1849 to find the first report of this club. Quite a large number of people—both players and administrators—have been responsible for the club's success, but one of the most important is undoubtedly Frank Smith, the secretary, who has done, at times, the work of half-a-dozen to keep things going. I have played on the ground many times, and when visiting with the British Empire side, I always saw the signs of Frank Smith's brilliant organisation. Frank used to be quite a performer himself. In 1924 he played for Bucks as a fast bowler with considerable success, and when Douglas Stott was away during the War, Frank acted as deputy captain.

His proudest moment? Not on the cricket field but when, in 1947, the club completed the purchase of its delightful ground in Chalvey Road by paying off a bank loan contracted in 1929.

Doug Stott, a great friend of mine, is my idea of a real club man. A member of the club for twenty-five years, he does a tremendous amount of good for cricket on and off the field. He has played for Bucks, and not many years ago was a more than useful fast bowler. There was no better slip fielder in the game.

Canon A. G. P. Baines, until his death in 1949, was president for over twenty-five years. He was an all-round sportsman, being a county footballer and cricketer. Harold Roberts, chairman of the club committee for fifteen years, succeeded Canon Baines, and Arthur Hill took over as chairman.

Dr. Ralph Weaver Adams, a life member of the committee, had, to his great regret, to give up the game through illness, but his interest never flags. Another former player, Charles Lloyd, is now treasurer. He used to be a regular fast-medium bowler.

The club's three visits to Devonshire on tour have produced these 'highlights': Frank Edwards, at sixty, took all 10 wickets against Royal Naval Barracks; Hastie hit a hurricane 'ton' at Brixham and lost seven balls, and Lawford, in conversation at Devonport, requested an admiral to 'Pass the cheese, mate'!

A scoop for *Aspro Club* in 1950 was the arrival of Ben Barnett, Australian Test player, who in 1949 was transferred from the parent Company in Australia to work at Slough. He plays regularly for the club side.

But he is by no means the only good cricketer in the team. A. Hayhurst, W. Yates, J. Birrell, N. Butler, and K. Butler all turn out for the county. Albert Hayhurst was captain of Reading Football Club before the War, and for Aspro has never failed to take 100 wickets a season. Bill Butler has been Aspro's stock bowler since the start of the club, and his two sons, Norman and Ken, are both promising cricketers. Both play for Bucks.

W. Parry, a very steady batsman, celebrated his fortieth birthday by hitting a century—the first he had ever scored. I doubt whether he had a birthday present that gave him more pleasure.

The present chairman and captain of the club is N. C. Blackman, who was one of the original members in 1928. He is regularly in the top six of the club's batting averages. P. J.

Halsey, vice-chairman, captained the side for several years, and has on several occasions topped the batting averages.

Aspro's first tour was made in 1936, when they went to Paris. They liked it so much they went again in 1938. The normal batting order was ignored on these occasions, being revised by the captain in ratio to the hours of sleep obtained by the players the previous night. It must be recorded that the opening pair performed on those occasions as Nos. 10 and 11.

Aspro toured again in 1950—the first time for twelve years—but this time they went to South Devon.

Bletchley Town's ground was completed in 1898 and the first match played in June of that year, when Sir Herbert Leon, owner of the ground in those days, raised an XI to play Mr. Rothschild's XI. The present treasurer, J. H. Fennell, played in that match. At the age of ninety-two, Mr. Fennell is not only extremely active, but still keeps the club's financial affairs in a very healthy condition. There are thirty-five playing members.

Minor Counties' championship matches were played on the ground until 1933. Sir Herbert Leon died in 1927 and after the death of Lady Leon in 1937 the estate was broken up and the cricket ground purchased by the Bucks County Council, which granted Bletchley Town C.C. permission to use it as its private ground.

A. E. James, better known to some as a Sussex professional, was a club member when selected to play for Bucks in 1946. Since, of course, he has been playing for Sussex. Leslie Hall, who has passed the 1,000-run mark in each of the post-War seasons, has, since 1946, also taken a lot of wickets. The 1950 skipper was J. F. Smithie, and vice-captain, J. Beech. R. G. Pollard is the hard-working honorary secretary.

If one meets a *Beaconsfield* player, then one knows he really does live at Beaconsfield, because the club restricts membership to residents within approximately four miles of the local railway station. The ground at Wilton Park is owned by Colonel F. J. Du Pre, D.S.O., joint president of the club; the other is Lord Burnham.

In 1927–28, when Bucks was top of the Minor Counties' table, Beaconsfield could turn out a complete XI of members who had played for the county. One of them, R. H. Rutter, then the county fast bowler, was appointed first XI captain in 1948, and in 1949 took well over 100 wickets for an average of 11·50. He is still captain.

First C. H. H. Shaw (1942–46), then K. Wood (1947–49), have been the post-War secretaries, in succession to the late J. G. Montague, who held the job from 1929 to 1941. He died in 1943. Captain of the club is C. V. Raffety.

Datchet plays in the shadow of Windsor Castle, on property attached to Datchet House—formerly owned by Sir Lionel Cust, Custodian of Antiquities to H.M. King George V. The estate was subsequently purchased by Irving Ascher, the film producer, and is now owned by Sir Eustace Pulbrook, chairman of Lloyds for so many years.

The highlight of Datchet's season is the annual match against Herbert Sutcliffe's XI in August, which has been included in the 'list' for the last sixteen years.

Oliver Battcock has been captain of the club for the past five years, and he needs little introduction, having skippered the Bucks Minor County team for a number of years. He is also a member of the M.C.C., Incogniti, and several other clubs.

Picked for the Minor Counties *versus* Yorkshire in 1949, this evergreen bowler took only a few wickets under 300 in the same year, which is a feat in itself in any class of cricket. As an opening new-ball bowler he has few equals on his day, and in 1950 he took 9 for 7 runs against Burnham.

Wally Gage, by the way, likes playing against Bracknell. He took 7 for 42 against them in 1948 and 6 for 19 in 1949.

President of the club for the past twenty years is C. E. Killick, while W. H. Gage, now secretary, has been a member for twenty-two years and an executive member for eight.

In this colourful side is Geoff Brown, one of the openers, whose best 1949 innings was 90 not out against Chertsey, and Wally Gage, a quickish new-ball bowler, who told me about a match against West Drayton.

On the way to the opponent's ground, it seems, six or seven of the Datchet side were directed to a ground near-by. They changed and were having a knock-up when some of the opposition arrived. At 2.30 the skippers tossed, and Datchet elected to bat. As the two opening batsmen were padding up, another group of cricketers also arrived on the ground. After a lot of talking, the Datchet men found that they had almost begun a match on the wrong ground and against another side altogether!

Datchet has other county men besides Battcock. N. F. Dracopoli has played for Middlesex second XI and is a 'regular' for Incogniti; B. J. W. Hill has played for Bucks and also for the M.C.C. He is a master at nearby Eton.

J. Mayhew, Oxford University Blue, is another who has played for Buckinghamshire. He has been first choice for wicket-keeper for the club for some years. All-rounder B. H. Crawshaw had a great season in 1950 and W. Vowler headed the batting averages.

Another Eton master, C. H. Taylor, who has played for Datchet, played for England in the tour of Canada, and has captained Leicestershire. A first-class bat and a good spin bowler, he cannot play often for the club because of his duties at the College. A. S. Barker, a 'regular' for the Stoics, opens the Datchet bowling, his best figures being 9 for 36 against Harrow in 1948, but muscular trouble has kept him out of the side recently.

Boyne Hill, in Berkshire, celebrated its diamond jubilee in 1950. This is one of the clubs that have different captains for Saturday (W. H. Jennings) and Sunday (R. W. Ingram) XIs. Fifty-six of the eighty members are on the playing strength, and when they played The Tramps in 1949 they had Godfrey Evans of England and Kent keeping wicket for them.

There must be something in the air—or the cricket—conducive to longevity at Balls Park, *Hertford*. Hertford president, George Nicholls, who was an all-rounder, is one of three of the 1883 side still alive. W. C. Hunt, now just on seventy and with thousands of runs and wickets to his credit, is still playing.

And surely these clubs in Hertfordshire offer perhaps the best example of the real old 'country house' cricket, so typical of England in the years before the First World War? Not that Herts has a monopoly by any means, but its bigger clubs, such as St. Albans, Hertford, and Welwyn Garden City, still play on these 'family grounds'.

Hertford is known to have played Ware in 1788, but it was the squire who put local cricket on the map. Balls Park—in the Faudel-Phillips family until the death of Sir Lionel in 1944, when the County Council bought the estate—was the first home of the club. Then it was named Balls Park C.C. The club transferred to Hartham Common, but about 1853 returned to Balls Park as Hertford C.C. The pavilion was built in 1899.

Naturally, the club provides many of the Hertfordshire XI, including A. V. Grubb, L. Wright, J. Winter, F. Allen, and R. V. Marquis. Left-hander Winter, as 1949 club captain, scored over 1,000 runs; another left-hander, Grubb, was club captain from 1936 to 1945, and in 1949 spin bowler Allen took 250 wickets for the club. He also played in Birmingham League cricket.

An equally fine Hertfordshire record is held by *St. Albans*, which plays in Clarence Park. It, too, provides county players, and has done so fairly consistently for the past forty years.

Indeed, J. E. Holt headed the county bowling averages for 1947–1948–1949. Another county man, D. V. Cooper, always does well for the club, and secretary F. Pavey is that most popular figure with the 'locals'—a hitter. President is C. H. Rabone; captain, his son, S. H.

Don't tell all the other clubs who have been in existence for 200 years or more—but St. Albans claim to have been founded in 1666! Three hundred coming up!

They would not tell me the name of the player who, when fully dressed after an away game, pulled a chain in the changing rooms. Apparently it was not the chain for which he was looking. It operated a shower and he was right under it.

There is a section of Herts known to cricketers as the 'Grimsdell country'. Arthur Grimsdell, former sports international and now a director of Watford F.C., has been with the *West Herts C.C.* for many, many years. He still plays the odd game of cricket, and kept wicket for the county until 1948. His son, 6 ft. 5 in. Harlequin rugby player Alan, is now captain, and West Herts too, have a current county player in Dickie Bennett.

Latest innovation—and one heartily applauded by the county committee, according to Hertfordshire C.C.C.'s secretary, Major H. G. Lay—is the provision of coaching twice a week for boys. The scheme, begun in 1949, is for boys, nominated by their headmaster, from each of the local schools. Major C. J. S. Mitchell is in charge.

.   .   .   .   .

Welwyn Garden City's ground at Digswell Park was originally the private ground of a country house which is now part of Sherrardswood School. So picturesque, in fact, that many North Londoners go out there by car on Sundays in the summer.

I wrote of the co-operation between the club and the town in Bexley, Kent, but it is outdone by that at Welwyn. The best example, perhaps, was the club's twenty-fifth anniversary, when those firms with premises at the Garden City supported the club celebration week in style, and directors assumed responsibility each day as hosts to the visiting teams. The 'week' was an outstanding success.

The prime mover was J. F. Eccles, managing director of Welwyn Garden City, Ltd., but the 'tie-up' with the club was made much simpler because R. L. Reiss, then club president, was on the board of the same company, and is now on that of the Development Corporation that at present controls the private estate of which the club ground is part. Reiss was with the cricket club when it was formed in 1921, and for many of the early years was first XI captain. He was the first to be elected a life member.

Since his term, Geoffrey Bulloch has been captain. Carnill is a family name at Welwyn, and Denys Carnill, useful left-hander and slow right-hand bowler, is the Oxford hockey Blue and now a county and international hockey player. L. O. Bateman, a regular county player, is perhaps the club's best bat. Carnill and Bateman headed Herts county batting averages in 1950.

A recruit in 1948 was G. Youngson, Scotland player. He was not known at the club and, having told them that he was a bowler, was included in the second XI practice game. Actually he topped the first-class averages in 1947, but he turned out for the second XI match—just that once!

In 1950 the first club match ever televised was played on Chipperfield Common with Welwyn in the field.

It is amazing how many cricketers have been associated with *Abbots Langley* in some way or the other for fifty years or more. G. F. Simons, now president, has also held the offices of honorary secretary, vice-president, and captain. B. T. L. Cooper is another whose name has long been seen in the records, for at the age of eleven he was the first XI scorer, and has been honorary secretary since 1926.

E. J. Pascoe, now vice-president, was a useful bowler in

M

his time. Until his recent retirement, he was for forty years a master at the village school.

L. Swallow, whom some of you may remember as having played for Hertfordshire at the age of eighteen, topped the club batting averages in 1950, and is a prolific scorer.

R. Crownshaw is another county cap and first-rate bowler. Another minor-county player is R. G. Simons, son of the president. As wicket-keeper he won his county cap and followed in the footsteps of Arthur Grimsdell. E. J. Lambkin, captain for several years, is an all-rounder who bowls leg-breaks.

Unfortunately, the minute books of the club go back only to 1909. Before that they were either lost or not kept at all. It seems, however, that the club has been in existence over 100 years, and seventy years ago an issue of the parish magazine shows that the M.C.C. and Free Foresters were entertained at Abbots Langley.

Abbots Langley has a lot to show for its encouragement of the juniors—boys between the ages of twelve and fifteen. At least three have subsequently been awarded their county caps.

During a club match, I'm told, the then first XI skipper (I must not hold this against Lambkin) had to stop the game to deal with an unruly spectator whose language was somewhat blue. Having escorted the spectator off the ground, he shouted to him as he went out of the gate, 'Clear off, and stop that —— swearing!' That skipper, I must mention, was in tremendous voice.

In 1949 the club entertained a side for Eddie Watts, of Surrey. It was his benefit year, and the side, of course, consisted of Surrey county men. Laurie Fishlock had a similar courtesy paid him by this Hertfordshire club in 1950. At least 3,000 people come to Gallows Hill Lane to watch these matches.

Barnet, founded in 1893, played on the site at the bottom of Barnet Hill where the Odeon picture palace now stands. In 192 the club was allotted a railed-off portion of the local playing field on a twenty-one years' lease, which has now been renewed (after a lot of anxiety, I may say) for a further seven years.

Indeed, it would have been less than justice if an extension had been withheld, because, after the ground had been commandeered during the War, fifteen members were faced with meadow, no groundsman, and a dilapidated pavilion. So dilapidated, in fact, was the pavilion that when an M.C.C. side arrived complete with flag, during a Barnet 'week', there was no flagstaff on which to fly it. After some discussion there was a compromise, and the flag was draped round a post on the verandah. All, I am glad to report, is now in first-class order.

T. H. Nicholson, president and chairman of the committee, looked after the interests of the club during the War, and when cricket began again in 1946 he personally interested many of the local residents, and is chiefly responsible for relieving the anxiety of Barnet's treasurer, B. G. Sweet.

They do things well at Barnet, I know—I've been there and seen for myself. Perhaps it is because they have separate committees exclusively for the ground and for refreshments. Their president, T. H. Nicholson, runs the former and L. J. Grant the latter. R. Hibbard looks after the bar, while John Gaywood is general secretary.

J. L. Cartwright is first XI captain and their left-arm bowler is J. W. Perman, who joined them from Upper Clapton. Another to join them more recently, 1949 to be exact, is G. F. O'Connor, from the Hayes (Kent) club. Batsman-*cum*-wicket-keeper is F. H. Dix; E. N. Shearly and D. E. Pearce are fast-medium bowlers. Old Aldenhamian, A. H. M. Bradley, hit over 1,000 runs in 1949.

Here's a good example of a sporting vice-president. He offered the treasurer 1s. a run over ten. The signal went out to the home umpire faster than from any jungle tom-tom, and being a very reasonable sort of chap he ensured that the treasurer was in for a longer time than he had ever dreamt possible. He made his highest score of the season—and the club funds were better off by 30s.

Hemel Hempstead is lucky to have former Gloucester captain B. H. Lyon. There is little doubt that he will draw large crowds, particularly fortunate in this case, because at the start of the 1950 season the club's pavilion fund was well 'in the red'. He raised a county-strength side to play the club during the season in aid of this fund.

Old Boys' sides like, if possible, to stay near the 'parent' school, and the *Old Merchant Taylor's* is no exception. When Merchant Taylor's School moved from Charterhouse Square to Sandy Lodge in 1933, the O.M.T.'s transferred from Teddington to Durrants, Croxley Green, with their cricket and rugby football clubs. Their comparatively new pavilion is a pleasant mansion, built in 1866–67, and their practice wickets are as good as 'the middle'.

Sir William Palin Elderton, K.B.E., is now president, in succession to the late Herbert B. Hays, who held that office from the club's inception in 1912 until 1947—thirty-five years.

There have been many well-known O.M.T.'s. It was 'The Old Bird' (S. W. Goble), J. P. Jamieson (an outstanding captain), and Robin Wells who formed the club. S. A. Trick, one of the finest bats in London club cricket in his day, also played a big part in starting it off. Trick played for Essex. His nephew now plays for Glamorgan. Others playing then include G. H. and P. M. Vasey, T. A. L. Welch, H. H. Bowen, B. Hull, and F. W. M. Draper, one of the former captains of the club.

Nowadays, with their 100 playing members, the O.M.T.'s turn out six Saturday teams. The captaincy, since 1936, has remained in the hands of L. W. T. Turner, who is still an outstanding bat and fielder, despite his being a member of the XL club. He scored 920 runs in 'Saturday only' cricket in 1949.

H. L. Greer is an outstanding personality. He has played for the first XI for thirty years and seems to have mastered the art of 'festina lente' so far as cricket is concerned. He has taken over 1,000 wickets for the club. Now match secretary, Greer goes on and on. For five years, immediately before Turner took over, he was captain of the club and a very prominent batsman. Truly an evergreen cricketer!

D. O'N. Hodson, the honorary secretary, is said to be the only personality in the game around whom any club has built a bar! He is a great worker and organiser. In former years he was the club's best wicket-keeper, but between the wars captained one of the junior elevens to 'bring them on'. Don Hodson will still be remembered for his innings of 118 against Midland Bank in 1934, when he made full use of his unique 'swivel shot'.

D. M. Parry, a Cambridge Blue in the early 'thirties, has been unable to turn out regularly, but when he does play is still a forceful bat. F. F. Spragg—master-mind of rugby at Oundle School for the past twenty-five years—has often played for the club.

Mainly for geographical reasons, K. G. Williamson and D. W. Piper, both opening batsmen, have not been able to turn out regularly for the club. The latter is greatly missed as a change bowler, and may be out of the game for some time with a bad back injury.

Williamson has scored over 9,000 runs for the O.M.T. club. During the War he served in the Transvaal, and organised a fortnight's leave tour of the Cape for R.A.F. personnel in November, 1944. For his services he was elected a member of what one might call the 'Free Foresters' of South Africa—the Black Bats' Club of Cape Town. When the War was over he remained in the Union for a further six months, and opened the batting for the most famous South African club of all, the Wanderers of Johannesburg.

C. W. Writer is another all-rounder and a Conference 'cap'. Neither J. W. nor G. W. Weston has been able to turn out regularly lately, but 'J. W.' did a grand job as team secretary in the difficult years of 1947 and 1948.

Those still on the spot include G. W. Booth, H. Harold, and C. D. Eden, who was match secretary in 1936.

R. F. Sharp is one of the club's most promising 'new-ball' men since the War, and W. A. Gluck (wartime Oxford Blue) is a really hostile opening bowler.

Free Forester R. B. Hawkey, an aggressive cricketer who had a trial for Cambridge, helps the club regularly, as he is now an assistant master at the school. He had a fine batting season in 1950.

R. Ostler, the honorary treasurer, was the first captain of the 'second' first XI, begun in 1948. A big-hitter, if ever there was one, he once hit a 6 over the guns at Armoury House against the H.A.C. to complete a fine 'hundred'. He also holed out into a bedroom off the Dover Road, when hitting the Royal Marines bowlers all over the place at Deal. That was during one of the annual tours of Kent.

A. F. G. Hayzelden, the club's 'greatest-ever' bowler, was one of the outstanding fast bowlers of London club cricket between the wars. He played for Essex, and apart from the fact that he took 100 wickets in Saturday cricket in six different seasons, has many fine performances to his credit. He will always remember best, I should imagine, his hat-trick to finish a game in the last over against the Nondescripts. No. 11 (George Hickson), the third victim, had other ideas, but in spite of having the screens moved, the first ball he received shattered the stumps.

One man the O.M.T.s will miss is groundsman W. Cooper, who after twenty-five years' service has now joined the Lensbury Club. His preparation of wickets at Teddington and Croxley Green was quite outstanding.

I don't suppose many clubs have seen the opposition turning up to play on a coalcart, but that happened to *Totteridge* during the last War. A charity match had been arranged in aid of the Red Cross. The opponents were led by the Western Brothers. They and their team arrived on a coalcart drawn by a tractor. They were dressed in clothing more in keeping with a Will Hay act. The match duly started, but was soon held up by a panto-mime horse, which carried out fantastic evolutions at the wicket. The game proceeded, but Kenneth Western suddenly found he could bat, and the game almost developed into a timeless Test. However, Totteridge finally won, and £150 was raised for the Red Cross.

Excellent matches in more serious vein are watched by a large number of local inhabitants on the attractive ground near Totteridge Green. The ground has been in use since 1919, and was purchased by the Barnet U.D.C. in 1938, when a long lease was granted to the club. Previously, since its inception round about 1880, the club had used various grounds in the village.

Most consistent batsman of recent times is the skipper, F. C. Baker. He is also a good slow bowler, who has taken a large number of wickets in club cricket. During World War II a dentist, Wilfrid Foster, led the side very successfully. Foster is an excellent fielder in spite of his diminutive stature.

A great deal has depended on E. Bradbrook, both during and since the War. He is a left-hand, round-the-wicket bowler who maintains a good length with great accuracy for a long time on end. He has also been responsible for scoring a large number of Totteridge's runs. E. F. C. Haymes is another good all-rounder, without whom the club would fare badly and who, on fast wickets, can be a devastating bowler. He has been a member of the club for twenty years. Brothers J. and G. Firth are also of outstanding merit. They are both all-rounders and, by the way, excellent footballers. C. J. Child is the veteran fast-medium bowler and right-hand bat, and Vic East has been batting for the club for over twenty years.

Before the War and for one season since, Lt.-Col. R. I. Musson was skipper. He is a brother of two other well-known cricketers— 'F. W.', the Lancs amateur 'keeper, and the late Squadron-Leader R. G. Musson who led the R.A.F. sides. 'R. I.' (Bob to his friends) was a good batsman and a great leader. He is still on the committee.

W. J. Braine is the club's secretary. Chairman is J. A. Town —one of Totteridge's oldest supporters. President is F. A. H. East (Herts C.C.), who succeeded the late Lord Hewart of Bury.

Chapter Eight

THE GROUND

Temporary or permanent?—Wicket—Practice pitches (concrete, etc.)—Pavilion—Score-box—Score-board—Scorers—Public facilities—Encouragement of 'locals'.

A GREAT deal has been written about ways of improving your cricket, the best equipment to choose, what to look for when watching the masters in action, and the background of the game. But little or no attempt has been made to discuss the amenities and facilities of the grounds on which week-end cricketers play.

Clubs face tremendous difficulties every playing season. Some have pitches on recreation grounds, where the wickets receive scant attention and care, and the outfield is lucky to get an annual cutting. More fortunate clubs own their grounds, but far too many of them are still requisitioned, despite the lapse of time since the War. Other clubs, though their grounds have been de-requisitioned, face the loss of them altogether to the municipal authorities or under the Town and Country Planning Act.

Whatever the position of your own club, the fact remains that in Great Britain as a whole there are just not enough grounds. Of those there are, the majority could be improved considerably. The standard of English cricket cannot be raised if the wickets and grounds are not improved.

On commons, parks, and recreation grounds I see dozens and dozens of promising batsmen and bowlers, but what chance have they to develop their promise? Week in, week out, they must play on the same rough piece of ground—on a wicket marked out in May and probably not rolled more than once a fortnight.

Since the War, many local councils are doing much more to help, but the task is beyond them. What is needed, in my view, is a central body charged with the sole responsibility of improving British cricket grounds—a body to which local councils would be responsible and from which it would accept instructions. In some countries—Australia, notably—a great deal is done to help clubs with their ground problems. There is far more room there, I know, but even so they go to considerable lengths to ensure that wherever there are pitches, those pitches are good ones, on which youngsters can practice without fear and so improve their standard of play.

Nothing I say can possibly change the position regarding your own ground. If your club owns the freehold, or has been able to lease the land for a long period, then you must consider yourselves extremely lucky. If, on the other hand, your club must either share someone else's ground or use a public recreation space, then your main target for the future is a playing place of your own. And, whatever the problems and difficulties before you, go all out for it. Until you do, your club, its fixture list, its standards of play, and, indeed, its attractions in general, can never really develop.

I spoke earlier of clubs that still have their grounds requisitioned. In cricket, as in other expressions of active life, you must fight to improve what you have, but you must fight even harder to hold on to it. Here, to my mind, is a classic illustration:

In 1942 the Forest Hill Cricket Club in London lost its well-appointed ground and spacious pavilion: overnight, almost, it was turned into allotments. Over seven years later, after the most strenuous efforts had been made by the club itself and by the Club Cricket Conference, Lewisham Borough Council decided to relinquish it.

Tony Harris, the Forest Hill secretary and skipper, foreshadowed that, though they regained possession in March, 1950, cabbage stalks and stubborn weeds would make cricket impossible until the 1951 season, so that, at best, this well-known club lost its ground for well-nigh ten years.

And even then the freeing of the ground did not gain the Council's assent without protest. A Socialist Alderman said that it was unfair that 139 people should be deprived of allotments for the benefit of fifty cricketers. Well, I am not interested in political propaganda, but I am in cricket, and as a cricketer I ask, How can we expect our great national sport to flourish against indifference of that kind?

Another of the bigger clubs to suffer in this way has been the Private Banks Cricket Club. This is an old-established body that ranks among the top flight of London's clubs and has an excellent ground at Lewisham—neighbours of Forest Hill, in fact. There was another years-long struggle to get just two of their six acres derequisitioned.

It is not my intention here to say anything about the wicket. That is the sole prerogative of your groundsman. *He* should be the expert who knows how to prepare and nurse it. It is the duty of your club committee, though, to see that you have as good a wicket as possible. At any time, at slight cost, well-established firms will always send a representative to take a sample of your ground's soil and recommend what fertilisers and treatment the grass should have to get the best out of it.

In my opinion, it is well worth the outlay of the odd guinea or two to get such first-class reports and suggestions. I have often advised clubs to adopt these measures after complaints that their wicket was not as good as it should have been, or that it was breaking up from the first ball bowled. The results, always, have been worth while.

However, I admit that every groundsman has his feelings, and to call in outside advice may lead to embarrassment. So always discuss the idea of doing so with your groundsman. He will be the first to acknowledge that, while he is the doctor, a consultant may have to be called in to see whether the ground needs special treatment.

Practice wickets and nets are very important. So many clubs have wonderful 'squares' and yet ignore their nets, allowing their members to practice on unsatisfactory playing surfaces. The Australians have been emphasising for years that no real value can be set on a poor practice wicket—the contrary, in fact.

For all-the-year-round practice, a number of clubs have invested in concrete pitches, over which coconut matting is laid. This provides a reasonably good 'stump-high' wicket, but there is one big disadvantage. The bowlers' end becomes very badly worn after only a few practices, and deep footholes make it dangerous. The stump at the bowlers' end can be moved a matter of several feet both ways, but only as a temporary expedient. The only satisfactory way of maintaining the bowlers' end is to re-turf at regular intervals, or, ideally, to have more than one practice wicket, so that when the new turf is settling down on one wicket, another is in use.

During the winter of 1949–50 the London County Council experimented with cork, peat, and matting surfaces for their concrete pitches. An asphalt surface was laid on the pitches at

Hackney Marshes in Essex, and sixty-one games were played. At Blackheath, a rubber surface was tried out, and at Hampstead Heath a wood-compound surface. Clubs found that none of these gave much help to the bowlers, and, on the asphalt surface, the destruction of cricket balls reached an alarming level.

Several experiments have been carried out with different surfaces. A comparatively new and quite 'natural' type of practice wicket is formed by a thick layer of ashes over which crude oil is poured and allowed to set. After the whole has been well rolled, matting is laid on top. It is claimed that this surface is satisfactory for both bowler and batsman.

London University, at their Motspur Park ground, experimented with a bituminous surface to their concrete pitch. Specially manufactured, it is claimed that although the ball 'dents' the wicket each time a ball is bowled, these dents can be rolled out after the pitch has been watered. Quite like a normal wicket, in fact. This is almost the best I have struck, and must be similar to the Essex experiment in artificial surfacing.

'Precast' concrete pitches are made up of a number of pre-cast concrete slabs which are fitted together by bolts. These pitches can be taken up and replaced as required. Now, I understand, the slabs are to be made with an artificial surfacing. Previously, they have been covered by coconut matting, which could be half-length or whole-length, depending on the number of slabs used. The 'natural surface' quest has been going on for many years. This method, it is claimed, is the answer.

But no matter what kind of practice wicket is favoured, your dressing-rooms should glow in letters of fire and gold with the reminder that the playing surface itself must be as good as, if not better than, your match wicket.

Many clubs are fortunate enough to have well-appointed pavilions. Others hope to build or re-build as soon as restrictions are relaxed, and to them I would say this:

Your committee, if it is not itself responsible for the erection of the pavilion, must insist on seeing and approving the plans before building begins, otherwise it may well be found—when it is too late—that the design could have been better.

A good example of how *not* to build a pavilion—for cricket, anyway—can be seen at the BBC ground at Motspur Park. There, some twenty years ago, the BBC built for the club what was considered as good a pavilion as the country could show.

In the main the object was achieved. There are large dressing-rooms, an excellent lounge, a fine billiards room, a bar, kitchens, shower-rooms and plunge bath, and a spacious hall.

The one and only point that was entirely ignored was that the whole pavilion faced the wrong way. From no point on the ground or first floors can the wicket be watched on the first XI, second XI, or third XI wickets! No planning now can rectify that mistake.

So be warned—no pavilion should be built on your ground unless your committee has approved the blueprint.

The type of score-board and score-box used varies with practically every ground. The majority of clubs remain content with the blackboard and plates. More prosperous clubs run to special score-boxes with numbered rollers, as good or better than those seen on county grounds. East Molesey and Guildford, two of the bigger London clubs, have even more advanced score-boards, resembling some of the magnificent Australian boards.

And here, a fervent aside. While it is not necessary for ordinary club cricketers to have a super-complicated calculating machine and three bright boys to work it, I do think that the score-boards on most of our county grounds are a disgrace to the game. It would be comparatively simple for these boards to have spaces added to show the spectator what is going on and enable him to pick up at least some of the threads. As it is, you must know the players to stand a chance of being any wiser at the end of a day's play.

It is interesting to note, though, that it was not until 1744 that a detailed score-sheet made its first appearance, and even then the method of the batsman's dismissal was not always recorded. It was not until 1846 that a score-board was installed at Lord's. The Oval followed suit two years later.

Trent Bridge, Nottingham's county ground, is to have the first 'real' all-in score-board. It should be quite a revelation in this country, but no novelty to Australians.

Back to the club. When constructing a new score-box, ensure that the scorer's line of vision is unimpeded and that he can see all points of the ground. Time and again one hears the plaintive bleat of the scorer, 'How was he out?'

Not every club has sufficient money in the kitty to be able to buy, or have built, an elaborate score-board. Alex Kemp, for years Harefield's indefatigable umpire, told me he had been working for a long time on a simple and comparatively 'cheap-to-make' contraption, which would serve the purpose better than the old telegraph board and tin plates. His recipe is: Obtain three boxes made of ordinary pinewood—two of which are 2 ft. 6 ins. by 10 ft. 4 ins., and one 10 ins. by 8 ins. Then you need fourteen rollers, each 11 inches long, made out of $\frac{1}{2}$ inch round wood. These rollers should be reduced at each end to $\frac{3}{8}$ inch, but one end must be longer than the other to allow the fixing of a handle. You should then get seven strips of calico 8 inches wide and 5 feet long, dyed black; white numbers 0 to 9 are painted on six strips, and 0 to 11 on the seventh—the latter is for the 'Number of Wickets Fallen' column. Holes, $\frac{7}{16}$ inch, should be bored in the top and bottom of the boxes for the ends of the rollers to be held in position.

A frame is then wanted for the front of the boxes, to give the necessary 6 ins. by 8 ins. apertures for the figures to show through. The three boxes may then be mounted on the conventional telegraph board.

Here's some more advice for clubs with their own grounds. In my opinion little, or at least insufficient, is done to encourage local residents to support the club and watch its matches. More often than not no seating is provided, and only one ground in a hundred offers the spectator a cup of tea or other amenities.

Some grounds are private, and the question of better facilities for the public does not arise. But, in general, I am convinced that if a real honest-to-goodness effort could be made to provide just a few simple amenities, attendances would be bound to increase.

Provision of facilities for the public, too, helps finance. Clubs that (so far as the Ministry of Food permits, of course) provide tea for spectators makes more money—a point of value in these financially difficult days. And don't forget programmes can carry advertisements, and that these become more valuable as circulation increases.

Where ground leases or other covenants permit, a small sum for admittance may be charged; other clubs rely on a collection. But whether admission is charged or not, the fact remains that few clubs do enough to encourage local supporters. Yet 'local' people can be a club's best friends. They can bring it into being, help to keep it going, and from their homes come the players. Why, therefore, neglect them?

Chapter Nine

EQUIPMENT

Club equipment—Personal kit—The club bag—Screens—Covers—The groundsmen.

HERE'S a warning to cricketers with cars who drive without a reasonably full set of tools. Sooner or later—in my experience, sooner—they will find themselves in a position similar to mine one sunny morning a few years ago.

I was captaining the Club Cricket Conference XI against the M.C.C. on the ground of the Kenley Cricket Club. Some five or six miles from my destination a front tyre burst. I had a spare wheel, of course, but when I took it out I found it was flat. I looked for my pump, then remembered lending it to a pal some three days earlier.

The first car I signalled for help contained a somewhat short-tempered gentleman and a pump that didn't fit the valve of my tyre. The second vehicle carried the local grocer and a pump that *did* fit. He obliged and went on his way. Then I looked for my wheel-brace and jack, but both were missing. More fuming, frustrating delay, ending only when an A.A. Scout came along. I arrived at Kenley only five minutes before the start of the match. As skipper, I should have been there at least thirty minutes beforehand. The moral is plain. . . .

Most of us become very lazy about personal equipment, too, and don't open our cricket-bags from one Sunday evening to the following Saturday afternoon (unless we happen to remember that our trousers want cleaning).

Care and maintenance of personal kit is of paramount importance. I am not going to suggest how to clean boots and pads, or oil bats, though even these elementary points seem to need stressing at times.

What I want to emphasise is that only by looking after your kit conscientiously and regularly will you avoid unfortunate 'situations'.

The classic story in this context is of an incident in the 1905 University match. Cambridge was dismissed for quite a low score. Oxford led by 101 runs on the first innings. At the second attempt Cambridge fared even worse, mainly owing to the excellent bowling of W. H. B. Evans—one of the best all-rounders ever. At one time they were 77 for 6 wickets, and the result seemed assured.

Then Evans burst one of his boots. Another pair was found for him, but playing, let alone bowling, in borrowed boots is asking too much. He just could not reproduce that sensational form with the ball and Cambridge batsmen L. G. Colbeck (who scored 107) and MacDonnell began to hit the Oxford bowling all over the ground. Cambridge totalled 264 in the second innings; Oxford, although requiring only 164 to win, failed by 40 runs.

The precaution is clear: two pairs of boots in the bag are far better than one. This may not be possible for everybody, but every player can at least check his boots at the end of every game and have any necessary repairs done before he plays again— especially if he is a bowler.

Don't have too many studs on your boots, but see that those you have are in order, and that none is missing; see, too, that the laces are strong and that you have a spare pair in your bag.

An ideally-fitting boot allows you to wear two pairs of thick socks. My preference is for a light boot, but bowlers may want something stronger. I also like to have an old pair of boots 'rubbered'. I can use them for batting and for fielding on dry days. They take the 'jar' out of the ground.

So much for boots; here are some more personal 'kit rules' that experience has taught me always to obey:

The Bat.—Never use it in the nets when it is new unless the wicket is good and the bowling sensible. In any case never, never use it at the end of your knock in the nets, when you are sent down 'a few to hit'.

Immediately after the game, scrape off any mud on the bat.

Never oil the splice. It will loosen the handle.

Don't over-oil the blade. After the first oilings, before the bat is used, just smear a film down the face, sides, and along the bottom.

Always check that the rubber handle is glued on securely A loose grip costs wickets.

Batting Gloves.—These should fit comfortably. If you are like me and often have your knuckles rapped by the 'quickies', try the 'sausage' type of glove, worn with undergloves of cotton, rather than the rubber spiked type.

Pads.—These, too, must fit comfortably. Otherwise the straps and buckles will make it difficult—and painful—to run. And *never* 'have a knock' anywhere without pads.

Cap.—A cap too small may give you a headache; a cap too big may come off when you are chasing the ball.

Protector.—Never—repeat, *never*—go in to bat, either in the nets or in a match, without wearing a protector. Ignore the cheerful optimist who assures you, 'That's all right, chum, I don't wear one and I've never been hit!'

I well remember a school match in which one of our best batsmen forgot this rule. He had made 78 runs and we needed only 20 more to win with 5 wickets standing. Then he was hit, assisted from the wicket, and was unable to resume. We lost that game by 8 runs.

It is not only foolhardy not to wear one. You are not playing for your side if you don't.

By the way, clean socks help to keep feet fresh and prevent their tiring so quickly, and I find powdering the feet is well worth while.

Those are just a few tips that help. There are countless others. Many of us have our own superstitions, too—such as always putting on the left pad first, or using the same bat every match. They are excellent for morale and confidence. Don't let anyone talk you out of them!

The great trouble these days about personal equipment is the cost. D. R. Jardine, former Surrey and England skipper, contends that purchase-tax is driving cricket off the village greens. Costs are becoming prohibitive for many club and village teams. It is not, says Jardine, a question of State aid, which, to many at least, is neither practicable nor desirable: 'The question rather is one of active State discouragement by means of the purchase-tax.'

He pleads for removal of purchase-tax on all outdoor team games: 'Such games make a fair contribution to the Exchequer, apart from keeping people fit. We want a nation of players rather than a nation of watchers. To make the game as cheap as possible goes some way towards realising that ideal.'

The M.C.C. has always done everything in its power to secure some relief from the tax. Indeed, increased costs and some scheme to combat them was one of the questions for the M.C.C. committee of inquiry set up in 1949.

Some clubs, so much more fortunate than others, have bats, pads, gloves, etc., in the 'club-bag'. It is the club committee's duty to ensure that this equipment is always up to standard— just as the individual has a responsibility towards his own gear. So often Committees fail here, though. I know. I've seen some of the 'club-bags'.

As far as the rest of the club's equipment goes, perhaps the most important is to have the right cutters, rollers, and accessories. That goes for screens and score-boxes as well.

I have already made the point in Chapter Eight, but I repeat that the score-table or, if you are lucky, the score-box, should be situated in a position from which the scorer can see everything without having to lean forward or sideways.

Covers for the wicket are not nearly such a luxury as many people think. To my mind, in this country they are a necessity. I well remember G. O. ('Gubby') Allen, the former Middlesex and England skipper, bringing a strong M.C.C. side to Motspur Park soon after the end of World War II. It had been fine the week before the match until late on the Friday afternoon, when down came the rain, which, although not at any time heavy, gave the ground a good soaking. The wicket, always fast-drying, had been watered plentifully during the early part of the week. By 10 a.m. on the Saturday—the day of the match—the wicket was under water, although the outfield was 'reasonable'.

The sun came out in fits and starts, but we were not able to make a start until after lunch. Even then it was a 'mudheap'. The game ought never to have been played, as the 'square' was cut up more than was good for it.

Gubby Allen said he was surprised to find a ground so well equipped in other respects lacked 'covers'. In consequence, our committee approved the provision of 'covers' for the first XI 'square'. They were made comparatively simply. Four sections were built, each measuring 18 ft. 6 ins. by 7 ft., and made up of a strong metal framework with sloping roof mounted on four small, but wide-section wheels. Over these frameworks were stretched tarpaulins of slightly larger dimensions. The ends of the two end sections were covered in to prevent driving rain from getting on to the pitch. The gaps between sections were covered by ground sheets.

N

Although these are days of high costs—quite a large sum of money was involved in the making of the covers, simple though they are—they proved one of the most useful acquisitions we have ever had. They are wheeled on during the Friday, when rain is about, and left on until the Saturday, when they are removed any time between 8 a.m. and 2 p.m., according to the weather. If it is doubtful we keep them on, after the final cutting and rolling, until just before the game is due to start. (I mention this because I feel there is no necessity for the club cricketer to be too rigid about the rules governing the use of 'covers'.)

All clubs should do all they can to raise funds for 'covers', even before other seemingly important requirements. They will pay a dividend within a year or two.

Among the things the committee should and must do is to ensure that the groundsman keeps all the mechanical equipment well serviced and maintained. One often finds that this all-important aspect of the groundsman's work has been neglected.

In consultation with the groundsman, the skipper should always make a point of inspecting the 'square' and picking out next Saturday's wicket. The majority of groundsmen will appreciate the interest shown, and will not regard it as interference. But never tell the groundsman his job. He knows it inside out, otherwise you would not have appointed him in the first place. Let him get on with his job, and give him advice only when invited to do so.

It is his job to maintain the bats and pads and keep the new balls, and, during the winter months, to look after the tarpaulins for the 'covers', repair the gear, repaint the scoreboard, and, if you are lucky enough to have them, whiten the screens. Your groundsman's conscientiousness and hard work will make or mar the following season. And remember, he likes encouragement just as much as you or I.

Chapter Ten

THE PLAYER

Club membership—Team selection—Encouragement of the young idea—
School—Club—County—The inquest.

DON BRADMAN once said, 'When I was a very small boy, cricket was to me the most wonderful game in the world.' For me, also, it was the only game.

I well remember playing imaginary games of cricket in my first school note-books, with my favourite team (it was Surrey, then!) on one side and another county side, the opponents, on the opposite page.

I scored on a large piece of squared paper, with each of the little squares containing either a number or a letter to represent runs or the various ways of getting out. Dotted about were the letters 'c' for 'caught'; 'b' for 'bowled'; 'st' for 'stumped', and so on, plus such things as 'no ball'; 'wide'; 'bye'. A pencil, with eyes shut, jabbed into a 'square' would tell me how the batsman or bowler had fared.

I expect most of you have played that game, or something like it, during your schooldays. Often my imaginary games were more important to me than the real ones on the county grounds!

I was lucky. I had a father who, although not a good cricketer himself, was a first-class sportsman, and played a very good game of tennis. He gave me every opportunity, and before I was ten years old was encouraging me to practise and have coaching. Without question it was this help and encouragement that enabled me to learn cricket properly. In this game, more perhaps than in any other, one really must start at the bottom.

The importance of training the youngster the right way cannot be over-emphasised. Coaches are only just beginning to realise this. Until comparatively recently their attitude was, 'Here's another youngster.' To-day they seek prospective Bradmans and Comptons when they are really young—not after they have gone to their senior school or college.

The 'young man' must be trained in the art of sighting and hitting a ball. Any kind of ball—with almost anything for a bat.

I again refer to Bradman, and nowhere is there a better example of a boy's training himself very early in life. His first bat was an old stump; his ball an old golf ball. It is obviously much more difficult to hit a golf ball with a stump than a cricket ball with a bat, but Bradman is convinced that this early training and playing with such a small ball stimulated his eyesight and taught him instaneous reaction.

It is unwise to start worrying small boys with grips and strokes. They are not strong enough. All that will come later.

As he grows up a boy demands a 'real bat', but, as when purchasing shoes, mum's advice can be heard in the background: 'Don't forget, dear, get it big enough for him to grow into.'

The result may be a beautiful bat of real English willow, but almost inevitably it will be two or three sizes too big. This is all wrong. The boy may well overtax his strength in attempting to use it. The sensible thing is to buy a bat—any kind of bat—that is the right size. Postpone the day for purchasing the 'real thing' until he has stopped growing so quickly. Then it will last two or three seasons.

It is the same with the young bowler. He should never bowl the full twenty-two yards, even in the backyard. Fourteen or sixteen yards is enough, and he can then learn to value accuracy in his bowling, assess 'direction', and conserve energy. After all, direction and length are the first essentials of bowling, so youngsters should start by concentrating on them in the easiest and best way possible.

The training of youngsters and their encouragement is so very important to the game that I want next to discuss the schoolboy cricketer—the potential 'week-end' recruit.

Assume he has reached school XI standard. This is a testing period. Whether he joins a club and later—let us hope—achieves county standard, depends so much on the atmosphere around him and the encouragement he gets. Let us assume he is lucky, his parents keen on cricket, he himself anxious to go far in the game. As soon as he leaves school, if not before, he must join a club. Here he may have several choices. He may belong to a large business organisation, which has a thriving sports club for which he can play, or he can join a local club. Before deciding, he should take care that he joins a friendly crowd, whose social activities are as progressive and well-organised as the cricket. One cannot over-emphasise the importance of joining players one finds congenial and who will accept you as one of themselves.

Nets in April will be the ex-schoolboy's first practical experience of the club game, and here—for the first time in his life—he will realise what a gulf there is between 'school' and 'club' cricket. Later on he will appreciate the similar gap between 'club' and 'county' games.

The main difference between 'school' and 'club' is, of course, physical. When I first joined my old boys' club I was quite at a loss. It took me a season or two to get used to the change. Everybody was most friendly and helpful, but the fast bowlers all seemed to be bowling much too fast, and the batsmen hit the ball much harder than anything to which I had been accustomed.

Sometimes the transition from school to club cricket may be more gradual and gentle. For instance, J. N. Crawford, while still at school and only seventeen years old, not only played for Surrey, but finished the season at the head of the bowling averages, taking 44 wickets for just under 17 runs each!

But there have never been many Crawfords about. The best recent example is Ian Bedford, of Middlesex, who has now returned to big cricket after completing his national service in the R.A.F. He was sixteen when he had his first county game as a spin bowler.

The most phenomenal schoolboy performance, I think, was for Clarke's House against North Town, on the Clifton College ground in 1899. A. E. J. Collins scored 628 not out in a single innings, spread over five days! For a boy, a wonderful example of will-power, strength, and determination.

However difficult other, less gifted boys may find the higher standard, there are always the 'old hands' of the club to bring them along and make them feel and become real assets to the side. This, above all else, in my opinion, can give young men the confidence so essential early in their 'club' careers. With courage the 'teen'-old player will often perform outstandingly in senior company, if he can stand up to it. *But he must have encouragement.* Just a word at the psychological moment is the thing, and I can prove it.

I was playing for my school XI against Cambridge Crusaders in 1932. The late Kenneth Farnes was then striving for his place as fast bowler in the Cambridge side, and he was making the ball lift most unpleasantly on a wet wicket. It was fast bowling for any class of cricket, let alone against schoolboys, and he had

hit one or two of the opening batsmen. I was certainly none too
happy, but my cricket master, realising the position, whispered
in my ear as I went in to bat: 'Nothing Farnes can send down
will frighten you.'

All the way to the wicket I kept saying to myself, over and
over again, 'He won't frighten me. He won't make me run away.
He won't frighten me. . . .' I got quite a few badly-needed runs.

What had happened was that for the first time in my life I
had gone in to bat with the fixed determination that neither
Farnes nor anyone else would frighten me, or get me out, no
matter how he bowled.

I've never forgotten that lesson. And I pass it on now with
all the emphasis I can. The offensive spirit is essential. The bowler
must be attacked. Cultivate this 'offensiveness'. It will help the
change from school to 'club' cricket and is invaluable in county
matches. And, more—this spirit *must* be instilled in future English
XIs.

Having had his form assessed at the nets, our new 'junior' is
picked for one of the club teams—the second XI, perhaps. After
a spell of success some youngsters—and, indeed, older men who
ought to know better—cannot understand why they are not
promoted to the first XI. Always remember the problems of the
selection committee—and what a thankless job it has.

A bowler is sometimes retained in the second XI after a good
performance the week before because the first XI bowlers also
did well and cannot be dropped. Or the second XI may have a
strong fixture, for which the best side must be on duty. There are
many reasons why the selection committee might not promote a
player who has done well (or, indeed, not drop one who has been
doing badly). And no responsible committee can be expected to
explain in detail its decisions—if it did, the argument that
would inevitably follow would make its job an impossibility.
So don't blame the committee or individual members of it.
They select teams for the club—not for the gratification of
individual players.

About those 'inquests'. Up to a point, discussion is a very
good thing. But it should never be allowed to develop into
argument. And to hear one player tell another that by dropping
'that catch' he lost the match—and it is done, believe me—is
one of the worst things that can happen. Discussion on tactics,
especially about the changing of bowlers, positioning of the field,

and the batting order is to the benefit of the side. But destructive criticism—never.

Above all, don't allow your players to dissect the match in a heated manner in front of your opponents. Always remember the precept King George V placed on his desk: 'Teach me to win when I may and, if I may not win, then above all, I pray, make me a good loser.'

I think the gap between club and county cricket less wide than that between school and club, and I must say I much prefer the club to the county attitude to the game. But then, of course, I do not have to play for my livelihood, which makes all the difference.

Even without 'points' to stimulate a result, it is more often the club than the county that goes flat out for a win, and not play merely to avoid defeat. In club cricket, sporting declarations are the rule, not the exception. But, I must admit, defeat in club cricket does not mean one of the official 'inquests' with which professionals have to contend.

The rather apathetic attitude adopted by many county players, especially towards the end of the season, can be attributed to playing six days a week. But I was horrified when one county skipper said to his team after the opposition had been dismissed for just over 300 runs, 'Well, boys, I only want four points [first innings lead] from this game!' That was forty minutes before the end of *the first day*'s play of a three-day match!

The professionals, too, are more fussy about the light and the weather. Naturally enough. As I said before, it's their living. And their standard of cricket continues to rise.

But there are quite a few club cricketers who are of equal skill. It is just that they cannot spare the time for county cricket. What better examples in recent years than the Alexandra Park cricketer, Len Newman and, more recently, Henry Malcolm, South Hampstead all-rounder, who has played so regularly and so successfully for the C.C.C. XI? Malcolm's temperament is ideal for the 'senior' game. He has infinite patience; his concentration is intense and unwavering. If the youngsters we have been discussing use him, or his like, as their model, they won't go far wrong.

Chapter Eleven

THE PLAY

Wicket-keeping — Fielding — Running — Backing-up and calling — Net practice—The slip machine—The bowling machine—Skippership—Field placing—Umpiring—Do's and don'ts.

IN sport, as in any other sphere of life, the star is no different from anyone else, except that he or she shines in one particular way. And why? Because, ninety-nine times out of a hundred, he has learned how to take pains—how to pay acute attention to detail. It is 'detail' in the cricketing sense that I want to deal with here.

First of all, wicket-keeping. Get hold of, and read as many of the very good books on 'keeping as possible. Wicket-keeping is a most exacting job and demands a great deal more physical exertion and concentration than most people think. It is a key position; so keep fit. Never stand 'up' to a fast bowler unless there are very good reasons for doing so. By standing back you are *always* going to accept more chances. Never stand half-way. If you do the good length ball will be rising, and the short one will come to you half-volley. The over-pitched ball might do anything.

Another elementary point, often ignored by the club 'keeper, is to move up to the wicket—if standing back—to take the fieldsman's return to the wicket. Always get there before the ball is thrown back. Apart from the practical value of doing so, there is a psychological value. At the end of a long tiring day in the field, everything possible must be done to keep up morale, and the 'keeper, next to the skipper, must show the way. In any case, returns should always be made to the top of the stumps. If fieldsmen are allowed to throw in to the 'keeper wherever he happens to be standing accuracy will be lost.

Finally, see your pads do not rub or chafe, and that your boots are comfortable. Nothing will make you lose your concentration more than uncomfortable boots or painful pad straps.

Now fielding. Never be content with standing where *you* think you should be. Always check that you are in the right place.

When in the field, always keep your eye on the skipper in case he wants to move you quietly. The captain may not want the batsmen to know that you are being moved. Always back up and *always* start moving in with the bowler, at mid-on, mid-off, cover, extra cover, third man, and from all 'deep' positions.

If fielding close to the wicket—especially at 'cover'—practice throwing the ball back underarm. And it is impossible to spend too much time on the slip machine. A book for fielders to read? *How To Play Cricket*, by Don Bradman. After what a number of authorities on the game have had to say, this book is a revelation.

Batsmen lose most runs between the wickets by not backing up and not calling. You are normally not taught to be a good runner, but it is something so easily self-taught and needs, as usual, interminable practice. You don't need to charge down the wicket like some galloping steed when you are supposed to be backing up. Just move back behind the wicket, and when the bowler comes up to deliver the ball move with him side by side. After he has bowled, keep on going a few paces until you have seen whether there is going to be a run or not. If not, then turn round and move smartly back to your crease so as to avoid being run-out yourself. Many club cricketers do not bother about regaining their ground quickly enough. I have often been lucky in running a batsman out when he has been backing-up too far.

When calling—and don't forget, the striker normally should call for every hit in front of the wicket, and the 'backer-up' for anything behind it—do it in a clear, business-like voice. You needn't shout your head off, but make it obvious to your partner what you intend to do. And always run that first run as fast as you can—you may make room for another one! With experience and practice comes the art of 'judgment'. To be able to judge a run at all times is extremely difficult, but keenness and practice will bring 'judgment' automatically in time.

Urge groundsmen to move the practice wickets as soon as they become worn or cut up. Batting on a bad net wicket does more harm than good.

There is a tendency among club players to 'overdo' it in the nets. As they manage to get to the ground only once a week they naturally want their money's worth, so they stay in the nets for two or three hours and get overtired. The value of practice obtained when moderately fresh is often wasted by staying on too long.

The latest challenge to bowlers is the newly-invented bowling machine. Compare it, with its motors, dynamos, and buttons, with an earlier 'rubber-band' automatic bowler shown alongside in the plate facing page 97. Manufactured by the 'Eureka' Engineering Company, but not yet in mass production, each machine costs about £250.

In the old machine the ball is held in a leather cup, attached to the end of a long wooden arm. This arm is held back, against the fairly strong tension of stout elastic cords, and released by the player operating it. It was, quite naturally, somewhat inaccurate, and no spin could be imparted to the ball.

The new 'automaton', with its levers, knobs, and springs, can be set to bowl twelve balls in succession at a required speed, although the fastest, I believe, is not above fast-medium. It can impart almost any amount of spin. When once set, the ball will always pitch in a beaten-zone of approximately six-inch diameter. Such a machine for every club would be invaluable, as batsmen could practise weak strokes indefinitely.

As I mentioned, cost is the difficulty at present, but if enough clubs were interested to make mass production worthwhile, the makers tell me the price would be more than halved.

If a bowling machine could help the vast majority of club cricketers to play spin bowling, then it would be worth its weight in gold.

Many excellent club batsmen will not use their feet and get to the pitch of the ball. They prefer to remain fixed to the crease. Denys Wilcox, the former Essex captain, emphasises that, if facing a good spin bowler, never play back. Always play forward with a defensive stop shot and smother the spin. To prove his point he usually recalls a question put to 'Tich' Freeman (England and Kent) a few years before he decided to retire. Asked how long he was going on, Freeman replied, 'As long as they play back to me.' He was well into the forties, then!

Now the captaincy. The skipper of any side must be given wholehearted co-operation, obedience, and loyalty. In return, he owes a lot to the side as a whole and to the players individually. His job by no means starts or ends on the field of play. He is often chairman of the committee as well, which involves innumerable other duties. To a captain I would say: Never ignore players when it comes to taking decisions, and always consult the vice-captain during a match. Change the batting order when the

situation demands it. Keep a bowler on only if he is continually
getting wickets.

In a Test Match against the Australians, Toshack, the slow
spin bowler, found the wicket was 'right up his street'. Bradman
called upon him to bowl. By lunch he had bowled seven overs
for no runs, but had not taken a wicket. At lunch, Bradman had
a word with him. Afterwards, in spite of having more runs
knocked off him, Toshack started taking wickets, and ended up
with something like 6 for 70-odd. It was wickets Bradman wanted,
not merely the keeping down of runs.

Keep the young, fit, and fast members of the side for such
positions as cover, mid-off, third-man, and short-leg—especially
third-man. Always give a 'real young 'un' a good trial, say six
matches.

Like batting, the best umpires have to concentrate on *every*
ball. The moment they lose that concentration they give bad
decisions. Some of the best club umpires are 'old men': a few of
the really competent ones over sixty years of age are Jim Mowate,
of the BBC (and a regular choice of the C.C.C.), M. W. Yemm,
Albert Beadle (both connected with 'Old Coulsdon'), and Joe
Filliston, who umpires for the H.A.C. and the University of
London.

Frank Chester, the most famous umpire of this generation,
has this to say about the 'profession', as he calls it: 'The main
essentials are knowing the laws of the game, concentration, good
hearing and eyesight, and the ability to show fear or favour to
no one.'

'Guard' should always be given over the middle stump, not,
as you see so often, from just outside the wicket or from where
the bowler bowls. Sometimes, though, the right-handed batsman
will ask for his guard from where the bowler delivers the ball,
especially when he is facing a left-arm or right-arm round-the-
wicket bowler. The umpire should always comply with such
requests.

I don't suppose anything causes more discussion and controversy in the pavilion after the game than the l.b.w. decision—
especially nowadays, with the new rule in existence. (Frank
Chester, by the way, is firmly of the opinion that the new 'off-
side' rule should not be enforced in club cricket, chiefly because
the majority of week-end cricketers do not understand it—nor
do some of the umpires.)

Here are some tips that may help: If the umpire is convinced that 'Yes' is the answer to the following queries then the batsman should be given *out*: (1) Would the ball have hit the wicket? (2) Did the ball pitch in a straight line between wicket and wicket, or to the off of the batsman's wicket? (3) Was it part of the batsman's person that first intercepted the ball, other than his hand? (4) Was that part of the batsman's person between wicket and wicket when the ball struck it?

The best umpires are those who make the least mistakes, but one thing I do want to say—and this applies to nearly every club player: no matter what decision the umpire gives, whether your side is batting or fielding, always accept it in good humour, without word of complaint and above all without showing, in any way, that you yourself didn't agree with it. This is a *must*. Good batsmen, often the top-flight players, spoil themselves by offending in this respect. To me, querying the umpire's decision, even by a sly glance or facial expression, makes that player a bad sportsman, a bad batsman, and a 'little man'.

An amusing story is told about Bill Reeves, the well-known county umpire, who has earned for himself the reputation of knowing more funny cricket stories than anyone else. The incident took place in a Hampshire *v.* Glamorganshire match. A new young bowler named Spencer had been introduced into the side. During the match he got a bowl, and was put on at Bill Reeves' end. Off the last ball of one over he hit the batsman smartly on the leg and shouted, 'How's that?' 'Not out,' replied Bill, and promptly called, 'Over.'

On his way to square leg, Bill summoned young Spencer to him. 'Why not call me 'sir'?' he said to the bewildered youth. 'You'd stand a better chance!'

A little later the same bowler appealed again. 'How's that, sir?' 'That's better,' replied Reeves with a smile. 'That's out!'

I am not going to deal with the subject of batting, for as I have said before, this is *not* an instructional book on how to play cricket. Nor am I going to discuss the mysteries of bowling. There are far too many good books about both these arts.

There are, however, a few 'do's' and 'don'ts' which, although heard of before, tend to be ignored or forgotten altogether. Here they are:—

Bowlers :

(1) Don't sulk when things aren't going your way.
(2) Always take a sweater on to the field, unless it is an exceptionally hot and windless day.
(3) Never bowl short or down the leg side.
(4) Always field for the 'other bowler' as you expect him to field when *you* are on.
(5) Try to carry a spare pair of boots.

You want brains and character to make a good bowler. Brute force and ignorance will get you nowhere.

Batting :

(1) Never lose your concentration.
(2) Never call 'Yes—No—Wait', when it is your call.
(3) *Never* play for yourself: *always* play for your side.
(4) Always run that first run as fast as you can.
(5) Never run down the middle of the wicket.
(6) Never bat without your 'box'.
(7) Don't forget that only second-rate batsmen are impatient, but all are vulnerable.

Chapter Twelve

THE CLOSE SEASON

Winter activities—Keeping fit—Cricket schools—Winter coaching—The season in retrospect and prospect—The A.G.M.—The cricket dinner.

WHAT does 'The Close Season' mean? Does it mean that from the last match in September until about the middle of the following April cricket is a back number? Or that its arrival is the signal to transfer to a winter sport and forget cricket for six months?

Well, if it does, then in my view it's the wrong meaning.

Just because the last game of the season has been played, cricket doesn't fizzle out like a damp squib. On the contrary, winter activities of players and officials are important—and necessary.

The club fixture secretary must confirm matches for the following season. The honorary secretary must arrange agendas for the winter committee meetings, and keep all members informed of what is going on behind the scenes. The honorary treasurer must balance—or try to!—the club budget. There is never a real close season for club officials. They do nearly as much in the winter as they do in the summer. They must review the season, sum up next year's prospects, and arrange dates for the two all-important annual events—the annual general meeting and the cricket dinner or supper.

And the player? First and foremost, to my mind, he must keep fit. Not nearly enough cricketers—county or club—keep really fit enough to avoid some very hard work three or four weeks before the start of a new season. If you are an all-the-year-round sportsman there is nothing to worry about. If not, then take up some kind of winter exercise and *make* yourself play regularly. Football, hockey, or squash-rackets will keep you in trim.

After Christmas try to arrange indoor cricket practice at one of the schools. In the south of England that is easier said than done, perhaps. There are far too few indoor schools and, almost without exception, those we have are inadequate. In and around the London area we have fewer than half a dozen of these schools for hundreds of thousands of cricketers. They are useful for a batsman to get his eye in after several months away from the game. But for the bowler—unless he takes no more than a few paces' run up to the wicket—they offer only a chance to get his arm turning over again. On this I always quote the case of C. B. ('Bertie') Clarke, of the West Indies, Northants, and, I'm glad to say, the BBC Club. One winter Bertie bowled a great deal at an indoor school, with, perforce, a shortened run. The result was that the whole rhythm of his run was destroyed, and it was not until the middle of the following season that he began to bowl really well again.

Some clubs book regularly at these schools, from October until grass wickets are playable again. Personally, I think it better to have a rest from cricket after a full season, because so often cricketers—good and bad—go stale. It is almost impossible to play one game ceaselessly without becoming so. Concentration plays a vital part in cricket—and I challenge anyone to maintain concentration at peak for twelve months out of twelve. To those who disagree, I instance many famous players who have themselves decided that they must take a full winter's rest from the game.

I agree, however, that clubs are sometimes forced into an October to April season of indoor cricket because it is the only way to ensure they have a net in March. My own club offers a good example of this. We find—naturally enough from the proprietor's point of view—that clubs who are prepared to book nets right through the winter get preference. 'Part-timers' are out.

In my various contacts with clubs in southern England I am continually being asked why there aren't more of these indoor practice pitches. Only recently I received a plea for something more to be done about this state of affairs by some of the clubs in the Bromley (Kent) area. Their nearest school at present, I believe, is at Wandsworth, in Surrey.

I think, indeed, that there's a fortune to be made by establishing a ring of really good cricket schools all over the country. Provided the wickets are perfectly laid, that the run-back for bowlers is adequate, that the tops of the nets are not too low, and that good changing rooms with hot showers are installed, the schools couldn't go wrong—and their promoters would be doing a great service to English cricket.

For the youngster, whether at school or not, winter coaching is essential if he wants to get on—but he must have the right coach. But remember, because the coach has been, or still is, a first-class county cricketer, it does not follow he is a good coach. There is an art in passing on what you know, and we are not all gifted that way. So choose your coach carefully. Then arrange to have at least a dozen lessons before the season opens. Get him to concentrate on your weak spots—whether at bowling or batting. He may not eradicate faults, but he will tell you where you go wrong. It is up to you, then, to practice and practice and practice.

Many people cannot get professional coaching. They should ask their experienced club members to give them the right kind of practice. They are not professionals but, through experience, they will be able, quite often, to explain where mistakes are being made.

Mass practice is a comparatively new art and obviously of tremendous importance to schools. At least the rudiments of stroke play can be given as a preface to individual net tuition for boys of promise.

The latest and, in attendance at least, the most successful winter school was held as an experiment at Westcliff-on-Sea in 1950. But it was a school with a difference: it offered not instruction for players, but instruction for coaches. This was so well supported that Middlesex had a similar school, in conjunction with the Council of Physical Recreation, at Bisham Abbey, Marlow, Bucks. This, however, was not so well attended. Both were three-day courses, with accommodation and meals at very moderate cost.

At Westcliff, seventy-five instructors, including seven women, attended the course, at which lectures were given by D. R. Wilcox, former Essex skipper; Peter Smith (Essex); Trevor Bailey (Essex); Frank Chester, on umpiring; Harry Crabtree (Essex and C.C.C.), on mass practice; Douglas Insole (Essex and Cambs), on fielding; Bert Lock, the Oval groundsman, on the care of the pitch, and Herbert Strudwick, on wicket-keeping and scoring.

Representatives of the M.C.C. Cricket Inquiry Committee were so impressed by the Essex school that they may recommend a nation-wide scheme on similar lines. Whether to have a permanent school or a team of travelling instructors is just another

J. F. H. Tyler (Southgate) batting in the centenary match between Hornsey and Southgate, played at Lord's. The former Rugby International, R. S. Spong (Hornsey), is keeping wicket, and F. E. Whitehead (slip) and G. J. Williams (gulley) are waiting in hopeful anticipation

Manchester and District Cricket Association *v.* Club Cricket Conference. Played at Urmston on June 21, 1947. The C.C.C. won by three wickets

Back row, left to right: F. Cross (Worsley, Umpire), W. G. Swann (Urmston), A. E. Fletcher (Heaton Mersey), G. B. Brookes (Whalley Range, twelfth man), E. R. Comradi (Bury), I. A. Kennedy (Chorlton-cum-Hardy), T. Watts (St. Helen's Recreation), R. T. Chadwick (Cheadle Hulme), P. Westerman (Hounslow), C. C. H. Buss (Weybridge), F. Farrington (Bolton, Scorer), J. Seward (Malden Wanderers), G. Potter (West Surrey), R. G. Warren (Guildford), L. G. Bishop (Crofton Park), R. Shutt (Cheadle Hulme, Umpire)

Front row, left to right: F. Saint (Wigan), G. Gates (Chorlton-cum-Hardy), G. H. Wigglesworth (Didsbury), D. W. Dutton (Castleton), W. N. Tonge (Bolton, Captain Manchester and District C.A.), A. C. L. Bennett (B.B.C., Captain C.C.C. XI), H. P. Crabtree (Westcliff-on-Sea), H. J. J. Malcolm (South Hampstead), K. J. Smart (Sevenoaks Vine), R. G. Elmsley (Ashtead) point the Committee have to determine. But whatever happens, more will be heard of this 'school for teachers' idea.

Holding an inquest on the past season, if done in the right way, can be helpful and instructive. A good scorer can help enormously here. Statistics and averages are inanimate things, but do help to assess a player's worth.

For instance, if a batsman averages over a thousand runs for two or three years and then, one year—given approximately the same climatic conditions—does not even top the '500' mark, it can be assumed that some radical fault must have developed. He needs someone to point out where he has gone wrong. That is one use of 'figures'. And, anyway, they are of great interest to the individual player. But I agree they must always be used with discretion when making decisions about team building.

A very necessary routine duty during the winter is the improvement of the ground, pavilion, and equipment. Expenditure on these items can be agreed at the annual general meeting.

As many club members as possible should attend the A.G.M. Usually, members are apathetic: to find 50 per cent of them present is exceptional. Yet it is *their* money that is going to be spent on improvements. And, of course, there are the new officers to be elected. There is no way of ensuring a good attendance. All the secretary can do is to announce the date well in advance and send a reminder to everyone ten days before the day. Most secretaries, however, already do this, with little response.

The cricket dinner or supper is always something to look forward to during the winter; this is the time when cricketers add to their repertoire of 'stories'.

Two I heard at recent dinners both concern fast bowler Harold Larwood, now living in Australia.

It appears Larwood was spending a September holiday at a small village and, one day during his stay, he was waiting for the local cricket match to start. Several of the team hadn't turned up and Larwood, who was unknown there, was persuaded to play.

After the opponents had scored quite a lot of runs, the local skipper asked Larwood if he bowled. 'Yes, a little,' replied Larwood modestly. 'Have a go then,' said the skipper.

Larwood took the ball, set a field, but took only a five-yard run instead of usual twenty-five-yarder. The first ball hit the batsman on his leg—a plumb blow. 'How's that?' queried Larwood. 'Not out,' said umpire. The next ball, the batsman got

o

a touch and was caught in the slips. 'How's that?' shouted
Harold. 'Not out,' said the umpire. Larwood later knocked all
three stumps out of the ground and turned to the umpire with a
smile, saying, 'I nearly got him that time, didn't I?'

On another occasion, when Larwood had again been asked
to make up the side, the village blacksmith was batting. Harold
was asked to bowl. His first ball whistled past the batsman's ears,
but he never moved. 'No ball,' shouted the umpire. The next
ball the same thing happened. 'No ball,' again yelled the umpire.
So it was with the third ball. Again the umpire shouted 'No
ball!' Whereupon the blacksmith, who still hadn't as much as
moved his bat out of the block-hole, looked at mid-off and said
in a loud voice, 'I knew 'e never 'ad the ball all the time!'

Perhaps a 'sausage and mash' supper is preferred to a four-
course dinner. It certainly cuts the costs, and the same object is
achieved. My club recently adopted the idea of holding the
annual supper in the pavilion on the evening of the first trial
match—that is, at the end of April. In that way we know that
at least forty-four players besides umpires and club officials won't
have to make a special journey for the occasion.

I like to think of a cricket dinner as a real celebration. As
they said at a Slough (Bucks) cricket dinner:

> When the game is over,
>   and drinking has begun,
> We'll all drink together,
>   as if we both had won.

Chapter Thirteen

AMONG THE LEAGUES

Organisation of League cricket in Yorkshire, Lancashire, the Midlands, and South Wales.

AS I have already shown, 'week-end cricket' means one thing in the southern counties of England and something quite different outside them. In the North, the Midlands, and South Wales especially, the club cricket that matters is competitive cricket.

The quality of the grounds of the best clubs up North are the equal of any in the South. Indeed, a number of them stage county matches. In the far North and in the North-West there are, of course, climatic differences. The 'green' wicket is common, and this naturally gives bowlers a much greater chance than they normally get in the South.

An object lesson for the southerner is the organisation and results achieved by league cricket in Yorkshire, where no club cricket, as we know it, is played.

One look at the Yorkshire team that nearly won the County Championship in 1949 explains why Yorkshire has never had to worry about a ground staff. Every single member of the side was a product of the league-cricket system, which traditionally provides the highway for advancement for any young player to the highest grades of the game. So long as this method works to send talent to the top, there will be no prospect of any change.

Careers of such players as Frank Lowson, Test trialist, Willie Watson, England footballer as well as cricket star, and Harry Halliday, another grand batsman who used to play wartime cricket with me in the British Empire XI, to pick out only three at random, show how Yorkshire goes on producing the goods.

Lowson is the son of a former Bradford second-division footballer who learned the rudiments of cricket in the back streets of the city. Then he went the way of so many other Yorkshire lads by putting down a few shillings to join the local Sunday

211

School club before he had left school. He was still only fourteen when he moved one stage upwards by becoming a member of the Bowling Old Lane Club in the Bradford League.

Bowling, one of the historic clubs of the county, brought him on gradually in its second team until at sixteen he was ready for first XI trials. From there he moved up again to the Yorkshire second side, to gain more and more experience until, at twenty-three, he was completely equipped to become Len Hutton's first-wicket partner and win his county cap. From the time his talent became obvious he was under the watchful eye of Ernest Holdsworth, a Bradford man and ex-local cricketer who is chairman of the Yorkshire County Cricket Sub-Committee, in the same way as other potential 'hopes' were being watched by Mr. Holdsworth's colleagues.

Watson went on a rather different path, but the essentials were the same. He spent his boyhood at Paddock, a Huddersfield and District League club, where Percy Holmes also learned his cricket, with valuable coaching by the local professional, Edgar Varley, and the captain, Herbert Robinson. Then a word in the right quarter, and a call to the pre-season net trials at Headingley, and then first-class attention by George Hirst. These were the preliminary steps to fame for Watson.

Halliday is another Hirst *protégé*. He had shown some talent with Pudsey St. Lawrence, Hutton's first senior club, when he was summoned to the nets at Bradford. There Hirst told him to forget his fast bowling ambitions and concentrate on batting. Again the word went round that here was a youngster a bit out of the ordinary, and old-timers Herbert Sutcliffe, Benny Wilson, and Emmett Robinson got busy on the polishing process at their winter 'school' in Leeds.

That's the way it works in Yorkshire. A hint that even one of the most minor league clubs has a star in the making is enough to get the machinery working. A district representative on the County Committee will look him over, and the suggestion will be made that here is a likely 'prospect' for a senior club in one of the *élite* combinations. If the boy still progresses in this higher company, he will go down on the county records, and get his invitation to the net practices where the sorting out process comes along. After that it is a case of back to Saturday-afternoon league cricket until the time comes for a second XI trial or a summons to serve as twelfth man for the county team to get the atmosphere of championship matches. Then it is all a question of an opening and ability.

It is the great strength and organisation of the league game that provides the frame for the network that allows no player of real promise to be overlooked. He may come from the sparsely populated East Riding, like Vic Wilson, or the Lancashire border, like Ken Fiddling (one of the most likeable of fellows, with whom I have played a lot of cricket for Northants), but if he is any good at all the chance will be there.

It could scarcely be otherwise when the close official link between the county and the leagues is borne in mind. At the time of writing, the President of the *Yorkshire Council*, biggest and most powerful local organisation of clubs, is Clifford Hesketh. On the county committee are: Jack Taylor, Barnsley captain; Fred Popplewell, ex-Guiseley and Bradford batsman; Edmund Jackson, Yorkshire Cricket Federation president, and Clifford Green, ex-Council president. Both Mr. Holdsworth and Mr. Green, along with Clifford Hare, another long-service member of the county committee, also serve as Federation chiefs.

The title 'Federation' means exactly what it implies. It is no more than a loose link-up of more than forty district leagues, founded in 1929 to develop friendly relationships between these competitions and to safeguard clubs' interests in matters affecting their grounds. Most positive results on the playing side have been the running of tours to the South for under-eighteen Yorkshire boys, which have served as a useful jumping-off ground for such lads as colts Trueman and Whitehead, as well as Brian Close himself.

There are not many leagues outside this extremely well-run organisation. Members range from the senior Bradford, Leeds, Huddersfield, Airedale and Wharfedale (with their two really picturesque grounds), Yorkshire Council, North Yorkshire and South Durham League, to Sunday School and workshops competitions.

They cover the country, too, from the Cleveland and Teesside League in the north to the Sheffield and District Association in the south, the Craven and District League in the west to the Bridlington Amateur League in the east. All share alike in the Federation's work of combating unfair increases in rate assessments and protecting grounds from the hands of local councils seeking sites for housing estates. Such threats were warded off at

Gildersome and Drighlington, two village clubs between Bradford and Leeds, through direct action that such modest organisations would find it nearly impossible to carry out themselves.

In the long run, of course, the power of the Federation
depends on the strength of the leagues out of which it is comprised. Here there need be no uneasy feelings. The chief organisations, headed by the Yorkshire Council with its eighty-eight
members, go on from strength to strength. Although the Bradford
League has captured most of the limelight through its policy of
introducing stars, particularly in wartime, the Council, unwieldy
as it is, still ranks as the premier organisation in most respects. It
covers an immense area and ranges from the powerful city and
town clubs at Sheffield, Leeds, Hull, York, Dewsbury, Batley,
Scarborough, Halifax, Castleford, Pontefract, Rotherham, Doncaster, and Barnsley, to tiny villages and works clubs of the
Darfield, Elsecar, and South Kirkby Colliery type.

Significantly enough, size does not mean everything. During
the 1940s, only Hull (in 1947 and 1949) was able to break the
monopoly of championship successes by such small clubs as
Swinton, Hanging Heaton, and Shiregreen, and the welfare clubs
attached to Hemsworth Colliery, Hickleton Main Colliery, and
Salts (Saltaire).

The Council, which has developed steadily since its formation
in 1903, decides its championship on a play-off basis among the
leading four clubs at a specified date towards the end of the
season. With its huge size, it has been found convenient to include
within its framework such 'inner leagues' as the Heavy Woollen,
South Riding, and Yorkshire, and separate sections for Bradford,
Halifax, and Pontefract. Even so, there is a tendency for clubs to
prefer a 'free-lance' system of arranging their own fixtures along
the lines adopted by Barnsley, Harrogate, and Scarborough.

Saturday-afternoon and midweek evening cricket it may be in
the Council, but the standard of much of it is high. In 1948,
J. A. Richardson, the Scarborough captain, reached a season's
aggregate as high as 1,242 (average 82), and in 1949 C. Pawson
(Hemsworth) followed his example in attaining four figures for
the year. An interesting sidelight on individual performances is
that in 1949, Arthur Bastow, ex-Huddersfield and Bradford
League professional fast bowler, headed the bowling averages at
the age of fifty-five with a total of 58 wickets.

The *Bradford League*, founded in 1913, has twenty-two members in two divisions run on a promotion and relegation system. In contrast to the widespread area of the Council, it is concentrated within a ten-mile radius of the city, and includes suburban teams as well as small town and village clubs.

Enterprise under the guiding hands of such men as J. J. Booth and W. H. Foster has always been the keynote of this League's affairs. The first forward move came in World War I with the attraction to the leading clubs of such players as Sydney Barnes (Saltaire), Jack Hobbs (Idle), George Gunn and Charlie Llewellyn (Undercliffe), Frank Field and Sam Cadman (Tong Park). The same trend was repeated in World War II, when Eddie Paynter, W. W. Keeton, Charlie Harris, Cyril Washbrook, Arthur Booth, Bill Copson, and the Pope brothers all starred in the League.

With the retirement of Paynter and Learie Constantine, much of the glory has been dimmed again in the post-War years, although Arthur Wood, ex-Yorkshire and England wicket-keeper, is still going strong.

An oddity in the Bradford League annals is a claim to have set up a world's record for local club cricket with a gate of £753 and an attendance of 14,000 for the Priestley Cup final at Park Avenue, between Keithley and Saltaire in 1921. Receipts of three figures have been attained in several earlier rounds during the past nine seasons.

Like the Bradford League's Priestley Cup, the *Huddersfield League* has its own knock-out competition for the Sir Charles Sykes Cup, which dates back to 1920. It is not the oldest cup of its kind. That distinction goes to the Heavy Woollen Cup, first offered for competition in 1883 to the Central Yorkshire League clubs centred on Dewsbury, which are now a *bloc* inside the Council. However, the Huddersfield and District Cricket Association, from which the present Huddersfield League sprang, has the Lumb Trophy competition, which was begun in 1887.

Huddersfield's twenty-four clubs, among them the historic Lascelles Hall, regarded as a rival to Hambledon in cricket lore, are on the Bradford pattern with a two-division plan.

They rank as one of the most prolific 'nurseries' for the Yorkshire county side in providing players of the calibre of Schofield Haigh, Lees Whitehead, George Hirst, Wilfred Rhodes,

Ephraim Lockwood, Percy Holmes, and, more recently, Alec Coxon, Willie Watson, F. Jakeman, and Eric Leadbeater. Dalton, still a prominent Huddersfield League club, dates its formation back to 1831.

Leeds has been less prominent than some of the smaller centres. Its local league of twenty-two clubs is growing in prestige, although something of a 'working-man' atmosphere retards progress. Hunslet, going back to 1888, stands out for both ability and enterprise in laying out money to secure a professional of the calibre of Arthur Mitchell, ex-Yorkshire batsman.

A feature of cricket in the North between the Wars was its cheapness. For a subscription of little more than a guinea, Leeds offers a cricketer the pleasure of playing at Headingley, a pavilion seat for Yorkshire and Test matches, and a stand ticket for all the Leeds Rugby League matches—games which are played on the ground behind the pavilion. Combined cricket and football grounds, by the way, are common in Yorkshire: Sheffield and Bradford in one code and Leeds and Huddersfield in the other all have them.

It is worth noting that Leeds, like Sheffield, rarely produces a player of county standard. Most members of the present Yorkshire team are drawn from the Bradford and Huddersfield Leagues, along with the Council.

Although Sheffield is recognised as the biggest supporter of county cricket, its own local game is not included in the front rank compared with the West Yorkshire 'giants'.

Few people outside the immediate localities know anything about such organisations as the Barkston Ash, Bradford Mutual Sunday School, Craven, Doncaster, Halifax, Pudsey, Rotherham, and Wetherby Leagues, but they all have a rôle to fill. Some have occupied it for half a century, and they will go on whether they throw up a star once in a lifetime or never. It is such 'unknowns' that provide the foundation of the county's cricket might.

From Yorkshire, naturally and inevitably, to Lancashire.

It is not surprising to find that interest in league cricket is a feature of sporting life of Lancashire. In the southern half of the county, the Lancashire and Cheshire, Liverpool Competition, Manchester and District, all attract keen support and considerable rivalry, while farther north, the Central Lancashire and Bolton Leagues draw large attendances each week.

Among the best known in the country is the *Lancashire League*, which caters for the east and north-east section of the county and has a proud record of achievement in keeping a high standard.

The League was founded in 1890 at a meeting in Accrington (still the venue of the monthly management deliberations), and was first called 'The N.E. Lancashire League', and thirteen clubs—Burnley, Nelson, Colne, Bacup, Todmorden, East Lancashire, Enfield, Church, Haslingden, Ramsbottom, Lowerhouse, Accrington, and Rawtenstall, and, a month later, Rishton—were admitted. In February of the following year, Todmorden withdrew.

A further meeting took place in March, 1892, when the present title was taken, and the same year Bury joined, but withdrew after two seasons. Todmorden were readmitted in 1897.

At first, each club was allowed two professionals, but in 1900 a restriction of one professional was imposed and has been maintained since.

Much has been said and written about the introduction of professionalism into league cricket, but there is no doubt that the advent of a paid cricketer has widened the interest of the game.

In addition to attracting gates—which, with membership, are the lifeblood of the clubs—the professional man can be of tremendous assistance in the development of new talent, and coaching is often part of a pro's agreement. Even so, the vast sums paid out by clubs at present is still the subject of criticism. Colonial players of world repute are sought, and will come only if salaries are high and conditions favourable. But there is no doubt that the clubs, by persisting in a bold policy, have attracted gates and memberships.

Rawtenstall has a membership of over 3,000 out of a 27,000 population, and enthusiasm is tremendous.

Contrasts in salaries paid to-day compared with the early days are interesting. Cecil Pepper, the Australian all-rounder, now with Burnley, is reputed to receive something approaching £60 a week plus collections for '50s'. In November, 1949, Lowerhouse, one of the smaller clubs, met with disaster when its club and committee rooms were destroyed by fire, and salvaged from the ruins was a note-book of the treasurer of 1894. Items included

—'Hardy's wage, £3 10s. 0d.; Brown's wage, £2 10s. 0d.', and these two were professionals!

Spice is given to the League programmes by the 'Derby' matches, which, given a fine day, attract 'gates' of approximately £300. The rivalry between Nelson and Colne has to be experienced to be believed, and at one time was fierce rather than keen.

The boundary wall between the neighbouring authorities, Accrington and Church, was the object of the whitewash and paint-brushes of 'artists' of the winning side when the two clubs met; and when Cecil Parkin was professional for Church, supporters used to invade Accrington with pieces of that popular Northern cake—parkin—fastened in their buttonholes, just to show which team they favoured.

Rivalry is deadly, too, in the Rossendale Valley (home of Bacup, Haslingden, Rawtenstall, and Ramsbottom), and at Rawtenstall, before the War, there was an old custom, kept for many years, that if Rawtenstall won, rockets were sent up to let the town and outlying villages know their team's fate.

One of the League's most prosperous clubs is East Lancashire, whose ground at Blackburn is one of the finest in the organisation, and has been the scene of several minor county engagements. Perhaps the most famous club is Nelson, which achieved national prominence when it signed as professional, Ted Macdonald, the Australian fast bowler, who later played with Lancashire. Later it achieved further distinction through the engagement of Learie Constantine, whom many still consider to be the finest professional ever to throw in his lot with the Lancashire League. He proved a tremendous attraction, his all-round brilliance not only helping to put Nelson at the head of league affairs in the League and Worsley Cup (a knock-out competition started in 1919), but brought spectators flocking to Seedhill, Nelson's well-appointed ground, and to any other ground on which he was playing.

One of Learie's finest feats was the taking of 10 wickets for 10 runs against Accrington in May, 1934. Alf Pollard, the Nelson captain, bowling from the other end throughout the innings, had only one run knocked off him.

Eddie Paynter, former England and Lancashire left-hander, learnt his cricket with Enfield, and Bacup, another 'cradle', had five players taking part in county cricket at one time immediately before World War II.

Haslingden has produced Leslie Warburton (Lancashire C.C.), a consistently high scorer in the Ribblesdale League.

One of the most promising amateur batsmen was Tommy Lawton, the great England and Notts County centre-forward. He played cricket for Burnley when in his teens and was noted for his rapid scoring. In a game against Enfield in 1936 he hit 87 not out in 64 minutes, but one of the most amazing partnerships was one of 164 between A. Dobson and B. B. Fitzjohn ('Bly') in 56 minutes in 1937 against East Lancashire.

Todmorden, the club on the borders of Lancashire and York-shire, at one time had the distinction of being able to boast that a bowler could start his run in one county and hit the wickets in the next, for the boundary between the two Red Rose rivals ran across the ground! Todmorden has always been a strong side, and in 1937 and 1938 won the Worsley Cup in successive seasons. Among its professionals in more recent years have been Fred Root (Worcestershire), the late George Macaulay (Yorkshire), and Stanley Worthington (Derbyshire).

Another Derbyshire player who had some remarkable perform-ances in the Lancashire League was the late A. G. Slater. In his spell with Bacup he once took 9 for 9 including 4 wickets in 4 deliveries. He later moved to Colne.

In addition to playing as professional, Slater was responsible for coaching, which produced some of the best players in the League, among them Fred Hartley, now professional for Church, and one of the best all-rounders to have played outside county cricket.

Just as the Rossendale Valley area is one of the hotbeds of enthusiasm, so is the Accrington district with the clubs Accrington, Church, Enfield, and, on the Blackburn side, Rishton. A peculiar feature is that the Accrington ground is in Huncott (formerly a village in its own right, but now a ward of its bigger neighbour), Enfield ground is in Church, and the Church ground in Oswald-twistle. Jim Bailey, of Hampshire, had a remarkable season as professional for Accrington during 1937, having eleven innings of over 50 including six successive half centuries.

The railway runs by the Accrington ground, and a home player used to boast that he once made the biggest hit ever: he landed a ball into a waggon moving from the railway sidings, and it was recovered at Blackpool!

Competitive cricket was suspended from 1914 to 1918, but it was decided to carry on as best they could during World War II, and no doubt this has helped to develop young players. There may be moans from former players, a goodly proportion of whom sustain their interest in the League by serving on club committees, that the game is not as good as it used to be, but attendances are great, and a particular feature is the drive to encourage schoolboys, with professionals officially as coaches. This is proving successful, and Bly tried to keep winter interest a few years ago by holding an indoor practice at a local hall.

The *Lancashire Junior League* is for the second XIs, and here again the development of junior talent is to the fore. It provides a valuable source of experience to boys in their teens who can profit by the inclusion of older players of league experience, one of whom is the skipper.

A new step has been the introduction of a competition for 'A' teams in which boys of from fourteen to seventeen or eighteen years are members. It was first tried in 1949 and five clubs competed, Lowerhouse being the winners.

The 1949 season was referred to as the year of the Australian invasion, for no fewer than half the clubs had professionals from 'down under', and most of the others had professionals from other Dominions. Whatever criticisms were offered, the Australians and their colleagues from other parts of the Empire proved a popular investment, despite the high wages.

The nearest approach to southern club cricket, but in atmosphere only, is the Lancashire League. It is so very much a 'family affair', and it is not unusual to find father, a former player, serving on the committee of a club, having one or more sons playing in one of the club's teams, while 'the wife' is a member of the ladies' committee and probably doing her bit in the tea-room on match days. Similarly, many clubs get valuable assistance from the work of the 'tea-room ladies', and it is not uncommon for club treasurers to receive over £1,000 in a season from this source.

Rules governing the League are strict. For instance, no club can 'poach' the player of another club, otherwise a fine can be imposed, and the player accepting an inducement for the securing of his services is disqualified for such a period as the League committee decides. 'A player offering his services for a consideration to any League club, except as a professional, shall be immediately disqualified,' is another rule.

All amateur players are registered and must possess a birth qualification for the club for which they play, or must have passed the whole of their youth from fourteen to twenty-one years of age in the town. Another qualification is that of residence in the district for not less than twelve months immediately preceding the registration date.

An amateur cannot be registered for more than one club at a time, and may not transfer his services to another league club for which he possesses, or may acquire, a qualification except by applying to the League, stating the clubs concerned and the reason he requires a transfer. The matter does not end here, for the League, through its secretary, then finds out whether the player's club objects to the transfer. If there is an objection, it must be stated; if not, the transfer is granted.

The League does not permit any Sunday matches of any sort to be played on its clubs' grounds. Games are confined to Saturdays or on midweek days during holiday periods, and it is not surprising to hear of players travelling back early from their holidays in order to turn out with their particular club, a sure indication of the enthusiasm and team spirit that mark the whole conduct of play throughout the League.

Nelson swept the board in 1928, when they won both the Senior and Junior championships and the Worsley Cup competition; in 1949 East Lancashire accomplished the same feat.

Here again the interest evoked in youngsters who have the determination to practise and the enthusiasm to continue plays its part, and in many areas schoolboys are encouraged to join their club and take part in practices. Some clubs arrange matches between boy members so that their progress under actual playing conditions can be noted by the expert eyes of committee men.

Some boys have their introduction into League cricket when still in their teens and often go on to serve their club as an active playing member for as long as twenty-one years. Usually such a period of loyalty is rewarded, on application to the League management committee, by a testimonial fund.

The *Ribblesdale League*, which extends from East Lancashire to the west coast of the county and includes two Yorkshire clubs, Barnoldswick and Settle, was founded in 1892, and now comprises sixteen clubs which fulfil twenty-two fixtures. Of eight initial clubs, only Whalley, Read, Clitheroe, Barnoldswick, and

Settle remain members, although Padiham re-formed and joined again for 1950.

Blackpool has won the championship eight times, Whalley twelve, and these two are the only ones to head the table in three successive seasons.

This League is noted for the diverse character of the clubs taking part. They range from large centres such as Blackpool, St. Annes, and Morecambe, to villages like Read, and it was a source of widespread satisfaction and encouragement to the smaller towns that Read accomplished the feat of winning the championship in 1949 for the first time in its history. Incidentally, Read made a great show of this worthy performance, and greeted its team when they returned with the cup in festive style, with bonfires and gay decorations, the whole village being *en fête*.

Here, again, each club has a professional, without the big fees paid in the neighbouring Lancashire League, but the cricket is none the less entertaining. In some instances, the professionals have come from the Lancashire League, but in others were formerly more the successful amateurs. A club like Blackpool, with a ground on which Lancashire plays occasionally, can afford to pay more than a small club. But this only makes the village clubs keener to win.

The *North Lancashire League* stretches from the Scottish border to Morecambe on the Lancashire coast. Most of the clubs have a professional; but these men do not gather the princely emoluments of their brethren a little farther south. Just after the War, the BBC Club, touring in the North-West, met three of the leading North Lancashire League clubs, and perhaps this gives some sort of test of the comparative standards of Southern club cricket and the Northern League game. The BBC was beaten in fairly close games with Barrow and with Kendal (whose professional then was Peter Greenwood, now one of Lancashire's most promising all-rounders), and swamped Dalton, mainly because of an orgy of 6s by L. H. Phillips. The test, of course, was not very definite. For example, the northern sides were more at home on the 'greener' wickets, and there was a touring atmosphere about the games, although all were keenly fought—as I can testify!

And now we turn south again—to the *Birmingham and District Cricket League*, which was founded in 1888. It has been one of the most successful organisations of its kind in the country, and sprang from the Birmingham Cricket Association.

Both Warwickshire and Worcestershire, the first-class counties, have benefited by the promising talent that has been discovered and encouraged by the League. Eric Hollies, the England and Warwickshire spin bowler, and Charles Palmer, the England and Leicestershire all-rounder, to mention only two still actively engaged in county cricket, are products of Old Hill, a club that has also provided many grand players for Staffordshire. When not available for Worcestershire, Palmer, against whom I have played several times, generally spends his Saturday afternoons away from Bromsgrove School, assisting Old Hill.

The League, which consists of ten clubs, covers three counties —Warwickshire, Worcestershire, and Staffordshire. Members of the League are Moseley (1884), Aston Unity (1868), Mitchells and Butlers (1882), all Birmingham; West Bromwich Dartmouth (1834), Stourbridge (1835), Dudley (1840), Kidderminster (1850), Old Hill (1884), Walsall (1833), and Smethwick (1875).

Grounds generally are well laid out, with good accommodation for spectators. Crowds in the Black Country are better than in Birmingham, and up to 5,000 have been attracted to needle matches, though the average for all games would be under 2,000.

First president of the League was a Walsall and Staffordshire player, the late Fred Cozens, who held the office for forty-three years. Since 1931 there have been a number of presidents, mostly men who were still playing or had played in the League.

During the sixty-two years of its existence the League has had only three honorary secretaries: the late Harry Grosvenor Hill, a solicitor who played for Handsworth Wood, an original member-club that had to drop out owing to ground difficulties in 1920 (1888–1909); the late Sir C. Herbert Smith (Moseley) (1909–20)—he had also been president; and J. A. Lones, of Mitchells and Butlers (1920–49). Lones had T. Clarke as honorary assistant secretary and treasurer during the twenty-nine years he was in office. Both resigned at the end of 1949. Lones was president 1932–34 and in 1945.

The clubs have always played forceful and attractive cricket. Attack has been the batsman's main objective. Proof of this is that the highest score ever recorded in the League was made by

Bernard Forrest, now the Old Hill honorary secretary. Playing for Old Hill against Walsall in the second division on May 24, 1931, he hit up 243 in 105 minutes. Highest score in the First Division is 197 by W. E. Merritt, the New Zealander and Northants player, while playing for Dudley against Smethwick on September 7, 1940. That season Merritt scored an aggregate of 878 to equal the record of H. O. Kirton (Mitchells and Butlers) set up several years earlier. Merritt's all-round performance that season was the best ever in the League, for besides his 878 runs he took 80 wickets.

The 1950 League president, H. W. Homer, former captain of Old Hill—a club he has been associated with since 1912—scored an aggregate of 854 runs in fifteen innings in 1928. This was a record until it was broken by Kirton. Homer, by the way, retired as a player as recently as 1945. He had an average in league cricket of 30·40 per innings and 34·40 per season. Homer had also captained Staffordshire, and played for the Minor Counties against the West Indies.

The record match aggregate for the League was made at the Reddings, Moseley's ground, in 1919. Moseley made 329 for 5 wickets, Frank Stephens scoring a century. Walsall hit off the runs for the loss of 8 wickets. Pearman Smith, the Walsall captain, scored a dashing century in this remarkable match, which yielded 659 runs in just over 5½ hours.

No bowler has ever taken 100 wickets in the League in one season, but Eric Hollies came very near to doing it in 1940, when playing for Old Hill. His total was 99, which beat the 1937 record of 'Tich' Freeman by one wicket. Freeman's record was made when he was with Walsall, and it was against this club on the last day of the season that Eric wanted eight wickets to make the century. Watched by his father, who was the last of the League's lob bowlers and who still holds the second-division record with ninety-four wickets in a season, the England spin bowler had to be content with 7 at a cost of 56 runs. In the same season Eric captured 10 Mitchells and Butlers wickets for 21 runs.

While on the subject of records, I recall Aaron Lockett, the Old Hill and Staffordshire bowler and now county umpire, telling me of perhaps the best all-ten-wickets performance in the League. In this remarkable match, at Old Hill, on May 22, 1926, Stourbridge lost 9 wickets for 9 runs. Then the last man, Colin Moberley, also a well-known tennis player, hit three 4s. Two other players made two each and there were five extras. Eight failed to score. R. H. (Dicky) Williams, the Worcestershire player, one of the opening batsmen, was 0 not out. Lockett took his first seven wickets, including a hat-trick, for no runs.

Nearly thirty years earlier Stourbridge was dismissed by Kidderminster for thirteen runs, the League's lowest score until 1949, when it was equalled by Old Hill in a second division match. West Bromwich Dartmouth was the team to dismiss Old Hill for thirteen at Haden Hill, Old Hill's ground. Barry Hatfield, a seventeen-year-old bowler, making his *début* took 6 wickets for 3 runs.

Under the late M. K. Foster's captaincy 'Tich' Freeman, the old Kent and England bowler, then the club professional, helped Walsall to win the League championship in 1937 and to set up a record. It was the club's third successive championship. M. K. Foster, you may remember, was one of the famous Worcestershire family of cricketing brothers.

One of the most famous bowlers of all time began his career in the Birmingham League. He was Sidney Barnes, who played for his native Smethwick before and after he had entered first-class cricket. He was over sixty years of age when, before World War II, he was the club's professional. Then there was Fred Root of Dudley, who went to Worcestershire before going on to play for England. Dick Howorth was with Old Hill before he joined Worcestershire, and Warwickshire discovered Charles Grove when he was with Mitchells and Butlers.

Nowadays a number of well-known professionals are playing in the League. They are: Maurice Nichols (Aston Unity); Bill Merritt (Dudley); Arthur Wellard, formerly of Somerset (Kidderminster); Eddie Watts, Surrey (Mitchells and Butlers); Don Taylor, the New Zealand Test player, now qualifying for Warwickshire (Old Hill); Frank Woodhouse, formerly with Old Hill (Smethwick); Bill Andrews, Somerset (Stourbridge); T. F. Smailes, Yorkshire (Walsall); Alf Gover, Surrey, who headed the League bowling averages in 1948 with 89 wickets for an average of 9·03 runs (West Bromwich Dartmouth).

Families have been associated with many of the clubs, Kidderminster, perhaps, being the outstanding example. Besides the Tomkinsons, there are the Humphries brothers, Norman, H. G., and Cedric, who was killed in Holland in the War. All played for Worcester. Norman nowadays assists Devon in the Minor

P

Counties. The Gethins, W. G. (a president of the League in 1938) and Stan, and C. S. Anton and his son were others.

Walsall had the Seldon brothers, Mervyn, F. C., and R. G., the Oxford soccer Blue and now captain of Devon; Smethwick, the Docker brothers; Moseley, Frank and George Stephens, both Warwickshire players, and the Tylers; West Bromwich Dartmouth, the late Walter Perks, his sons, and his brother, and the Perrys, nowadays represented by club captain Eric, who has also played soccer for West Bromwich Albion and is a former Staffordshire amateur golf champion. Eric is still one of the League's best all-rounders. Aston Unity has the Hossells, J. J., senior and junior, still active in the club.

When Aston Unity won the championship in August, 1949, it was the club's eleventh triumph. Unity has been champion club eight times and shared the honour on three occasions—indeed, it was the first champion side in 1889. Wooden spoonists in 1948, it just beat Walsall, which occupied bottom place but one in 1947. West Bromwich Dartmouth, champion club in 1948, has won the championship nine times and shared it twice—a record now shared with Aston Unity.

Most of the credit for Unity's success went to Maurice Nichols and to the popular Jack Hossell (junior), who led the side for the first time after playing for Warwickshire.

Ken Gilson, the county hockey player, also delighted the crowds with his big hitting, which earned him fourth position in the League batting averages. There was nothing better than Gilson's 101 in seventy-five minutes for Unity against Mitchells and Butlers, after going in at the fall of the sixth wicket. Nichols, who had 69 wickets for an average of 12·23, occupied sixth place in the bowling honours list.

Mitchells and Butlers again headed the second division table, with Walsall as runners-up.

League clubs play home and away matches with one another in both divisions, each division playing its respective match on the same day. The matches are played between the third Saturday in April and the first Saturday in September. Three points are awarded for a match won and one point for drawn games. In the event of a tie one and a half points are credited to each club. Any dispute having reference to the interpretation of the Laws of Cricket is referred to the M.C.C. for settlement, but in other matters the League's decision is final.

Neutral umpires, approved by the League, are appointed to each match. Clubs pay each umpire 10s., inclusive of travelling expenses.

If both sides have completed an innings by 5.30, and either captain so desires, a second innings may be started, and play is continued until 7.30 p.m. If no other result is arrived at by this time, the result of the first innings will stand.

Only *bonâ fide* club members are allowed to take part in League matches, and are eligible to play for any one club during any one season. They must not be members regularly playing for another club outside the League.

There are a number of junior leagues in the Birmingham area. The *Midland Works and Business Houses*, perhaps the most important of these, runs seven or eight divisions. Leading clubs that have their own grounds include: Bakelite, Mitchells and Butlers, Revo Electric, Metropolitan, Hingleys, Averys Ltd., Lucas Ltd., Coombs Wood, Post Office Stores, Morris Cars, Chance Bros., Wolseley, Dunlop, Birmid, Hope Bros., Birlec, Reynolds Tubes, Wrights' Ropes, and Gaskell and Chambers. There is a system of promotion and relegation.

The largest competitive organisation is the *Birmingham Parks Association*, with over 100 clubs playing in about twelve league divisions on Saturdays, with another four or five divisions on Sundays. Promotion and relegation is operative. Runs for and against are shown in the League tables, and where points are equal, position is determined by run average per wicket. This League also runs a number of trophy knock-out competitions.

The *Birmingham and District Works Association* and the *Birmingham Industrial League* are also two very active organisations. The Industrial League, unlike most of the other Northern Leagues, plays on Saturdays and Sundays, and like the Works League, promotes knock-out competitions.

The *North Staffordshire and District Cricket League* records show season 1949, not only as the organisation's diamond jubilee year, but as one of the most successful from both playing and entertainment aspects.

After a dramatic struggle between those long-standing rivals, Porthill Park and Norton, the Porthill side topped the senior 'A' section with a margin of three and a half points over Norton.

Blythe Works, which lost only one match during the season,

was invariably too sound for the majority of the opposition with the exception of Bolton's, which finished runners-up. There was another close thing in the Junior 'A' section, where Leek and Longton fought out the honours, Leek winning by three points. This solid, all-round Leek XI has now won the title in four of the last seven seasons. There was an even closer fight in the Junior 'B' section, where the champion club, Betley, had all its work cut out to hold on to its title against the spirited Scot Hay team, which finished with the same number of points (fifty-four) as the champions. Both these sides won eighteen and lost four of their twenty-two games; none was drawn.

Porthill, which last won the title in 1935, owed a great deal to that solid batsman, F. R. Bailey, who topped the averages with 530 runs for an average of 27·9. His highest score was 160. Norton's G. Birch also had a good summer, with 320 runs for an average of 22·9. N. Roberts, the Bignall End star, figured well in the averages with 483 (highest score 92), and an average of 26·8. The consistent G. Sedgwick (Longton) finished runner-up, however, with 413 runs for an average of 27·5. H. Boon (Longton), R. Smith (Great Chell), H. Cooper (Nantwich), and G. Morrey (Longton) were also prominent among the batsmen.

Leek's B. Shardlow, who again figured in Staffordshire's Minor Counties side, headed the bowling with 100 wickets for an average of 6·2, although F. Taylor, the Stone Club's professional, set up an all-time record when he captured 131 wickets for an average of 6·6. Taylor took six more wickets than the previous record, established in 1911 by G. A. Wilson, who in those days was the Norton Club's demon bowler.

The century-makers were headed by F. R. Bailey (Porthill Park), whose 160 not out was easily the best of the season. Others to top three figures were G. Shaw (Silverdale) 111, and J. H. Ragsdale (Longton) 103.

Bignall End had two bowlers in the leading five averages— A. Burgess and V. Burgess. It was A. Burgess who scored a personal triumph against Knypersley when he took all 10 wickets for 31 runs. This match will always be remembered as a bowlers' day, for Knypersley's W. Boon brought off the hat-trick.

Professionals are allowed only in the two senior sections of the League. Senior 'A' clubs so equipped were: Burslem (A. W. Massey), Great Chell (R. Smith), Knypersley (F. T. Boulton), Leek (B. Shardlow), Longton (R. Norcop), Nantwich (K. Dean),

Norton (W. T. Nolley), Porthill Park (H. Hanock), Silverdale (S. Norcop), and Stone (F. Taylor).

In scoring 3,215 runs, Blyth, the champions of the Senior 'B' section, had nearly 400 more runs than any other team in the section. It had three batsmen in the first seven leading the averages, and T. E. Hawley, with a total of 693 (highest, 105), headed the list with an average of 38·5. H. Whalley and R. Dunkley were sixth and seventh. The names of Hollowood and the North Staffs League are synonymous, and T. G. Hollowood, runner-up in the senior 'B' section batting honours list, is only carrying out a tradition when his name figures among the records. He was the section's most prolific batsman, totalling 773 (highest, 124), for an average of 36·8. R. Dale (Audley) and F. Butler (Meakins) also topped the 600 aggregate, while Blythe's O. E. Braime and T. G. Hollowood—124 each—headed the century-makers' list. Others with three-figure scores to their credit were: S. Whitehurst (Bolton's), 116 not out; H. Whalley (Blythe), 116; K. Raby (Kidsgrove), 107, and T. E. Hawley (Blythe), 105. H. Jones (Meakins) led the bowlers with 44 wickets and an average of 7·3, with T. Woolley (Blythe) second with 65, average 7·4. L. Hall (St. Edwards) had the highest average bag with 93 wickets for 8·1.

The rules governing the North Staffordshire League game are laid out on the simplest lines, which no doubt accounts for the success of an organisation that covers such a large area.

Clubs in each of the four sections play home and away matches with the other clubs of their section. Should two or more clubs secure the same number of points, a play-off for first place will be necessary. The champions of the Senior 'B' section are automatically promoted to the Senior 'A' section provided that the promoted club's ground is, in the opinion of the League committee, of the standard required for Senior 'A' cricket. The club gaining the least number of points in the Senior 'A' section is relegated to the Senior 'B' section.

An eight-ball over is in force in all matches, and six runs are allowed for all hits that drop over and clear of the boundary fence or line.

Before leaving the provincial leagues, we must cross into Wales to take a brief look at the vigorous activities of the *South Wales and Monmouthshire Cricket Association*.

I. J. Thomas, its present secretary, tells me that it was founded in March, 1926, and nowadays it brings together clubs in the Swansea, Neath, Llanelly, and North Glamorganshire areas. Cardiff, Barry, Newport, and Blaina were among the original members, but have since seceded, owing to the relatively long-distance travelling they incurred.

Today the Association runs two divisions, with sixteen clubs in the first and fourteen in the second. There is no system of promotion or relegation, and the clubs in each division play one another in league matches only once every season, the venues being alternated each year.

For the first three years of its existence, the Association was chaired by H. W. Baxter, of Swansea. After seeing the new body safely through its teething stage, he was succeeded by J. D. D. Davis, the ex-Glamorgan county cricketer and centre three-quarter of Neath Rugby Club. Davis has held the office ever since.

J. C. Griffith-Jones, a well-known South Wales journalist— and known to many of us, too, as one of the pioneer sports commentators of the BBC—was the first secretary. Then came W. R. Morgan of Merthyr, and then the present secretary—he plays, incidentally, for Pontardulais Cricket Club. His assistant is Leslie Morgan of Briton Ferry C.C. E. Baber, of Bridgend, was the original treasurer; Thomas followed him, and remained in the office for nine years, when he swopped places with Morgan.

Many of the clubs now attached to the Association have long traditions of 'friendly' cricket behind them. I asked secretary Thomas what advantages they gained by entering his leagues.

'Don't get the picture out of focus,' he replied. 'We still play a great deal of friendly cricket; indeed, any one club can play at the most only fifteen league matches in the season. But, by joining the Association, they know their fixtures are sure and that games will start on time; they have the services of officially-appointed, neutral umpires; the Association's inspection system leads to improved wickets, out-fields, and dressing-room facilities, and they profit financially from better takings at the gate—after all, the competitive element *does* spice the game for the spectator! Players in affiliated clubs may qualify, too, for representative matches against the Glamorgan county side, the Pembroke County C.C., and opponents of similar calibre.'

I greatly wish I had the space to close this chapter by intro-ducing you to some of the outstanding players of these clubs—my friend, Wilfrid Goatman (who was born and brought up in that delightful village, The Mumbles), is convincingly loud in his praise of their abilities and prowess. But I have room only to record that many of the affiliated clubs have enjoyed the help of distinguished professionals—among them, Tom Gange and Harry Wrathall, of Gloucester; Jim Jones, of Somerset; Charlie Hallows, of Lancashire, and G. C. Macaulay and Percy Holmes of Yorkshire.

Chapter Fourteen

COMPETITIVE CRICKET

For and against—Opinions and views—The future.

IN the dictionary, the word 'competition' is defined as 'action of endeavouring to gain what another endeavours to gain at the same time; the striving of two or more for the same object; number or eagerness of those competing for something'.

But each of us cricketers interprets that in his own way. To one, it connotes a quiet, friendly game; to the chap next door, the grim earnestness of a Cup Final.

The word can be applied to those delightful, leisurely games on the village green on summer afternoons. The opposition, perhaps, are a few minutes late in arriving, so out comes the bat, and you have a gentle knock-up on a flat piece of the outfield. The match starts. You come in from the field to lettuce and cakes —or char and a wad! After tea, it's your side's turn to bat. You, yourself, are lucky during your first few overs, and manage to escape serious trouble. Perhaps, at the end of the match, you are the highest scorer and your side has won, and so to 'pints' at the 'local', where you chat with your opponents and discuss the game in all its aspects. . . . Maybe that's what 'competition' means to you.

Or it may mean next Saturday's Final in the local 'Evening Cup Competition'. The weekly net and fielding practices are intensified. Five minutes before the drawing of stumps your fast bowler puts paid to their No. 11, and you have won the Cup. You have the reward of a week's hard effort; the spectators have had good value for their admission money. . . .

Or it may mean taking part in one of the dour and almost hostile Northern League matches, in which no quarter is given and certainly none is asked. After many of the matches, there is no going to the 'local' to hobnob with opponents. The occasion is too serious for that. Frank Dolman, of the C.C.C. Council, who has played a great deal in league cricket, confirms that this is so. He told me that the whole atmosphere of the contest is against fraternising of this kind.

Well, whatever *your* interpretation of 'competition' may be, it is but a short step from the dictionary definition to the literal meaning of the phrase, so familiar to present-day clubs, 'competitive cricket'.

I drew an imaginary line across England through Ipswich—Bedford—Worcester, and found that, to the south of the line, honest-to-goodness village or club cricket is played, but to the north it is league cricket that interests our week-end cricketer.

Consider the position that exists below the line. The question came almost to boiling point in 1950 when one heard it asked on all sides, 'Competitive cricket, or ordinary club cricket?'

It was discussed on most grounds one visited, in the pavilion bars after the game, and by most of the cricket committees. The Press took it up, and the Club Cricket Conference was forced to consider whether or not it would permit clubs affiliated to them to participate in competitive cricket.

The C.C.C.'s rule 5 says: 'It shall be a condition of membership that no club shall be connected with any organised cricket league or other competition, except as defined hereafter . . . or take part in any form of newspaper, trade, or other prize competitions.'

Exceptions to the rule are: hospital cup competitions, inter-college competitions, inter-university competitions, or any other competitions of a wholly charitable character.

League cricket, in my view, is ideally suited to the northerner. His character, outlook on life, and temperament differ widely from those of his southern counterpart; he loves a gamble; he likes a game to be invested with a keen, competitive atmosphere; he wants the result to be a practical kind of triumph—something, for instance, that may make his favourite team League champions. It follows that increased support from spectators and bigger gates—with their benefit for club funds—can be anticipated when the club manages to climb higher in the championship table than in previous years. Hence everything is done in the league to attract the best available players, and so make the side as strong as possible.

More often than not, well-known international and county cricketers are lured away from the more arduous, six-day-a-week, county matches to the less strenuous Saturday-afternoon struggles. What is more, this can be very lucrative for the player, who may well pick up a £50 collection if he takes five wickets or more, or scores an attractive '50'. During the week he can devote his energies to a coaching job at one of the schools or clubs.

These star celebrities certainly draw the crowds. Many of the fine cricketers the West Indies export to us have joined league clubs: for example, E. A. Martindale, Frank Worrall, Learie Constantine, George Headley, Ellis Achong, Everton Weekes, and —the latest recruit—Sonny Ramadhin, the success of the West Indian tour of Britain in 1950. Other equally well-known cricketers from Australia, South Africa, New Zealand, India, and Pakistan can also be followed in the various leagues. And from our own country, such stalwarts as George Pope, Eddie Paynter, Alf Gover, Emmett Robinson, Bill Andrews, and Maurice Nichols have all at one time or another played in league elevens.

There is no doubt at all that these distinguished players have stamped their personalities indelibly on the northern game, with the result that the interest created among spectators, players, and officials has outstripped the more leisurely and friendly club and village games of the south.

We all know what a draw the Comptons, the Huttons, and the Washbrooks have been to county-cricket supporters. And so it is in the league, but with one vital difference—especially from the spectators' point of view: he is assured of seeing his idol play during the afternoon's play, instead of having to wait, maybe, all three days of a county match. Here the club game has something in common with the league. Unless it happens to be a representative two-day or three-day match (and these are becoming as rare as good fast bowlers), the performance is all over in the day—a decision is reached, and, as with the football fan, the spectator leaves the ground with a much greater sense of satisfaction.

While I must steer a middle course, many of my own cricketing friends are strongly in favour of competitive cricket.

Cricket writer Bruce Harris, for example, has often said that he advocates league cricket among southern clubs, and that it *will* come. One of his many reasons for giving it his support is most interesting, and one that those taking the opposite view must surely have difficulty in explaining away. Bruce contends, 'Yorkshire and Lancashire owe their predominant position in cricket over many years to the leagues, which nurture young professionals.'

Peter Goodall, who has spent many years writing about club

cricket, is emphatically on the side of competitive or 'progressive' cricket. He goes further than most. This is why he wants competitions:

> Club cricket, he says, has been played successfully for many, many years. More important, everyone has enjoyed it. But those were in the halcyon days, when club members had more money for the game—there were many more wealthy vice-presidents to help the clubs financially. And the players were *keen*.
>
> Now what has happened? Members have little or no money to help subsidise their clubs, and, most important of all, they do not seem to care whether they play or not.
>
> That is the root of the trouble. And those that have been playing for twenty years or more are not being replaced. Until sufficient interest is shown by the younger members—and that can be stimulated by competition—there will be no lowering of the average age of thirty-five in the club sides of to-day.
>
> So, in the absence of any alternative, it seems we must turn to incentive—that all-too-familiar word. As far as I can see, the only way to instil it into cricket is to copy football with their cups and points. Abhorrent, maybe. But what is the alternative?

What must be remembered, as far as I am concerned, is that I am a member of the council of the Club Cricket Conference—one of those, in short, who assisted the C.C.C. to form its decision against league or competitive cricket.

In May, 1949, the Conference gave a great deal of time to discussing the introduction of competitive cricket. A letter from George Parkinson, who was treasurer of Crompton Parkinson's (Essex) Sports Club at the time, forced the issue. He sought permission to run a league among Essex clubs—and this made the Conference act.

At times, discussion at the council meeting in May became heated, but the general feeling, after all opinions had been aired, was clearly against any change of rule. After this meeting, chairman Jack Cooper, who is one of the shining lights of Barclays Bank cricket on and off the field, made a statement to the Press. As a matter of fact, there was a great deal of talk among the councillors about whether they should say anything definite to the Press at all, but ultimately a considered statement was prepared. This statement, written by hand, was given to Peter Goodall, who happened to be the only Press representative who bothered to come along and who had knowledge of what was being discussed at the meeting:

> 'That this Council considers the introduction of competition cricket in the south is not in the interests of club cricket and that no alteration to the objects and rules of the Conference is necessary or desirable.'

Clubs then had a decision to take. Whether to accept this ruling, or, if they still wanted to pursue the idea of playing competitive cricket, to call an Extraordinary General Meeting of the Conference.

George Parkinson got support from enough Essex clubs to force such a meeting, and he called them together the same night that the C.C.C. had their meeting to discuss their future attitude to competitive cricket. That afternoon, Goodall ran a story in the *Evening Standard*, asking why the Essex clubs could not wait until the following day, when the Conference decision would be published, before making their decision.

Parkinson told Goodall later that his story had made the Essex representatives waver. Indeed, many of them ignored their promises and did not attend Parkinson's meeting. They even left him to find the money to pay for the hall himself. And that is why the Conference secretary never received the Parkinson resolution.

There was no doubt the Essex clubs had received a nasty jolt, but the C.C.C. was taking no chances. In July, a specially selected sub-committee of the main council drew up a memorandum listing the main arguments for and against competitive cricket, so that if the Essex clubs returned to the attack, or for that matter if any clubs had similar ideas, it would have most, if not all, the answers in support of the view that southern clubs in general opposed any departure from their normal game.

Now Essex was not the only county to come out into the open with strong views about the desirability of introducing this controversial innovation in the south. Sussex, too, was deeply interested, and under the guidance of the popular, knowledgeable,

and evergreen England and Sussex cricketer, Arthur Gilligan
—one of the three famous Old Alleynian brothers—had taken
the matter even further than had Parkinson. Arthur Gilligan's
efforts were, in fact, partially successful.

Gilligan conceived the idea of a league to play competition
cricket, but he had a hard time persuading the bigger Sussex clubs
that they should compete, because of the risk of their being
banned by the Conference. At their first meeting nearly all the
top clubs, as well as many others in Sussex, were represented. But
the more senior or 'established' of them backed out as soon as
they were told that the Conference would never approve.

However, with characteristic fighting spirit, Arthur Gilligan
persevered with his brain-child. In 1949, with the newly formed
Sussex Association of Cricket Clubs, they had a comparatively
successful season, although the calibre of the clubs taking part
was not as good as Gilligan would have liked.

Now, though I have never heard Arthur Gilligan mention
it, I myself believe he would have been far happier if the more
powerful clubs could have been persuaded to enter the
competition. But clubs like Middleton, Worthing, Bognor,
Hastings, Pagham, St. Leonard's, and Haywards Heath, which
at first showed interest in what was going on, made it quite
clear that they didn't want to have anything to do with the
scheme.

A project like this needs organising. Arthur Gilligan had some
willing helpers. For instance, E. Hardy, of the Eastbourne Club,
must have done a lot of overtime getting the secretaries together
and discussing the whole thing with them. They all had to bear
in mind that the difficulties and problems confronting one club
were not necessarily the same as those affecting their next-door
neighbours. For example, a collection may be taken at one
ground, but prohibited at another; or one of the interested clubs
may not have a ground of its own, and so 'home' matches
would have to be played on other club grounds. Yet, for
'admin.' purposes, one of these would have to be the 'home'
ground.

These were but a few of the many difficulties that faced this
bold, enthusiastic Eastbourne man.

But, whereas Arthur Gilligan's success story was only
threatened by the unwillingness of clubs to risk excommunication
from the C.C.C., Parkinson's Essex experiment was ruined by it.

Hardy backed Gilligan's argument that exclusion from the Club Cricket Conference did not necessarily mean the end of cricket. Nor has it. The Competition went on.

The winners in 1949, by the way, were Rottingdean, where some sixty years ago cricket was played on the famous Windmill Down. And that reminds me of a story. In one match, a full-blooded crack sent the ball rolling down the hill. The whole fielding side had to line up in relays to get the ball up the hill again and back to the wicket-keeper who, in a frenzy, hurled the ball at the wicket. It missed the stumps and eventually rolled down the other side where, summoned by frantic shouts from stumper and spectators, the fieldsmen climbed the hill, crossed over and repeated their relaying efforts. By the time the ball had been safely recovered, the two exhausted batsmen had notched 67 runs (and run nearly a mile!)

Many other men, prominent in sport, have come out into the open with their views.

Brian Valentine, for example. Wherever cricket is played the name of Valentine is almost a household word, for no more popular or likeable person has ever played the game. I personally have played a lot of cricket with him, but more often than not, against him—especially before World War II, when he used to come down regularly to the BBC ground.

From Press reports there seemed no doubt at all about Brian Valentine's views on the introduction of competitive cricket to the southern counties. Apparently he was in favour of the scheme as it could stimulate interest and keenness, and would help to raise the standard of club play. However, when I recently had a word with him about it, he asked me to say that he was very strongly against it. He couldn't see how it could be successful in the south as we don't play the type of cricket for it. He did think, though, that the counties should be split into areas, and that inter-area matches for the youth of the county should be arranged, in order to try to discover new talent. As you may have read, Brian is now chairman of the newly-formed Kent Association of Cricket Clubs, so we should soon see some results.

My friend Tom Pearce, of Essex—without doubt one of the most knowledgeable and enthusiastic cricketers of our time—told me this: 'I am still of the opinion that some kind of competitive cricket would be a great stimulus to club cricket even if it only got matches to start on time, and gave the declaring captain some idea of how long tea intervals would be, and when —in actual fact—the game was going to end.'

For another opinion, let us turn to H. M. Garland-Wells, the ex-Surrey skipper, whose views, in the main, I wholeheartedly share. There are few more interested and enthusiastic supporters of the club game in this country than Garland-Wells ('Monty' to his friends). Among his many activities for cricket, he is president and chairman of the Surrey Association of Cricket Clubs. This Association was formed during the winter months of 1946–47 by the Public Relations Sub-Committee of the County Cricket Club.

It was decided that some sort of co-operation between the county and the smaller clubs would be an all-round advantage. Monty almost immediately came out on the side of competitive cricket. He has told me, during several chats we have had on the subject, that he was very much impressed by the obvious swing of public opinion about the type of cricket played, and that the demand by some of the younger members of clubs within his Association was for a competition of some kind or the other.

In the Guildford (Surrey) area, for instance, some forty clubs participate yearly for the 'Flora Doris Cup'. This competition was formed by four or five men—including Mr. Wright, secretary of the Farncombe Cricket Club—to raise funds for the Surrey Cricket Club Centenary Fund. Since that fund closed, any profit —and there always is a profit—goes back into the game. Matches are played in the evenings and consist of twenty overs each side. Cranleigh has won the competition four times, Guildford once, and Farncombe once. There is no doubt that this Cup has aroused very great interest and keenness among players and spectators alike.

You may well ask why such well-known C.C.C. clubs as Guildford are permitted to take part. The answer is that it is considered to be too small a competition to worry about, and the existing Conference rules permit this type of competitive play.

'Monty' has made it quite clear that, in his opinion, if competitive cricket were introduced in the South of England, the standard of cricket would undoubtedly improve, and for that reason alone he would welcome it.

But this raises a most important question. Is the standard of village and club cricket indeed so low that it requires the stimulus of such an injection? There are many who think not.

John Arlott, cricket writer and BBC commentator, is one. He says:

I far prefer ordinary club cricket to league cricket. Now, obviously, such a statement needs considerable qualification. I realise that from the point of view of the spectator—particularly the spectator only partly educated to the game—league cricket is the most exciting form of the sport played in these islands. Nowhere else does cricket yield quite so much excitement quite so frequently. A few things, however, set me against league cricket, and they are faults not in league cricket itself, but in the relationship of the league game to cricket as a whole.

First of all, I am worried by the 'star' system, under which one outstanding professional player is liable to be the mainstay of the batting and the bowling, with his 50 runs or 5 wickets in a match. The matter is made to be of extreme, selfish, personal importance to him—inevitably, since 5 wickets or 50 runs yields him a collection among the spectators. This, obviously, distorts the balance of any eleven and prevents it from being a cricket *team*, reducing it instead to a company of 'star' and ten others. Consequently I am not altogether in favour of the dominance of the star and the effect it has, all too frequently, of preventing the early development of a young player. This, of course, means that league cricket does not develop and supply to higher cricket so many good players as it might.

My next ground for objection is that it places the spectator above the player—which must always be a bad thing. Above all, even the leagues—such as those in Yorkshire—that do not employ the star system, tend to rule out much of the sympathy and comradeship that less competitive club cricket can produce, by placing winning above all other considerations. This it is that drives the man to whom cricket is a life all too soon from the playing sphere, when ordinary humanity would say let him go on playing because of the happiness he derives from it. I should hate you to think, from what I have said, that I am completely indifferent to the matter of winning or losing a cricket match. Obviously no cricketer is worth his salt who does not go flat out to win. But, equally obviously, the desire to win and the enjoyment of the game must reach a reasonable balance—and much of this balance is attained before and after the actual hours of play.

I like to see a cricket match played hard, won hard, and lost hard, but once it is over I completely fail to see that the recording of a win for one side, a defeat for the other in figures, in print, or on a cup, makes any difference whatever to the game itself.

Finally, having heard what some of the county players and other well-known personalities think about it, let us see what opinion the ordinary club cricketer has on this important topic.

My usual end-of-the-season match is against Harefield, that delightful little Middlesex club to the north of Uxbridge. After one of these games, I asked Dick Wiles, the chairman, what he thought about the possible introduction of competitive cricket. Very quickly he became heated on the subject and told me he never wanted to see such a catastrophe occur to club cricket. His main reasons for being so decidedly against it are that teams would be inclined to stoop to any method of getting an opponent out; that you wouldn't get new members to join the club as they would never get a game unless they were very good players; that there seems to be a general drift towards knocking competition out of work and putting it into play.

Dick Wiles would like to see a halt called to this. He says, 'Put competition into work and leave the pleasure in our play.'

Well, he may have a good point there!

I asked H. H. Nicholson ('Old Nick'), another club cricketing pal of mine, who has played a lot of cricket in the north and has had four years in London club cricket, how he thought the game down here in the south compares with the league game.

He said: 'Let me emphasise that in my view there is no fundamental difference. But there are misconceptions—on both sides. In the North, there is a belief that the indolence of southern club cricketers is such that they do not even trouble to chase the ball to the boundary. The southern critic usually seizes on professionalism. This, they aver, introduces too keen competition, and that breeds practices that are "not cricket".'

However, to sum up, it appears that the opponents of competitive cricket say there is no need for the standard of play to be

Q

improved, as club cricket must not be regarded as the recruiting ground for county and Test-match players; that, ultimately, it would lead to professionalism—especially would this apply to the more wealthy clubs that could afford such luxuries; that it would be difficult for some clubs to take part in a competition owing to the leaseholds on their grounds; that clubs would not be able to choose their opponents; and, perhaps, one of the most important points of all, that it might tend to destroy the friendly, social atmosphere, traditional in this kind of cricket.

Those who argue for competitive games say that the standard of play would improve; that games would start punctually and there wouldn't be the same leisurely time taken over the lunch or tea intervals; that the counties would be able to select players for their sides more easily if tables and averages were published in the Press; that the keen atmosphere of competitive cricket would prepare the club cricketer more easily for the county game, when that honour came his way; that the standard of umpiring would improve; and that, from the spectators' point of view, a match is usually much more exciting and interesting when fought out under competition rules.

When, for my own part, I am asked what I personally think about this vexed and thorny topic, I find the question difficult to answer.

It is not that I haven't made up my mind (as you may have gathered by now!) but my position on the council of the C.C.C. necessarily imposes certain restraint. However, without wishing to cause any embarrassment, I have no hesitation in recording my views, and on this matter they are decided and strong.

I maintain that the introduction of some form of competitive cricket—not the league variety—would be a good thing for present-day club cricket. Was it not one of the better-known C.C.C. councillors who said, 'We must remember we are not now living in 1914?' And how right he was. Present-day development and tempo of life sometimes leave some of us behind. There are some who will not recognise that to-day things really are different, in spite of the wealth of evidence all round them! Why they love playing this head-in-the-sand game with themselves, I don't know. They fool no one except possibly themselves, and we get no further.

To them, anything other than the club cricket to which they have become accustomed and which they have played all their lives, means nothing, and they will hear of nothing to change a single rule.

But, with the changing times, they *are* going to get left behind. The type of cricket we play must also change, although how this change is to be brought about is, at the moment, a very moot point.

The answer may be competitive cricket. But I clearly recognise all the difficulties in organising and running such a project—for instance, at the outset, its administration must be voluntary, yet foolproof and efficient—and I am genuinely afraid that, with the general state of apathy prevailing to-day among club secretaries and players alike, it would be quite impossible to set up the necessary machinery to start off a big competition and keep it going smoothly. To my mind, there is no doubt that it would be a step in the right direction, but can we take it, and do we want to?

Now, it is only fair that I should put also the majority view, so here it is, in the form of a debate with that trenchant critic of the anti-competition diehards, Peter Goodall:

GOODALL: The Conference says that few southern clubs could afford a first-rate professional and coach, because there is no gate money. That is silly, because if they had a man of the standard they suggest, he could more than reimburse them for any outlay by coaching throughout the week at a fee, although this, I think, would be unnecessary because the few pounds that they would have to expend could be found by most clubs.

BENNETT: The one thing you've overlooked is that very few clubs would be in the position to take advantage of a 'through-the-week' coaching scheme. Also I don't agree that in these days clubs could afford the little extra that you talk about to pay a coach, and unless he is going to be a coach worthy of the name, and somebody whom everybody knows, like Compton or Washbrook, you will not stimulate interest and get the chaps there.

GOODALL: Then why do clubs pay, say, £1 an hour for nets at cricket schools, or individuals 10s. a half-hour for coaching at those schools?

BENNETT: That's a good point, but the number of cricketers who go to the schools for special coaching is very small compared with the large number of people who play club cricket. But I do agree with one of the points you made, in that a coach of some description would materially assist in raising the standard of play. For instance, in the early days of the formation of my own club we had two characters, both well known in their own spheres—Arthur Sellick, who played for Gloucestershire and Wiltshire, and Pat Beckett, who played for Ireland and a number of first-class Irish sides. They were both members of the club and took it upon themselves to coach our youngsters, with the result that in a few years the BBC not only had a cricket side, but a side that played a high standard of cricket.

GOODALL: The Conference is not prepared to push cricketers to play for their counties. They deny any knowledge of county cricket, in effect. This surely is of no benefit to the game. If there are cricketers of sufficient merit in their organisation, then surely they should do what they can to get them to play for England, never mind the county.

BENNETT: It seems to me that there has been some misunderstanding here because I am sure no member of the council, or anyone running the affairs of the C.C.C., would wish to do anything other than assist and help, in every way possible, a player who shows outstanding ability. But the Conference is a body formed to look after the affairs of clubs playing club cricket, and must devote its entire energies to furthering the causes of club cricket only. The counties can look after themselves, but at all times can call upon—and frequently do—any club cricketer to come forward for county trials, or even go straight into the county elevens.

GOODALL: The Conference itself admits its difficulty in excusing late starts, indefinite intervals, and so on. In fact, there is no excuse.

BENNETT: All I can add to that is that the Conference, long before I ever joined the Council, has always urged that clubs take no more than twenty minutes for tea and a minimum at lunch. It has made statements emphasising these points at Annual General Meetings, and in its handbooks. Yes, Peter, I thoroughly agree with you. In my opinion there is no possible excuse for these protracted intervals, and I am continually urging my own side, and my opponents, to keep to time.

GOODALL: The Conference claims that the Press prefers league cricket. As far as the Press itself is concerned, cricket is not all-important, and without doubt the papers would be full of interesting sports news in any case. It is said that the Conference considers club games receive inadequate publicity. I doubt the statement because in my experience of the clubs themselves—and I visit clubs throughout the summer (and in the winter, too) they nearly all maintain that they have no publicity at all. Why the Conference should think that newspapers want league cricket when there is plenty of interesting news and comment about the game as it is played now—but which seldom appears in the papers—is beyond me.

However, I am quite sure that should a newspaper decide to run a league of its own, it would attract at least twenty-five per cent of the best clubs playing to-day.

BENNETT: Obviously, the Press has been up against the paper shortage, and therefore far less publicity has been given to club cricket since the end of the Second World War than before it. My own cutting-book is proof of that. But I have in mind at the moment a news-letter by the clubs and for the clubs. This will give them greater publicity than they've ever had before—at least among themselves. Also, we are making another drive to interest the national Press in telling everybody more about us.

GOODALL: The Conference has many good reasons, it says, why competitive or professional cricket is neither necessary nor practicable in club cricket. First, it claims that in league cricket a club would not be able to choose its opponents. That hardly calls for comment. It is entirely up to the club.

Clubs might be barred, the Conference says, from competition because of their leaseholds. I cannot understand this, unless it means that admission fees would be barred by the terms of their lease.

The next claim is that the social side of league cricket is non-existent. That is also absurd. Consider how they get on in the North. And if you want a good time, go on tour and play Yorkshire clubs. Ten-to-one they play league cricket.

Now comes the question of 'veiled professionalism'. Without going into detail, I must agree that the Conference is right when it infers that such a state may exist in top amateur soccer. But has top amateur soccer suffered? Undoubtedly it is as good as, if not better than, pre-War, and in any case, there seems no need to assume forthwith that a similar situation—if such a one exists—would arise.

There is no doubt that I, as a supporter of some form of

competition, realise that this is the point where league cricket in the south is up against it. Establishment of league cricket inevitably means a complete—and I must repeat, absolutely complete—list of all players in the south of England. This, of course, would be a gigantic task, and nobody seems to be prepared to take it on. Even if a 'league committee' were formed, it could not afford at first to pay at least three people a reasonable full-time wage. Therefore formation of a competition must depend primarily and entirely on voluntary effort. This is, I'm afraid, not forthcoming —nor will be.

BENNETT: Yes—but before you go on, I must butt in and argue about one thing. To my mind the choosing of opponents is a most important factor in the argument against league, or competitive cricket—you have to play against other sides in the league, whether you want to or not.

The very nature of club cricket—especially in the south of England—is such that we have all grown up in the game knowing that we can play just who we like, where we like, and when we like, and this to my mind is one of the most attractive factors in the informal, friendly atmosphere of club cricket.

You say that you cannot understand how leaseholds on the grounds can possibly have any effect on clubs should they want to play competitive cricket. I am sure you will find that there are more clubs than you think that would be prevented by covenants from taking part in any kind of organised competition.

I hear you saying that in amateur football, not only is a charge for admission made, but collections are permitted. It must be remembered that this kind of football is played only on Saturdays. The answer may be, if competitive cricket is contemplated in the south, to play the league matches on Saturdays and stick to 'friendlies' on Sundays.

Another of your points concerns the social side. You say there is a friendly atmosphere in northern league cricket and that one has only to go on tour against the Yorkshire clubs to realise it.

My answer to that, having toured Westmorland, where nearly all play league cricket, is that when a southern club does venture up into their territory, the characteristic league atmosphere disappears and they regard the game as an ordinary friendly match, just as we know it in the south.

In any case, I can quote players with great experience of

league cricket who complain that the social side is non-existent. You say the reverse. I am sure that when points, cups, and money are involved, a much tenser, 'cut-throat' atmosphere prevails.

You more or less agree that professionalism, as such, would not be a good thing; I thus have no point to make, but I do want to stress that, in my own opinion, we must keep professionalism out of our Southern game.

The last point you make is also one on which you come over to my side. I, myself, cannot see how any organisation can be built up to run a league or leagues when apathy among secretaries, even now, is so rife.

GOODALL: The Conference says its clubs get umpires to officiate unpaid. This is admirable, when they can get somebody sufficiently competent. More often than not, however, the unpaid umpire is incompetent, and any club of standing that cannot pay ten or fifteen shillings a day for a good umpire should cease to play. Have a competent man—unpaid if possible—but surely the extra money must be made available if necessary. The game can be ruined by a 'quack'.

BENNETT: I agree with you, so far as 'clubs of standing' are concerned. You must not forget, though, that there is a very small percentage of 'clubs of standing' playing club cricket. There are thousands of village teams, and small country clubs, that rely entirely on voluntary assistance in every aspect of the game, including umpiring.

GOODALL: The job of league cricket is to improve the standard of the game as a whole. The thousands of clubs you talk of would be unlikely to be invited to join a league of the standing which I have in mind. After all, if their players are of sufficient competence they will migrate to one of those 'clubs of standing' you consider so few.

One last point. The support that the Conference officials give—when fighting against league cricket—to wandering clubs seems unjustified. As I consider that most wandering clubs already take all, and give little or nothing in return, further comment seems unnecessary.

BENNETT: Yet the wandering club does exist and, as far as I can see, will always exist, and there's no doubt whatever that they would be prevented from playing cricket at all if league cricket became universal.

.   .   .   .   .   .

Well, our argument ended there. But your opinions are as important as ours—so, I'll leave this colourful subject by asking a question. Think about it carefully, weigh up how it would affect you personally and your club particularly, and how it might affect your standard of play, then answer with a simple 'yes' or 'no'—is it to be *competitive cricket* or *ordinary club cricket* for you in the future?

Chapter Fifteen

THE CLUB CRICKET CONFERENCE

Function and organisation—Method of selection—Committee work—
Value of affiliation—Some C.C.C. matches and anecdotes.

THE Club Cricket Conference (C.C.C.) is not unique, but because it is the biggest of its kind—in membership, at least—I have chosen it as the best illustration of amateur cricket control.

It was founded in 1915, the second year of the First World War, which seems a peculiar time to begin a new cricketing organisation, but the War itself was directly responsible for what was then quite a new departure. Several of the leading London clubs thought that the formation of such a Conference essential to keep the clubs together, as the War had completely wrecked the general organisation of the game.

The purpose of convening the first meeting was to discover which clubs intended to remain active throughout the War. These could then arrange fixtures with each other. In other words, the initial idea was a sort of glorified fixture bureau.

At the first Annual General Meeting, on March 22, 1916, a very large number of well-known clubs already belonged to what was then called the London Club Cricket Conference. Established clubs like Alexandra Park, Malden Wanderers, Honor Oak, Ealing Dean, Parsons Green, North Middlesex, and many others of equal fame were represented. It seems membership of the Conference started at the top, and has since worked down.

Later on the Conference became known as the London and Southern Counties Club Cricket Conference. Sir Home Gordon, Bart., was the first president, and he appears to have taken the chair at all meetings during the First World War.

Since those days the renamed Club Cricket Conference has developed out of all recognition. The original rules remain basically unchanged. Additions and amendments have been made only to keep pace with modern conditions. Councillors and officials, too, have tended to remain in office for many years, even after their playing days are over.

Since the Second World War, however, younger men, who still play, have been elected: Eddie Ingram (Middlesex and Ealing); Ken Poulter (Sidcup); Con Davies (Middlesex and Alexandra Park); Ronnie Bryan (the former Kent skipper, Lloyds Bank and Beckenham); and I myself have had the honour to be nominated as one of Surrey's seven representatives. Mightily astonished I was to find, when I attended my first meeting, that I was one of sixty!

Member clubs are always asking what they get for their affiliation fee. Here's the answer. It enables the C.C.C. to maintain a cricket association to assist affiliated clubs in matters of general policy; foster amateur cricket on non-competitive lines; establish and maintain an emergency fixture bureau; maintain a register of approved umpires; collaborate and co-operate with kindred associations and local authorities in the preservation of private cricket and sports grounds; foster the provision of additional grounds and the reduction of rating assessments on private grounds; produce a handbook each year, which contains details of its member clubs, and to run 'trial' and representative matches.

Douglass Bruce, the C.C.C. treasurer since 1946, sums it up this way: 'The Conference exists to make life easier for more than 1,800 clubs.'

The Conference itself is governed by an Executive Council, consisting of: the president; the vice-president; the life vice-presidents; active vice-presidents (not exceeding ten in number); the chairman; the deputy chairman, and the honorary treasurer.

Then there are representative councillors from the various counties, a permanent secretary and, when considered necessary, representatives from other cricket associations.

The Council delegates much of its work to eight sub-committees: (1) Emergency; (2) General Purposes; (3) Finance; (4) Selection and Match; (5) Umpires; (6) Emergency Fixture Bureau; (7) Preservation of Sports Grounds and Rating; (8) Publicity.

Of these sub-committees, the week-end cricketer is more interested in the last five. So let's take a closer look at them.

Selection and Match: This has a chairman and twelve members, and the power to co-opt the selected C.C.C. skipper for the season if thought desirable. Obviously this Committee must meet more often during the summer months, when Conference trial-match teams and representative XIs are selected. But there is a considerable amount of work in the close season as well.

You all know the importance to your club of your selection committee. An efficient and well-run committee can make all the difference between a club's having a good or a bad season. It can help materially in raising morale in all the XIs.

And so it is with the C.C.C.'s Selection and Match Committee. The prestige and good name of the C.C.C. can be greatly affected by the manner in which its members do their work. I'm sure not many people realise just how exacting this work can be. Primarily, this Committee depends on every club affiliated to the Conference for information about the standard of its players, and for recommendations for higher honours.

You, through your own club committee, *must* keep the C.C.C. well briefed about your players. During the short time I have attended Selection and Match Committee meetings, I have been amazed at the number of smaller clubs that continually draw our attention to some outstanding performance by their members—and at the fact that the bigger and better-known clubs just don't seem to bother. They seem to expect the Committee to know all about every player playing club cricket. That is, of course, absolutely impossible.

I am continually on the look-out for promising material among the clubs, but councillors can cover no more than a few of the grounds and clubs between May and September. It is up to your club to see that the Committee does hear about the performances of players worthy of a place in trial or representative matches. My own club, incidentally, has been just as guilty!

Information received, together with what we already know about certain players and their ability, is sifted out in such a way that early in the season we are in a position to select players for the trial matches.

We are continually being asked for more trial matches, but if we did arrange more, they would have to be held mid-week—an inconvenient time for most players. The only alternative is Saturday, an obviously unpopular day from any club's point of view. They want their best men themselves, then.

From these trial matches we judge whether a player should be encouraged, held back for another year, or dropped out of our list of 'possibles'. And we judge not so much by the figures he returns at the end of the game, but by the way he has set about his job, the keenness he has shown, and whether he *looks* a cricketer.

Then come the representative matches. For the past few years, games have been played against the M.C.C.—sometimes twice a season—the Royal Navy, the Universities Athletic Union—selected from universities all over the country, but excluding Oxford and Cambridge—and the touring sides.

The notable exception to the last mentioned is that we have not played the Australians since World War II. They consider they have a tough enough tour as it is and now never include the minor counties or the C.C.C. in their fixture list. It is a pity they don't complete the cycle, especially in view of the interesting and anything but one-sided games we have played against the South Africans, the New Zealanders, the Indians, and the West Indies.

Selecting a representative C.C.C. XI is a mammoth job. Certainly we come in for criticism. That's good. We must have criticism—but for goodness' sake let it be constructive and helpful. Time and time again, we have been blown up by the Press, or by a club, for leaving out a certain player. Later, it is found that the man in question is either too old, doesn't belong to a club affiliated to the C.C.C., or is not in the top-flight of club cricket.

A good example of this occurred in 1949 before one of the representative matches. We were badgered from all sides to include a certain bowler from an out-of-London club. We did, but in the end discovered that, while one of the most delightful people one could wish to meet, he was, in his own words, an 'old gentleman'.

Most informed critics consider that on the whole the Selection and Match Committee does a good job. It could do better if every club made sure that the C.C.C. gets up-to-the-minute information about players worth a trial.

Umpires Committee: The C.C.C. keeps a register of approved umpires, which is at the disposal of any affiliated club, and has as its underlying object the maintenance of a high standard of club umpiring.

Any umpire can apply for registration. The C.C.C. secretary supplies the necessary form. If found satisfactory, he is placed on the register, and is entitled to wear—indeed, *must* wear—the official badge. From the reports submitted by clubs to the Conference, an attempt is made to assess each umpire's capabilities.

While this Committee constantly strives to raise the standard, to my mind club umpiring will never improve unless something is done to help prospective umpires. Among the umpires in top-flight club cricket, I have found the standard to be high—indeed, on occasion, higher than in county cricket.

We badly need a supply of younger men to stand at each end, but we must ensure that they stand there only after they have had instruction. Otherwise we shall never have an improved standard of umpiring in club cricket. Regular 'refresher' courses would need to be organised to keep them at concert-pitch.

My point here, of course, is not that young umpires are best, but that, like most forms of skilled effort, the umpire reaches a higher standard if he starts at a not-too-advanced age. So we find the successors to the veterans who set the standard for us to-day. Some of them—men under whose eyes it's a privilege to play—are well past sixty years of age.

Emergency Fixture Bureau: The Bureau was instituted to assist affiliated clubs to arrange substitute games when, for any reason, the planned fixture is cancelled.

Clubs without games on any particular day can ring up the C.C.C offices and ask for the names and addresses of clubs also without fixtures on that date. Six fixture applications will be dealt with during any one season free of charge. After that a special booking fee of 2s. is charged for each additional fixture arranged by the Bureau on the basis of 'No play—No pay'. It normally operates, by the way, from May 1 until the end of September.

During 1948, 3,691 last-minute applications were received by the Emergency Fixture Bureau, of which 1,928, or 52 per cent. were satisfied. A year later the figure had gone up to 4,301, of which 2,058 were accommodated (although it produced 4 per cent. fewer satisfied customers, in bulk the achievement was greater).

In addition to this service, the C.C.C. arranges two fixture meetings a year, of which several hundred clubs take advantage. At these autumn and early spring meetings, clubs display vacant dates on blackboards, and their representatives go round finding out what other clubs have coincident blank dates. Thus, in a short time, they can complete their fixture lists.

This drill is not quite as simple as might appear—at least not for the 'big-name' clubs. They, too, have their fixture difficulties at times, although not to the extent of the lesser-known clubs.

Often, however, a secretary finds himself with, say, two vacant dates. Now, if he attended one of the fixture meetings and offered his two dates for auction, as it were, he would be overwhelmed by lesser clubs, who complain long and bitterly that they find it impossible to join the band of—shall we say?—the 'select'.

What, then, is the embarrassed secretary of the A1 club to do? He cannot refuse everybody. He must agree to play what he considers the best of the fixtures offered. But imagine the consternation of his committee when he returns and says, 'I've fixed up for C3 on August 20 and B2 on September 7'!

The answer, of course, is that the 'A1' secretaries do not appear at the fixture meetings. In general, they prefer to take the chance of arranging their two vacant dates by sending letters on the offchance to clubs that they know will be 'acceptable'.

But that does not stop these meetings from being quite invaluable to the lesser lights. In fact, many rely on them to complete about half their fixtures.

Preservation of Sports Grounds and Rating: Since the end of World War II, a large number of clubs have been worried about their grounds from three points of view: (*a*) existing tenancies; (*b*) requisitioning; (*c*) the effects of the Town and Country Planning Act, 1947.

I asked Wilfred Waters, chairman of this Committee, to tell me something about its good work in helping clubs about these three problems. In the first place, he explained that any successes achieved were really a record of the great work carried out by H. G. Dorman, who was one of the members elected to the Executive Council at the first Annual General Meeting in 1916.

The Preservation of Sports Grounds and Rating Committee was formed in 1942 under the chairmanship of Dorman, who remained in that capacity until 1948.

As far back as 1919, a special advisory committee was formed. Deputations were sent to the Ministry of Health and the London County Council, and in 1922, clauses, which were incorporated in the Open Spaces Bill, were embodied in the Public Health Act of 1925. The Open Spaces Committee and the C.C.C. assisted wholeheartedly in the formation of the National Playing Fields Association in 1925, and there has been a very close link with the national body and with the London and Greater London P.F.A. The C.C.C. has had representation on the N.P.F.A. committees and the sub-committees, at the present moment through Wilfred Waters. This co-operation has resulted in the saving of many grounds.

In 1929, there was considerable agitation against the crippling rating assessments of sports grounds and the C.C.C. had much to do with the Playing Fields (Exemption from Rating) Bill (before Parliament in 1930). Unfortunately, this was rejected, but some relief was obtained by the recommendations of the Central Valuation Committee, which prepared a statement for the guidance of the rating and valuation authorities. Then in 1948 came the Local Government Act, which also appears to be having an adverse effect of the rating of these grounds.

Since World War II, the C.C.C., through the P. of S.G. and R.C., submitted a considered statement of evidence to the New Towns Committee, under the chairmanship of Lord Reith, and has also issued an explanatory memorandum on the Town and Country Planning Act, 1947, to all member clubs to assist them in safeguarding the position of their grounds. Many proposals for compulsory purchase by local authorities and education authorities have been opposed and evidence given at public enquiries. In such cases, it has been customary to work in conjunction with the National Playing Fields Association or the Greater London Playing Fields Association.

The results have been good. As examples: the spacious, fifty-acre Wembley ground has been saved by the efforts of the P. of S.G. and R.C.; with the assistance of the Greater London Playing Fields Association, the threatened loss of the Walthamstow Cricket Club's ground was averted.

Publicity : It is felt by the Conference that insufficient publicity is being given, not only in the Press, but to all affiliated clubs about its work, and particularly about the results of 'trial' and representative matches. In March, 1950, this committee—the old Publicity and Propaganda Committee having gone out of existence—was formed to remedy this state of affairs.

These Sub-Committees break the back of the Council's work, and from personal experience I can say that their efforts have put clubs in a very much better position than they would otherwise be.

I have tried to tell you briefly how the C.C.C. works on your behalf. The *C.C.C. Annual Handbook*, brought out at the beginning of each season and sent to each club secretary, tells you much more. It also includes, like all such publications, a survey of club cricket, on and off the field, during the previous season, the laws of cricket, and details of all Conference members.

More publicity about the activities of the Conference might well widen its sphere of influence. More publicity and propaganda is essential. I shall not feel happy until club-cricket publicity compares favourably with that given to amateur soccer and rugby. The only periodical with collated club cricket notes is *The Cricketer*, but pressed for space as it is, it offers, in my opinion, little of specific interest to the club cricketer. I think the time has been reached when the C.C.C. should publish regularly its own magazine or news-letter.

As I said at the outset of this chapter, the Club Cricket Conference is not the only body of its kind in the country.

The father of all amateur club cricket associations is the National Club Cricket Association, formed in 1946. This body handles all matters of national importance.

Several other conferences and associations exist to look after the clubs in their respective areas. A typical example of these organisations is the Midland Club Cricket Conference, founded by W. Leslie Jones of King's Heath, Birmingham, in 1947. Many well-known clubs belong to this Conference; they come mainly from the counties of Warwickshire, Worcestershire, and Stafford-shire. In addition, it has outposts in the counties of Gloucester-shire, Shropshire, Leicestershire, Northamptonshire, Hereford-shire, and Bedfordshire. More than 200 clubs, including public schools and grammar schools, are members. The organisation seeks to improve the liaison between schools and clubs and between the latter and the county clubs, who are giving their strong and enthusiastic support.

To encourage the juniors, these Conference clubs meet Conference XIs composed of players under eighteen, and are captained by such county players as Tom Dollery (England and Warwickshire skipper), or E. J. ('Tiger') Smith (England and Warwickshire 'keeper), who is now coach at Edgbaston. 'Tiger' Smith, incidentally, is one of the most active men in Midland cricket. For many years he has been President of the Midland Counties Umpires' Association, which provides umpires for league and friendly matches. Warwickshire discovered him as a youth of eighteen when he was playing for Bournville.

The Midland Conference, like its southern brother, has set up a fixture bureau, distributes cricket films, and arranges lectures for groundsmen and umpires. It also publishes a Yearbook, which includes a secretarial directory.

Many of the Midland Conference clubs have provided county players. Harborne, for instance, has the distinction of having provided three out of the last four Warwickshire captains.

Other organisations include the Manchester and District Cricket Association, and the Devon Club Cricket Association.

C.C.C. Representative Matches

I do not intend to set out here details and scores of the C.C.C. Representative XIs in their matches of recent years, as they can be seen any time in the *C.C.C. Handbook* for the particular year. There are, however, some interesting facts about some of these games that do not appear in the *Handbooks*.

Against the Royal Navy

In 1947 and 1948, we had the beating of the Navy sides, but could not quite press home our advantage. I consider it to be almost impossible to obtain a decision in a two-day match when the sides are evenly matched. In the '47 game at Portsmouth we had our chance when we dismissed the Navy in their first innings for 146, in reply to our 326 for 6 wickets declared. John Dewes (England and Middlesex), then a sub-lieutenant, opened, but was back in the pavilion with only one run to his name. Lieut-Commander Geoffrey Vavasour, one of the grandest sportsmen you could ever wish to meet, was out to a splendid catch by Jack Seward (Malden Wanderers) for 10, and the other Navy batsmen couldn't do much against Fred Smith, Sam Buss, and Henry Malcolm.

Then came misfortune in the form of a pulled thigh muscle for Peter Westerman (Hounslow fast bowler) and a strained Achilles tendon for Smith. With my two opening bowlers mere passengers, the Navy batsmen dug themselves in—John Dewes in particular with his 104 not out—and managed to score 225 for 6 wickets. Had our bowlers remained sound, we might have won.

The following year, at Whale Island, we played another draw. We shot the Navy out for 219, and then scored 307 for 9 wickets declared. The wicket was beginning to take spin in the

R

Navy's second innings. I persevered with Keith Walker (leg-spinners), Sam Buss (left-arm spinners), and Henry Malcolm (slow right-arm spinners). Lieutenant T. Weston, who scored a painfully slow 78 in the first innings, came to the Navy's rescue again in the second innings with a somewhat drawn-out 33. With Vavasour showing a welcome return to form (from the Navy's point of view) with an attractive 40, and Captain R. A. Akam, last in, getting 25, we couldn't quite get them out, although with 10 wickets down (12 aside), the Navy was only 80 runs in front.

The feature of this particular match was the Navy's hospitality, beginning with a cocktail party for the American Navy, which had just arrived at Portsmouth, and ending with a trip over some of the ships in the Reserve Fleet. Later, there were some high jinks in the Mess with our old friend 'Cardinal Puff', at which some of the C.C.C. players failed, until the beer gave out, and Epsom salts were substituted. Even later, ink writing appeared mysteriously on the Mess ceiling, but these were obliterated by breakfast-time next day!

Then came our great triumph against the Navy at Hastings in 1949, when we acted as hosts. Under the headlines, 'If Only Test Cricket Could be Played Like This', Peter Goodall, in the *Evening Standard*, had this to say, 'Here's an example to our Test players. The C.C.C. team, playing their two-day match against the Royal Navy, needed 158 to win in under $1\frac{1}{2}$ hours, yet won with 17 minutes to spare. It was a magnificent game, and one which I wouldn't have missed for the world.'

We mustered only 198 in our first innings, but Geoff Smith and Keith Walker drove the first nails well and truly into the Navy coffin. Together—Smith bowling at great pace, and with consistent accuracy, and Walker with his devastatingly fast leg-spinners—they put the R.N. back in the pavilion for a mere 75 runs.

In spite of the fact that the wicket was showing signs of wear, we enforced the follow-on. This time, Writer P. G. H. May, of whom we shall hear a lot more in the future, and Lieut.-Commander J. E. Manners (Hampshire), took the bowling by the scruff of the neck and for a time were complete masters. Keith Walker then got May l.b.w. for 85 and, as so often happens after a big stand, Manners followed soon afterwards for an excellent 79. Henry Malcolm then took the last three Navy wickets for 9 runs.

The rest you know. We were given a quick start, but at

33 both Salmon and Allan Rae (West Indies) were back in the pavilion. I was lucky, and grandly supported by Gordon West, truly a 'find', with 48 well-earned runs, we managed to knock off the runs for the first victory over the Royal Navy since the War. Unfortunately, the 1950 match at Plymouth was ruined by rain.

Against the Touring XIs

In 1947 we had a phenomenal match against the South Africans. It was a draw, and you may remember the high scoring. Never have I played in a match when by lunch-time the board read 311 for 1—as it did that September 6 at Guildford! Tony Harris was mainly responsible, and I don't suppose any of the spectators, or players, have ever seen before, nor are they likely to see again, such terrific hitting. The ball went off the Harris bat like a bomb. He bombarded the off-side so much that I continually had to change fielders over to the other side of the wicket to prevent their hands (and legs!) from being too bruised.

The C.C.C. replied grandly to the tourists' 402 for 1 wicket declared, with 313 for 4 wickets, of which Peter Wreford batted conscientiously and soundly for 50, and I was able to get 156.

But I still have nightmares in which Tony Harris appears with a huge club, smiting red-hot cricket balls at me from point-blank range!

Then, in 1949, the New Zealanders arrived. And a grander bunch of cricketers you will never find. We played them at Guildford on August 31. You may remember that Oxford alone had pulled down the N.Z. flag—on a wet wicket earlier in the season. At Guildford we had a perfect wicket to play on. The C.C.C. reached 217 for 6 wickets before the declaration. Before that, we witnessed a grand century by Henry Malcolm. His not-out effort was first class in every way. The New Zealanders opened their batting with F. B. Smith and C. C. Burke. George Pullinger (Essex) and Geoff Smith bowled with such hostility that both Burke and Smith were back in the pavilion for 8 apiece, and Cresswell, who followed, for 1. Then came a short stand by Martin Donnelly and Cave, before Pullinger bowled Donnelly 'all over the shop'. John Reid was tricked by Keith Walker for 11, Wally Hadlee failed to open his account, and Bert Sutcliffe was l.b.w. to Geoff Smith.

With 7 wickets down for just under 100, the tourists were

really in trouble, but Cave and Mervyn Wallace pulled them
clear of the threatened disaster and were still together when rain
put an end, five minutes before time, to one of the most exciting
matches I have ever played in.

On that showing, the C.C.C. side were worthy of all the very
pleasant things said about them in the Press and elsewhere.

In 1950, we had a most interesting game against the West
Indies at Kingston. It was one of the coldest days I can remember.
The result was a draw, but in the tourists' favour.

Against the M.C.C.

Between the years 1947 and 1950 in matches against the
M.C.C., the C.C.C. has won one, lost two, and drawn three. I can
think of only one incident worth repeating out of these six games.
It concerns the match played at Kenley on June 25, 1947. You
will remember that, in Chapter Nine, I told you how I had a
puncture on the way to this match and, as a result, arrived on the
ground only five minutes before play was due to start.

On driving into the ground, the first person I saw on the
pavilion steps in the distance was Frank Whitehead, the M.C.C.
skipper. Even from the other side of the ground he didn't look
happy. I shot out of the car, with Ken Ablack (BBC) who was
also playing, and quickly made my way towards the wicket
where I was joined by Frank, whose first words were, 'You're jolly
late.' (Or something to that effect!) 'Let's toss at once.' I dropped
my bag and spun the coin. Frank called correctly and decided to
bat. Hurriedly I changed and we were out in the field only a few
minutes after 11.30 a.m.

On the way to the wicket I was convinced we must do well
and trounce this M.C.C. side after having put up such a 'black'
by arriving so late. Never did I dream that things would go the
way they did. Jack Leiper (Woodford Wells) struck two shrewd
blows by dismissing W. H. ('Tag') Webster (Middlesex) and
Harry Sharp (Middlesex) in the first over. Neither of them had
scored. The M.C.C. never recovered from that shock and were
all out for a mere 81 long before lunch. Jack Dennis (Epping)
and Peter Wreford (Brondesbury) opened quietly and were both
not out at lunch-time with a few useful runs on the board.

Afterwards, they went majestically on until Jack Dennis was
dismissed for a well-played 54. R. E. Evans (Ilford) then joined
Wreford, and together they passed the M.C.C. total. Soon

afterwards, Wreford was out for 41, and I joined Evans. Evans got an attractive 54, Jack Meill (Mitcham) notched up 20 not out, and I managed to indulge in some big hitting at the expense of young Norman Hever (who later went to Glamorgan, and has done well as a fast bowler). Eventually, I declared at 292 for 3 wickets, and put the M.C.C. in again! This time they put on 73 for 2 wickets, but we had already scored a great victory—it was, of course, a single-innings match.

The only other annual matches the representative C.C.C. XI has played since the War have been against the Universities' Athletic Union—in 1947 and 1948 we won; in 1949 and 1950 the games resulted in a draw. We played the Manchester and District Cricket Association in 1947 and 1948, winning by three wickets in 1947 at Urmston, but the following year at Guildford the game was left drawn after rain had seriously interfered with play. Both these games against Manchester were thoroughly enjoyed and were played in a keen and sporting manner—I sincerely hope the fixtures will soon be renewed.

Chapter Sixteen

CRICKET IN THE COMMONWEALTH

Club cricket in Australia, India and Ceylon, New Zealand, South Africa, and the West Indies.

WHAT I want to do here is to show the difference in methods and organisation between Britain and the cricketing countries of the Commonwealth, and to explain why their attitude to the sport often varies quite considerably.

The organisation of the game in Australia follows similar lines in each of the States. Victoria, which, with its 2,030,000 people, is the State with the second largest population, gives us a typical example.

Junior cricket there is controlled by the Victorian Junior Cricket Union (V.J.C.U.), a federation comprising 38 associations with a total of 1,123 clubs and about 16,000 regular players.

Usually, an association consists of a number of clubs in one suburb. For instance, 38 teams compete in the Footscray District Association and 33 in that of the Coburg District. Then there are Church Associations: 45 teams compete in the C.Y.M.S. and 50 in the Eastern Suburbs Churches Association. Each have several grades. There are also industrial associations like the Footscray Industrial (18 clubs), and the Mercantile Association (30).

Most of Australia's best players have graduated from the junior ranks. Of the 1948 Australian Test team to tour this country, Miller, Ring, and Ian Johnson are all products of the V.J.C.U.; their first cricket caps were those they won by representing Victoria in the inter-State schoolboy championships (for boys from the State primary schools).

Australia's junior cricketers, unlike the English, have an abundance of playing-grounds. As suburban settlements spread from the cities, large areas are reserved for parks, gardens, and sports grounds. In some suburbs, twenty games of cricket can be played on a single wide stretch of open land, with paths and flags to mark the boundaries.

Junior cricket is played on matting wickets laid on pitches of concrete or prepared mud. Play can be resumed on these pitches after heavy rain which would cause the game to be abandoned on a turf wicket. The matting pitches favour the batsman after rain, though in normal conditions bowlers can get plenty of spin from them. The pace from matting is almost the same as from a medium turf pitch.

From junior cricket the most promising youngsters graduate to the grade or district competition, which is the real nerve-centre of Australian cricket.

Except when a touring side is visiting the country, Australia's Hassetts and Millers play only about six first-class matches in a season; their regular Saturday-afternoon games are played for their grade or district club—Carlton, South Melbourne, or whatever suburb they happen to live in.

Each district club fields five teams, the fourths and fifths having mainly boys in their teens. Players in all grades practice at the nets on two or three evenings a week, the youngsters receiving coaching from the club captain and coach, besides benefiting from association with senior players. Most important, they acquire the confidence that comes only from regular competitive matches.

Sometimes their rise is rapid. Ponsford began playing first-grade district cricket at fourteen years of age and Miller at fifteen. In 1939, Bill Johnston, a seventeen-year-old country lad, came to live in Melbourne and asked the Richmond selectors for a trial as a left-hand bowler. They put him in the thirds, promoted him to the seconds half-way through the season, then gave him a game with the first in the last match of his first season with the club.

His rise was unusually rapid. Usually, even exceptional youngsters are not rushed from lower to higher grades until experience has developed the confidence which will enable them to do themselves justice in senior company. The three brilliant brothers, Neil, Mervyn, and Ray Harvey—the first two internationals and the third an Inter-State batsman—each began grade cricket with the Fitzroy fifth XI when aged about fourteen. Each took three or four years to reach the first XI.

District officials are always on the look-out for talent, but there is no short cut to their favour. The captain of Melbourne Grammar or Scotch XI (the equivalent of England's public schools) is certain to receive an invitation to play with his district team. But so is the labourer's son who gets the hat-trick in the final of the State schools championship.

Organisation is much the same, though on a smaller scale, in country districts. In Victoria's larger towns, such as Ballarat and Geelong (Hassett's birthplace), there are senior and junior competitions in various grades.

There is not much 'village green' cricket in Australia. Even a tiny village doesn't content itself with a friendly game every year or so. It meets its nearest neighbours in the third round of the North-North-West Victoria Association, with two points for a win in the first innings, two qualified umpires, and a premier-ship flag, just as in the major competitions.

Eighty-five country associations are affiliated to the Victorian Country Cricket League, each representing from ten to thirty clubs. The big chance for country cricketers to reach the top is the annual 'Country Cricket Week', when some 600 country cricketers invade the capital to play knock-out competitions in four graded sections.

Another important match for country youngsters is that of the City Colts *v.* the Country Colts. Bradman, McCabe, and O'Reilly are three of many stars who have attracted attention in 'Country Cricket Week'.

Of course, organisation is not the only factor that enables Australia, with a population of 8,000,000, to compete successfully year after year with England and her 50,000,000. Behind the organisation are the gum-tree wickets in every paddock and the strips of concrete in every school playground. There is the sun-shine and the healthy outdoor living that the sunshine makes possible. There is the intense public interest, which impels as many as 88,000 people in a city of just over a million to attend a day's play in a Test match on the Melbourne Cricket Ground. Above all, there is the Australian character—the character that in 1882 enabled Australia to beat England at the Oval during their first visit to England. And that was only twenty years after the first English professional had stayed in Australia to teach the rough colonials the finer points of the game!

.   .   .   .   .

The Nawab of Pataudi once said that potentially Indians are the finest cricketers in the world. They have all the natural advantages; they are supple and agile; their eyesight is extremely keen; their climate enables them to play all the year round. But, for all that, cricketers in India are less fortunate than those in Australia; there is not the same intensive organisation, nor the same facilities for coaching and talent-spotting.

India, because of her vast area and far-flung cricket centres, has no uniform standard in club cricket. The first organised clubs, few in number, were mostly Parsee clubs, which came into existence almost a century ago in Bombay, the Parsee having been the first among Indians to take up cricket—as could be gauged from their ambitious projects to send teams to England for educational purposes as far back as 1886 and 1888.

But it was the European Calcutta Cricket Club—the second oldest cricket club in the world—that had the honour of first functioning as a club. That was as early as the 18th century. Civilian in character, it played cricket mostly against the Services people, who, incidentally, were the first to introduce cricket to India.

Enthusiasm for cricket spread rapidly, and towards the close of the 19th century, many clubs, from Bombay to Calcutta, from Peshawar, Rawalpindi, Lahore, and Delhi in the north, to Madras and Mysore in the south, came into being.

Club cricket is almost entirely amateur. In Bombay, the home of Indian cricket, the better clubs, mostly 'communal' in nature, often play a high standard of cricket, but Bombay suffers from a lack of first-class grounds. It is there that the Cricket Club of India, with its huge membership, plays on the magnificent Brabourne Stadium ground adjoining the club-house. But the Cricket Club of India (of comparatively recent origin, despite its all-pervasive title) is, for the purposes of cricket, only a local institution. Club cricket in Bombay was dominated in the past by the European Bombay Gymkhana, the Hindu Gymkhana, the Islam Gymkhana, and the Parsee Gymkhana, which, to-day, in spite of retaining their names, are non-communal.

Bombay sees some competitive cricket as well, run on a league system, in which many Test cricketers take part, among them now V. M. Merchant and D. G. Phadkar (who was sent to England in 1949 for special coaching). The standard in general is fair.

In Calcutta, there are some 100 clubs, and the number of good club grounds far exceeds that in any other Indian city. There is little competitive cricket in Calcutta, but the standard is fair and the atmosphere for club cricket the finest in India.

Madras, also, has a fair number of clubs that play on the league system. As in Bombay, the best players, including Test cricketers, figure in the club cricket of both Madras and Calcutta.

But the finest feature about club cricket in India is the friendliness that prevails in the scores of towns, big and small, that have now almost accepted cricket as the national game.

The Ranji Trophy matches are the highlights of Indian cricket, and are keenly followed all over the country. In the 1948–49 season, for instance, B. B. Nimbalkar's record-breaking innings of 443 not out for Maharashtra, against Kathiawar, was undoubtedly the peak of the season. He nearly beat Don Bradman's record of 452 not out, but Kathiawar conceded the match before he could do so.

In the same season the Board of Control experimented with the 'open' draw, as against a form of 'seeding', for the Ranji Trophy Championship. It proved attractive, since almost every competing team faced a new opponent, and the spectators at each centre had the benefit of watching new players.

Such clubs as Bombay (who won the trophy for the fifth time in 1948–49), Madras, Maharashtra, Baroda, Hyderabad, Holkar (holders, 1947–48), Bihar, Berar, Mysore, Kathiawar, and the United Provinces participate in this trophy. Maharashtra, incidentally, were champions in 1939 and 1940.

Apart from these Ranji Trophy matches, which are played for the Cricket Championship of India, there are zonal matches when clubs from each zone play one another. There is also an Inter-University Tournament, from which come many of the best-known Indian Test players and the All-India Schools Tournament. The zonal tournament is run by the Cricket Club of India as 'trials' for the selection of players for the Tests. In 1948–49, the contest was a triangular one, the South and the North having combined to form one team. The winners that particular year were West Zone.

.   .   .   .   .

'Get out now, let us see another man!' That is the cry that one hears after reaching a century in Ceylon, and this typifies their approach to the game. To the Ceylonese, cricket is, above all things, a sport. It provides him with entertainment, so that when a man has scored a century he must let the next fellow in to have his go.

Don't be fooled, however, by this light-hearted gaiety. Cricket is a game of skill to them. They take it seriously, and they expect the outsider to take his cricket seriously, too. When one remembers that, in 1934, F. C. de Saram, playing for Oxford, made 128 out of a total score of 216 (no other batsman made 20) against an Australian team that included Grimmett and O'Reilly, one is forced to take them seriously. That was the fastest century of the season, and over 100 of the runs were made in boundaries.

In Ceylon, the youngster begins his cricket at school, and eventually plays club cricket on one of the beautiful grounds mainly in and around Colombo. Some cricket is played in the 'out' areas—notably at Kandy and Galle—but most of Ceylon's club cricket is played in Colombo on Saturday and Sunday afternoons. There, the leading clubs are the Sinhalese Sports Club and the Tamil Club. One's memory conjures up names like Jayawickereme, Gunasekara, Coomaraswamy, when one thinks of this tiny island.

In the international arena, Ceylon, as yet, has not quite caught up with the other cricketing countries of the Commonwealth. But it has put up good performances against visiting sides. Situated as it is on the direct sea route between England and Australia, it sees all English and Australian sides, for each of these breaks its voyage to play in Colombo. In addition, Indian sides visit Ceylon periodically. Since the War it seems to have become the practice for whatever team is visiting India and Pakistan to spend two weeks in Ceylon.

. . . . .

In New Zealand cricket is the main summer sport. Its history is almost as long as that of the British colonisation of the country. The first settlers brought the game with them, and within a few years of the founding of the main settlements cricket was well entrenched.

The first games were played at the Bay of Islands about 1833— seven years before New Zealand became a Colony. The first fully-recorded match was played at Nelson in 1844, but two years previously the sport was already established in the young settlements of Wellington and Auckland.

Otago's first game was played on New Year's Day, 1849, with bats of New Zealand wood and balls made by the local shoemaker. Canterbury's first club was the Christchurch club, formed in 1851, within six months of the founding of the province.

The first inter-provincial match, Auckland *versus* Wellington, was played at Wellington in 1860, and the first international fixtures in New Zealand were played by Parr's All-England XI against Southland, Canterbury, and Otago in 1863–64. This tour was followed by Lillywhite's All-England XI in 1876–77. The Australians visited New Zealand in the following year, but it was not until 1894 that a 'Test' was played in New Zealand *versus* New South Wales.

Four years later New Zealand sent its first representative cricket team abroad, playing New South Wales, Victoria, and North and South Tasmania. The first Tests against an English team were with an XI sent by Lord Hawke, the Yorkshire captain, in 1902–03, both being won by the visitors. The first tour by an M.C.C. team followed in 1906–07. After World War I, New Zealand saw a succession of visiting cricketers from England, Australia, and South Africa.

The greatest single development in the game was New Zealand's promotion to international standing; this followed the first visit of a New Zealand team to England in 1927. In 1931 the M.C.C. granted the New Zealanders one Test, and subsequently three Tests. Three Tests were played in the 1937 English tour. The fine showing of the New Zealanders in their 1949 tour, and the fact that they held England to a draw in each of the four three-day Tests, is likely to result in four-day Tests being played in future.

Cricket, like other sports in New Zealand, is organised and democratically controlled on a national basis. With the rapid growth of the game, the need for a central body to co-ordinate the activities of provincial and district associations, and to control international tours and select New Zealand teams, became apparent before the turn of the century.

After the first Test—New Zealand *versus* New South Wales in 1894—the New Zealand Cricket Council was formed, with head-quarters at Christchurch. To-day, twenty-five provincial and district associations affiliated to the Council have a voice in framing its policy, which is carried out by a management committee elected each year.

In New Zealand inter-provincial cricket, which may be

likened to the English county competition, the premier trophy is the Plunket Shield, presented in 1906 for competition among the four major associations—Auckland, Wellington, Canterbury, and Otago. The shield was the gift of Lord Plunket, then Governor-General of New Zealand. The contest is on a competition basis, with six matches each season, each of the four associations playing the other three. The contest has now been extended to give the four main associations the right to select players from minor associations within their districts, but without disqualifying such players from taking part in Hawke Cup matches. (The Hawke Cup, presented by Lord Hawke in 1910–11, is a challenge trophy competed for by the minor associations.) The Redpath Cup and the Winsor Cup are awarded annually to the leading batsman and bowler respectively in Plunket Shield matches.

In addition to the matches for these trophies, the North Island *versus* South Island game is generally the main fixture of the season.

The fact that cricket is a game which lends itself to play by men well into their forties, and even fifties, has led to the growth of several smaller district organisations such as the Mercantile Cricket League in the Wellington area, which controls teams drawn from the staffs of business and industrial concerns, from State Departments, or the Christchurch and Auckland Suburban Cricket Associations, all playing 'village green' rather than 'Test' cricket.

Cricket is the main organised summer sport for schoolboys, and it is in the primary and secondary schools that they are made cricket-minded.

Cricket in New Zealand is cheap. In most cases, grounds are owned by local authorities, which charge low rentals, and a common method of meeting this charge is for each player to contribute 1s. to 1s. 6d. a game, in which event his club subscription is proportionately lower. But club subscriptions are kept reasonably low anyway: the overall cost to each player each season is only about £1 10s. for juniors and up to £3 for seniors. Club funds are used mainly to meet the cost of equipment.

New Zealand's two major sports, rugby in winter and cricket in summer, require similar grounds. In most towns the same facilities are available for both, and good stand accommodation is generally available for big-cricket fixtures. Among New

Zealand's best-known grounds are: Eden Park, Auckland; the Basin Reserve, Wellington; Lancaster Park and Hagley Park, Christchurch, and Carisbrook and the Caledonian ground at Dunedin.

.   .   .   .   .

My friend and colleague, John Arlott, was out in South Africa with the M.C.C. touring side in 1948–49. This is what he has to say about club cricket over there:

My first experience of cricket in South Africa was at a club match—in which five provincial and three Test players were engaged! Their club cricket is the most impressive of my experience, because, although it is highly competitive—they have, in Johannesburg and Durban, Saturday and Sunday Leagues—it is also highly social.

In all the big provincial centres—Johannesburg, Port Elizabeth, Durban, Cape Town, East London, Bloemfontein —there are well-organised leagues that include all the best cricketers in the district; in fact *all* the provincial players are also, and mainly, club players. The strongest leagues are those in Johannesburg and Durban, where the standard of play is much higher than, for instance, in English club cricket.

Cricket circles are the centre of summer-time social life and are, in most cases, sections of the huge clubs which are a feature of South African life. There is a strong loyalty to the clubs, which have aspects we in England do not normally connect with cricket. They tend to represent the opposite camp to that of the baseball players. There are, certainly, some players—O. C. Dawson, the Natal and Springbok all-rounder, is one—who play both cricket and baseball, but, in general, there is a very sharp and clear division between the players of the two games.

The leagues in the two main centres—Johannesburg and Durban—are so strong that either could produce at least three teams probably capable of beating any of the other provincial sides. Two striking examples of the standard of play are to be observed in the South Africa-Australia Tests of 1949–50.

At the end of the M.C.C. tour in 1949, I persuaded a young Johannesburg League player, Paul Winslow, to come over to England for the following summer because I thought he would profit from the experience and also because, if a special registration could be obtained, he would have been a very valuable member of the Hampshire county team. The registration was not approved, and S. C. Griffith, the Sussex secretary, gave him a season at Hove; he played for Sussex in friendly matches, acted as twelfth man, and played for the Club and Ground and local club sides. He returned to South Africa; went at once into the Transvaal side, and then into the Test team.

There are at least thirty other players in those leagues who would 'walk' a place in an English county side. Thus, Tayfield, Watkins, Fullerton, and Melle of the 1949–50 South African Test side are club players who, in the preceding season, could not command regular places in their provincial sides.

It would be very difficult to find happier cricket than this in South Africa. In general the grounds are good—with turf wickets—and the pavilions and club-houses magnificently appointed. The play is keen, yet there is an immense feeling of good fellowship; in all, they seem to have combined the best of two worlds—the competitive and the social—to a degree that we very rarely attain. This may well be owing to the fact that the cricketers are, first of all, fellow-members of the parent club—frequently an old boys' club—and cricketers only secondly and incidentally.

This club cricket spirit may be the root of the country's inability to win Tests, but they have, nevertheless, produced great cricketers and, perhaps more important, have managed to retain the good feeling that we always associate with club cricket even on the level of Test play—which may easily be a greater triumph.

.　　　.　　　.　　　.

The players from the three Commonwealth countries New Zealand, Ceylon, and the West Indies can be described accurately as club cricketers. From results, the West Indies can claim to be the strongest.

In fact, so much progress has been made by this body of 'week-end cricketers' that cricket lovers throughout the world eagerly await the result of the 1951–52 tournament between Australia and the West Indies.

In all the four territories in the British Caribbean—Barbados, British Guiana, Jamaica, and Trinidad—from which the West Indies cricket teams are usually picked, cricket is played on Saturday afternoons only (though, in recent years, Sunday cricket has been gaining popularity).

West Indies cricket is organised and competitive, and there are various grades of players. Professionalism is non-existent in West Indian club cricket, and even the groundsman, who is considered a professional, does not play for his employers, but for some other club of which he is a member.

Further, he represents them as an amateur in the strict sense of the word. The matches described as first class are spread over three Saturday afternoons, but the cricket season and the atmosphere of the game vary widely in each territory.

In Barbados, where there are some clubs almost as old as cricket in the West Indies, there is strong rivalry among four leading clubs—Pickwick, Wanderers, Spartan, and Empire. These club sides, and others, are fed both from school teams and from their own second XI teams.

It will be doing no injustice to Barbados to say that the player chooses his team according to his colour and his social status. Pickwick and Wanderers, for example, are exclusively white.

In the other Colonies, social status is the outstanding factor on which a player chooses his club. English club cricketers would be most unfamiliar with the distinct cliquishness which takes place after the day's play.

The Barbados Cricket Association regulates the Saturday-afternoon club competitions. All the 'first-class' clubs in this island have their own grounds and some sort of pavilion facilities. The colleges and secondary schools also from time to time play in the highest grade competition.

Dr. C. 'Bertie' Clarke, the West Indian Test cricketer, was selected to play for his island in an inter-colonial tournament whilst he was still at Harrison College. A few months later he was selected for the West Indies.

Frank Worrell and Roy Marshall were still at school when they were selected to play for Barbados. Another Barbadian, J. E. D. Sealy, in 1929–30, was at Combermere School when he represented the West Indies against England, and he went to Australia in 1931 while still a member of his school team.

Sunday cricket was hardly known in Barbados before World

War II. Recently, however, the Barbados Cricket League was formed, and during its brief life it has brought organised cricket within the reach of a far larger number of players than had hitherto been possible.

The League has already proved its value, for the team which represented Barbados against British Guiana in the Inter-Colonial Tournament in January, 1950, was selected after trial games of sides representing the Association and the League were held. A few of the League's players were chosen. Everton Weekes is a product of the League.

The Barbados Cricket Association selects the team to represent the island, and it also elects the two representatives who are on the West Indies Cricket Board of Control.

In British Guiana, Saturday cricket is organised on similar lines as in Barbados. Control is vested in the British Guiana Cricket Board of Control, which chooses the two representatives for the West Indies Cricket Board of Control.

West Indians would describe most of British Guiana's Sunday cricket as a 'fête affair'. The majority of the Saturday players journey to country districts to play against country teams. The cricket is of a good standard and exciting—and so is the food and drink! There is also a keenly contested, knock-out competition played over four Sundays.

Jamaica has the biggest population in the British Caribbean, and her cricket clubs receive far more financial support from spectators than in the other West Indian colonies—in fact, except at inter-colonial or international games, gates or even collecting-boxes are seldom seen in the Southern Caribbean.

Each Jamaican senior grade cricket club has its own ground and club-house. Jamaica has two international grounds—Melbourne Park and Sabina Park.

The Jamaican Cricket Association has entertained English county teams and other English representative sides—Lord Tennyson's XI, for instance—in addition to the regular visits of the M.C.C. representative teams that tour all the West Indies.

The Jamaican Cricket Association is the representative body of numerous cricket clubs. Each club sends an equal number of members and they elect the Jamaican Cricket Board of Control.

This Board organises mid-week and Saturday cricket, and it selects teams for Colony games. Sunday cricket is organised by different bodies. That, too, is competitive, but it is actually

S

designed for business houses and players who are not free on a Saturday afternoon—a few first-class clubs, however, enter teams in some of the competitions.

In spite of the fact that Jamaica seems to have far more competitions than the other States, their colleges and secondary schools take part in none. The schoolboys are denied early 'blooding' against experienced cricketers—an opportunity that boys in British Guiana, Barbados, and Trinidad enjoy.

Cricketers like Jeff Stollmeyer, Gerry Gomez, Prior Jones, and numerous others in the Southern Caribbean played for their colonies before they were twenty, and thus improved their chances of selection for the West Indies teams. George Headley played for the West Indies when he was hardly nineteen and had played competitive cricket from an early age.

Cricketers in Trinidad probably get more play than those in any other Colony. In addition to the Saturday club matches, there are also Sunday-morning and Sunday-afternoon games. Top-grade cricket is not confined to the towns—there are first-class clubs in the outlying areas. The credit for this must be given mainly to the oil companies, which employ many good sportsmen and encourage them to play.

Trinidad's cricket has many peculiar conditions. First, the game is played on what G. O. Allen describes as 'the dreadful mat'. But there are fewer spoilt games owing to rain than in turf countries. The 'mat' is made from fine jute fibre and is pulled over a hard, reddish, clay-type of soil.

There is no need to protect the wicket—if there are holes in the soil the groundsman fills them, waters the wicket, and puts on a very heavy roller. Within two hours the wicket is baked hard and shirt-front smooth, and the matting is pulled tightly over the wicket.

When it rains, the matting wicket plays much the same. The outfield is slower, but the ball is slippery—as it is in England. An experimental turf wicket has been made in the South, however, by an oil company, and has proved satisfactory.

Secondly, there is no cricket association as in the other Colonies. The control of club cricket is vested in various cup committees, but the Queen's Park Cricket Club selects the inter-colonial teams and chooses Trinidad's representatives on the West Indian Cricket Board of Control.

The third peculiar condition is one that every club cricketer will appreciate. In Port-of-Spain, where 60 per cent. of Trinidad's club cricket is played, only one club has its own ground. The two colleges—Queen's Royal and St. Mary's—also have their own grounds, but the others all play on the Queen's Park Savannah, where there are no pavilion facilities.

The Savannah is a wide, gently-rolling space of about 200 acres, in which are held horse-race meetings, football (amateur), cricket, ladies' hockey, and other games. On the north side of the Savannah is Government House and the Botanic Gardens Charles Kingsley described in *At Last*. The Savannah is a favoured residential district, and is the popular afternoon or evening 'walk' with Trinidadians. As the visitor passed along the 'pitch-walk' on any Saturday or Sunday afternoon he would see the soft grass speckled with hundreds of figures in white flannels and shirts— some thirty club matches would be in progress.

It is picturesque, certainly, but not very convenient for the cricketer: extra cover and deep fine-leg of two games can enjoy long conversations, and should it rain—well, they all begin involuntary training for the middle-distance races of the next athletic meeting!

It is a matter for wonder that West Indian week-end cricketers are able to hold their own when they meet players who play almost every day of the week.

Perhaps the different spirit that infuses the players accounts for it. At every opportunity and at any time of the year, wherever there are two or three West Indians there is a scramble for a bat and ball. There are many variations, but in essence it is cricket that is being played: 'Bowl for bat' in Jamaica, 'Bottom-house cricket' in British Guiana, 'Firms' in Barbados, and 'Pass-out' in Trinidad all mean that old and young are spending a quick hour in the 'development of the carpet drive'.

Any number and anyone may join in these games—'who gets the ball, bowls; who gets the batsman out, bats'. Like hungry sharks there are ten, twenty, thirty pairs of hands not more than five or ten yards from the bat waiting for a catch.

Learie Constantine describes in one of his books how his father, his uncle—both international cricketers—his brothers, and his sister used to play in their backyard.

The Imperial Cricket Conference's agreed definition of a 'first-class match' is 'a match of three or more days' duration between two sides of eleven players', etc. So it follows that only the inter-colonial tournament provides the West Indian player with first-class cricket experience before he enters into the international conflict of Test cricket.

Such is the spirit of cricket in the West Indies. The player plays the game for the love of it, without hope of reward other than the possibility of selection in the island's team for the inter-colonial tournament, and ultimately, perhaps, to play for the West Indies.

Chapter Seventeen

WHITHER THE BRITISH CLUB?

Possibility of changes—Value to the community—Future of club cricket.

BACK in the days of King Edward IV the lads of the village played a bat and ball game that their descendants came to know as cricket. They played it with intense enthusiasm—so much so that the King, fearing the sport would interfere with the serious business of archery, made the playing of it a crime and ordered the implements to be burned! Sometimes I wish as much enthusiasm was shown to-day.

I fear the threat of apathy to our sport, and I see too much indifference to the reasonable discipline we must all observe if the game is to have any meaning. Club cricket, in the south, any-way, is beginning to suffer from lassitude; it needs a stiff dose of something. But what? And who is to administer it?

We must be our own doctors, I think, and prescribe the treatment as well as administer it. Your remedy may well be as good as mine, but we may differ about the ingredients.

I may feel, for instance, that organised league cricket must be one of them; you, that our local temperament is against it. But—and here is one of the ingredients I do recommend—we could brighten up cricket by adopting a scheme similar to that tried out by the Press for the Rugby Football Union clubs during the 1949–50 season: they tabulated the results of some of the clubs, so that the Wasps v. Rosslyn Park game at the end of the season—when the Park were top of the table, and the Wasps only a fraction behind—became as keen as an international match.

Peter Goodall has already tried out something similar for cricketers, and clubs, while wary of becoming implicated in any suggestion of league cricket, were only too happy to co-operate. There is nothing against a table or series of tables to reflect the performances, and so the standing, of the clubs.

Here is another point. Whether, by the introduction of competitive or league cricket, we should produce better players for the counties—and England—is something on which one could debate for centuries. If it did raise the standard of play, do we want it? Would we really like to see the 'rabbit' being pushed out of his week-end game?

John Arlott is one of those who has decided views on this question. He gives me my climax by saying:

Because I am a cricketer—which means not only a player, because I can play very little now—and also a man whose life is tied up with the game, I am a *club* cricketer.

My three interests in club cricket are inter-related, although they seem so different. One interest is as a cricket historian, for earliest good cricket was played by small clubs —The Vine, Hambledon, Slindon, Farnham in Surrey, and Hartley Wintney. Then again, as a player, I found some of my happiest cricketing times with the clubs. Thirdly, and most important of all, I am interested in club cricket because it holds the vital character of English cricket.

Sometimes I am anxious for club cricket because I feel it may be threatened by an approach that may kill its character. Now, while I am convinced that England may beat Australia in the normal course by 1952, I also think it would be possible, from our greater population, for us to beat them regularly, but at a price which I, for one, should hate to contemplate.

We could do it by the methods followed in Australia, where the clubs play in leagues or grades, so that all their matches are competitive. Their aim is league victory and promotion to higher grades for the club. To this end young cricketers are highly coached, pitted against the finest opposition, and gradually developed first as State, and then as Test players. There is no room in any Australian grade team for a 'rabbit'.

Every cricket team in England could be allotted fixtures in a specific league; points could be awarded for wins; promotion and relegation systems instituted, and, no doubt, we should soon have a system of registration of players, with, inevitably—since the leagues themselves would play representative games—a dossier of the ability of every player, plus, of course, a transfer system. All this analysis of play and organised competition would obviously raise the standard of play in terms of *performance* and, starting at the bottom, it would build us a winning Test team.

But what a grievous price this would be to pay merely for winning a series of Test matches! Cricket grew up in England as the recreation of country craftsmen. It developed as the pleasure of many people of all classes. The greatest factor of all in English cricket has been the pleasure, the happiness, it has given.

Nobody who has ever *played* cricket with any pleasure would wish to see our games regimented to the end of winning a representative match. Test matches are good Press copy, and the castigation of English cricketers by those who know little more about cricket than what their papers tell them can be a fine armchair pursuit. It has provided many a hard-pressed journalist with a good set of headlines to revile England's failure to beat Australia. Highly-competitive cricket as a remedy follows as an automatic suggestion. This *is* obviously the remedy—if we place the honour of beating Australia above the pleasure of thousands of men all through the country in a game which they enjoy irrespective of—nay, often in inverse proportion to—their playing ability.

Introduce competitive cricket, weed out the man who is not worth his place in terms of performance, and what a strange sight English cricket will present! To begin with, half the men, who take the team to matches in their cars, will no longer be in the team at all! Much of the enjoyment, kindness, good feeling, and their joint product of happiness—win or lose—will be removed from this sport altogether. The happy 'rabbit', most lovable and rewarding of cricketers, will have to go. So will the irregular player, the man whose work allows him to play only rare but treasured matches.

When cricket places winning beyond its capacity to give delight then I, for one, have no desire to be associated with it any longer.

The Australians play their cricket in a naturally combative way. England, even in Test matches, could produce a Cecil Parkin, who sang as he ran up to bowl; a George Brown, who could convulse the entire team with one remark; a Maurice Tate, who spoke to everybody within reach; and a Patsy Hendren, with his unique gift for standing at second slip and making the wicket-keeper giggle.

Because I believe that men are more important than games, that happiness is more important than winning, I should like to see English club cricket remain exactly as it is, or perhaps even reject some of its competitive organisations and representative honours. Its most important ingredient is human happiness, which cannot be regimented.

So I end this literary innings. If I glance back as I leave the field, it is to remind you that *your* opinion on the value of competitive cricket will decide the future of club cricket in this country. But John Arlott is right: in the last resort, what matters is the happiness our game gives us.

THE END

INDEX